D0117710

Portraits
of Jesus

Portraits of Jesus

An Inductive Approach to the Gospels

Michael R. Cosby

Westminster John Knox Press
Louisville, Kentucky

© 1999 Michael R. Cosby

All rights reserved. No part of this book may be reproduced or transmitted in any form or by any means, electronic or mechanical, including photocopying, recording, or by any information storage or retrieval system, without permission in writing from the publisher. For information, address Westminster John Knox Press, 100 Witherspoon Street, Louisville, Kentucky 40202-1396.

Scripture quotations from the New Revised Standard Version of the Bible are copyright © 1989 by the Division of Christian Education of the National Council of the Churches of Christ in the U.S.A. and are used by permission.

Grateful acknowledgment is made to the following for permission to reprint previously copyrighted material:

Material on pp. 65–67 from *The Old Testament Pseudepigrapha* by James H. Charlesworth, Copyright © 1983, 1985 by James H. Charlesworth. Used by permission of Doubleday, a division of Random House, Inc.

Book design by Sharon Adams
Cover design © 1999 Eric Handel/LMNOP

First edition
Published by Westminster John Knox Press
Louisville, Kentucky

This book is printed on acid-free paper that meets the American National Standards Institute Z39.48 standard. ♾

PRINTED IN THE UNITED STATES OF AMERICA
99 00 01 02 03 04 05 06 07 08 — 10 9 8 7 6 5 4 3 2 1

Library of Congress Cataloging-in-Publication Data

Cosby, Michael R.
    Portraits of Jesus : an inductive approach to the Gospels / Michael R. Cosby.
        p.   cm.
    ISBN 0-664-25827-1 (pbk. : alk. paper)
    1. Bible.   N.T.   Gospels—Study and teaching.   I. Title.
BS2555.5.C67   1999
223'.06—dc21
                                                            99-32672

This book is lovingly dedicated to my youngest son,

Evan Patrick Cosby

His natural inquisitiveness provides a model
for enthusiastically diving into the study
of uncharted areas.

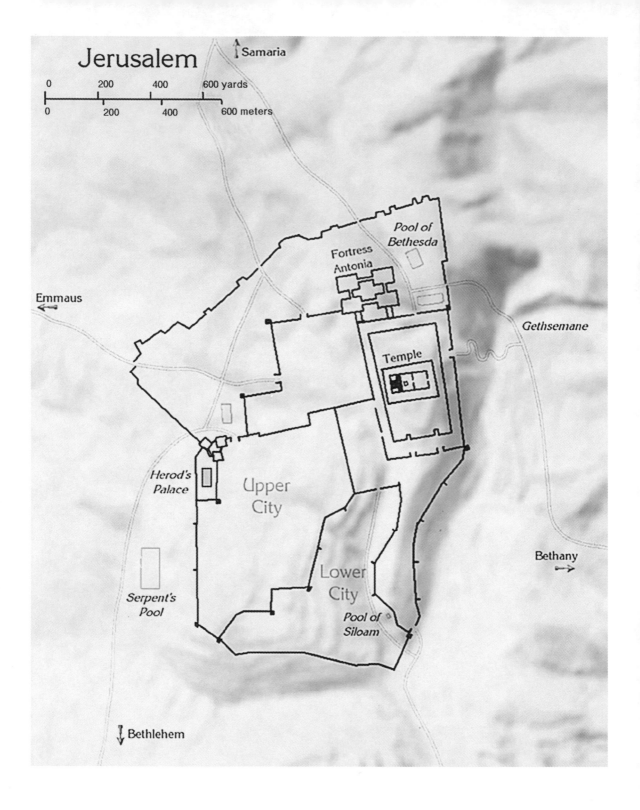

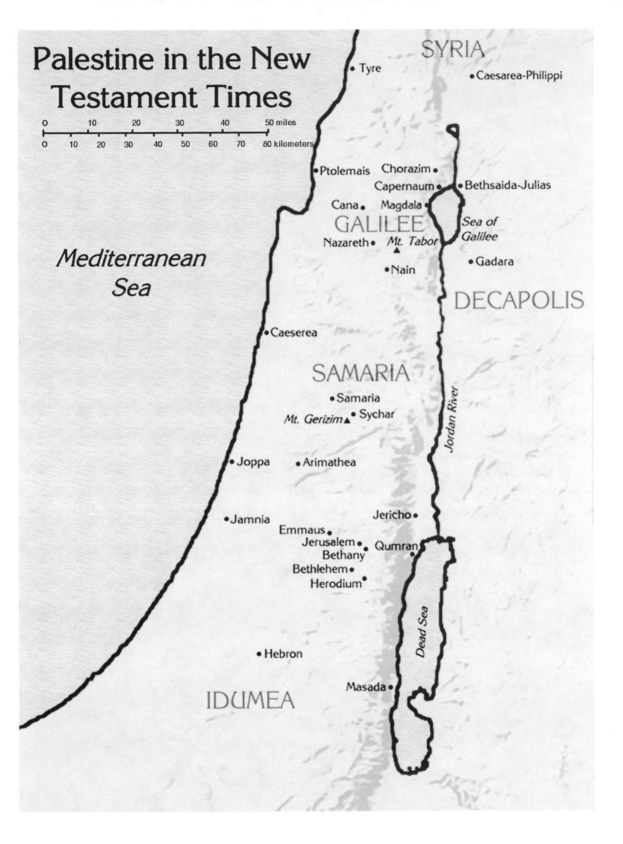

Palestine in the New Testament Times

0   10   20   30   40   50 miles

0   10   20   30   40   50   60   70   80 kilometers

SYRIA

•Tyre

•Caesarea-Philippi

•Ptolemais   Chorazim•

Capernaum•   •Bethsaida-Julias

Cana•   Magdala•

GALILEE   *Sea of Galilee*

Nazareth•   *Mt. Tabor* ▲

•Nain

•Gadara

DECAPOLIS

Mediterranean Sea

•Caeserea

SAMARIA

•Samaria

Mt. Gerizim ▲ •Sychar

Jordan River

•Joppa   •Arimathea

•Jamnia

Jericho•

Emmaus•

Jerusalem•   •Qumran

Bethany

Bethlehem•

Herodium•

Dead Sea

•Hebron

Masada•

IDUMEA

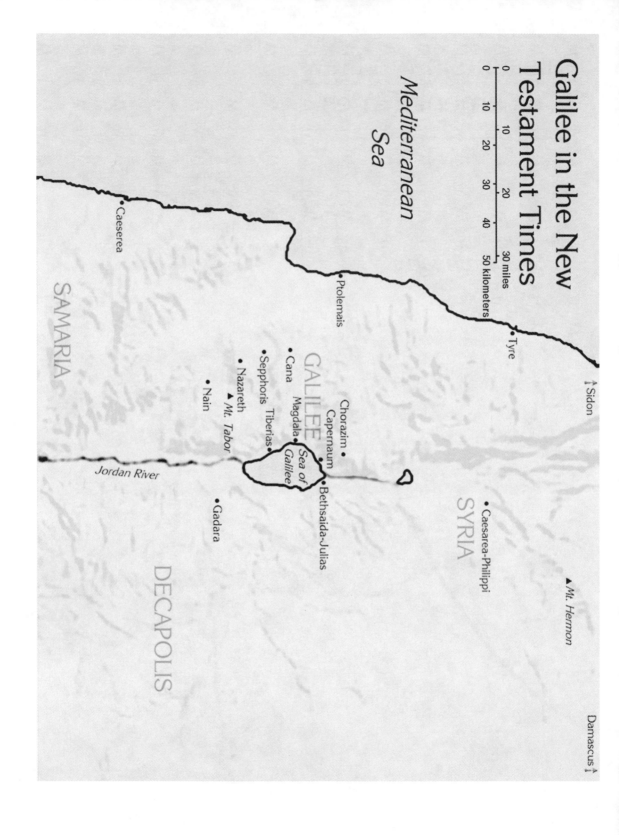

Galilee in the New Testament Times

0 | 10 | 20 | 30 | 40 | 50 kilometers
0 | 10 | 20 | 30 miles

Mediterranean Sea

Caeserea

SAMARIA

Ptolemais

GALILEE

Chorazim •
Capernaum •
Sepphoris Tiberias •
Cana •
Magdala •
Sea of Galilee
• Bethsaida-Julias
Nazareth •
▲ Mt. Tabor
Nain •

Jordan River

Gadara •

DECAPOLIS

Tyre •

↑ Sidon

SYRIA

Caesarea-Philippi •

▲ Mt. Hermon

Damascus ↑

Contents

Contents

Contents

1

The Rewards of Inductive Study of the Gospels

Years ago, while an undergraduate at the University of Montana, I attended a seminar called a "Bible Study Dig In." This weeklong study of Mark 1—8 opened what was for me a new world of inductive Bible study. I experienced in a captivating way not only how challenging but also how rewarding biblical study can be. Each of us received a copy of the Gospel of Mark, typed on 8½-by-11-inch paper, double-spaced, with wide margins. There were no paragraph divisions, no verse markings. We had only the text of Mark and line numbers down the left side of each page, indicating every fifth line so that we could keep track of where items were located by page and line number. The leader called this approach a *manuscript study,* and the purpose was to remove external guides, such as study-Bible notes, and force us to focus on what the text said.

Our somewhat eccentric leader, Paul Byer, who pioneered these studies of the Gospel of Mark, had bushy eyebrows that he brushed straight up. With childlike enthusiasm he almost skipped around the room, urging us to see every meaningful detail we could discover. We studied our manuscripts individually, then gathered in small groups to compare what we saw, and then met in a large group discussion led by Byer. We noticed vivid aspects of the Gospel author's writing style. We saw that the order in which Mark's stories are arranged has significance, and we started acting like detectives, searching for clues to solve a mystery. Byer's enthusiasm was contagious, and soon we hardly noticed those wild eyebrows; we were too busy trying to crack the code.

Had I spent the week instead listening to a good scholar deliver lectures on the Gospel of Mark, I am confident that my life would not have been changed significantly. I probably would have been impressed with how brilliant the scholar was, and I most likely would have returned home with a notebook filled with lecture notes. But I doubt that I would have left with the belief that I, too, could see the intricate connections between stories in Mark's Gospel. What made the week so life-changing was the way in which *we* became immersed in the study of the Gospel. The *excitement of discovery* caused many of us to return to our campuses and want to duplicate what we experienced at the "Dig In."

We did not know we were practicing a form of literary criticism; we just knew we were having a great time trying to discover what we believed Mark was seeking to communicate about Jesus. We did not know we were learning how to do exegesis, nor did we know how dangerously subversive such study can be. When you seek to discover what the text says, instead of reading into the text your own theological bias, you might begin to conclude that you need to change some of your existing beliefs.

At that time, I assumed that a careful reading of the text alone could unlock the clues to correct interpretation. I did not understand much about cultural anthropology, and I knew nothing about the sociology of knowledge. It didn't occur to me that ancient Mediterranean people saw reality differently than I did, and that only by learning more about their world would I be able to do successful detective work on individual biblical books. I didn't fully appreciate that authors write within particular sociological settings and presuppose many shared understandings of the world with the people for whom they write. I didn't realize that if I do not share these cultural views, I can easily misunderstand their words. I was unaware of the vast number of documents written by ancient Mediterranean authors that are found in the Old Testament Pseudepigrapha, the Dead Sea Scrolls, and such collections as the Loeb Classical Library. I had little idea of the relevance an ancient historian like Josephus might have for understanding the Gospel of Mark.

The interest generated through inductive Bible study, however, led me to such discoveries. Seeing things for myself instilled not only the necessary confidence but also the curiosity to look for details I had not seen before. The thrill of discovery established a pattern of looking closely, of not being content with pat answers or regurgitated data. I wanted to see it for myself, and this attitude carried over into my other course work at the University of Montana. It also shaped my approach to education.

Professors are painfully aware that students too often read only what is necessary to prepare for exams. Unfortunately, in Biblical Studies classes this means students often end up reading books about the Bible but not the Bible itself. I became aware of this during my doctoral work at Emory University, while assisting a very capable professor in teaching a course called "Biblical Literature and Faith." For this introductory class, he used a good introduction to the Bible as his textbook and in the syllabus assigned readings from both the Bible and the textbook. As I graded the exams, however, it became obvious that the students were reading only the textbook. I determined that when I began teaching my own classes, I would devise some way to ensure that my students would read the Bible and see for themselves what it contains.

No matter how good the textbook, no matter how responsible the information it contains, it can never replace reading the Bible itself. People cannot move beyond the novice stage in Biblical Studies, or in any other field of literature, as long as they rely completely on secondary sources. There is no substitute for a careful, inductive analysis of the text, and I have found that students prefer this approach over reading someone else's analysis.

The first time I taught "Life and Teachings of Jesus," I used a standard text and received a less-than-enthusiastic response from my students. The book assumed that its readers already knew a significant amount about the Gospels and were ready to interact with critical issues of historical investigation. This was not a good assumption for my students. Unfortunately, the author answered questions that they were not yet ready to ask and that they did not perceive as important or legitimate. The issues the book addressed bewildered them, and they became frustrated and then bored with it. In itself the book was fine, but before my students were ready to interact with its contents, they needed a good, intensive study of the Gospels.

Many good books are available that explain the central themes of Gospel authorship, dates of writing, theological agendas, and so on. But when students see such issues for themselves as they study the Gospels, they become much better prepared to interact with the analyses of competent scholars. Until, by sufficient encounter with the biblical text, they see for themselves the issues involved in Gospel interpretation, they never adequately understand or appreciate scholarly books on the life of Jesus. My

"Life and Teachings of Jesus" class therefore became a careful analysis of all four Gospels, and this manuscript began to take shape. My students became aware of scholarly methods of studying the Gospel narratives not from reading descriptions of them but from implementing these methodologies. The results are far more satisfying and convincing.

This book provides the resources needed to study the Gospels inductively. To complete the assigned readings, one has to look carefully at the Gospel stories. *Instead of giving what I believe to be the correct answers, this book provides the tools needed for you to find answers for yourself.* The focus is on reading the Gospels, not descriptions of them; and the questions, maps, explanations of historical matters, quotations from other ancient sources, and exegetical helps interspersed throughout the book are designed to enhance your reading of the primary text.

Although the book does not seek to duplicate the environment of a "Bible Study Dig In," its observation questions, notes on cultural backgrounds, and questions focused on the significance of Gospel passages will help you discover the meaning of the stories in their ancient Mediterranean context and also ponder their relevance for life today. This combination of academic rigor (the detective work of seeking to uncover the Gospel authors' intended messages) and vital interest in the relevance of the text for today (personal reflection and application) does justice to the intent of the first-century authors who wrote the Gospels. The Gospels are, after all, documents of faith that address important issues of belief and practice. Taking their messages seriously will challenge not only your historical views of Jesus of Nazareth but also your personal beliefs on the best way to conduct your life. In other words, you simply will not be able to complete this journey of historical discovery without having your opinions of Jesus changed in some ways. And you will not be able to reflect on the significance of his teaching and lifestyle without wrestling with their relevance for your own life and for society as a whole.

Jesus of Nazareth profoundly affected the course of human history, and the Gospels are the primary sources for studying his life. Carefully analyzing each of these accounts to discover its unique presentation of Jesus is therefore indispensable for those who desire to know about this person who is the focus of Christian beliefs. Obviously there are many conflicting views of Jesus, and there is little hope that people on a broad scale will reach a uniform set of conclusions about him. Different presuppositions, questions, and methods lead to different conclusions. But behind all of these stand the Gospels, and no one can make responsible

The Rewards of Inductive Study of the Gospels

decisions on the person of Jesus without first carefully studying these primary sources.

FOUR GOSPELS—ONE JESUS

From the earliest encounters with Jesus no two people perceived events identically, and the stories of Jesus include the perspectives of the storytellers themselves. Each of the four canonical Gospels gives a unique portrait of Jesus that reflects not only how its author understood Jesus but also the author's intended message to his audience. The *Evangelists* (= Gospel authors) did not write scientific histories of Jesus Messiah but accounts intended to influence the beliefs and behaviors of those for whom they wrote. The resulting differences among the Gospels have been known from an early time in the history of the church, and Christians have explained them in a variety of ways.

Evidence shows that in the second century C.E. some Christian leaders were studying the Gospels carefully, noting many differences among the accounts of Jesus. Scholars such as Irenaeus saw these distinctions as signs of the fullness of God's revelation in Jesus Christ. Writing about 180 C.E., Irenaeus explained that each Evangelist focused on a different aspect of Jesus' person and ministry, and he assigned the four creatures from Revelation 4 as symbols for the four Gospels.

> Around the throne, and on each side of the throne, are four living creatures, full of eyes in front and behind: the first living creature like a lion, the second living creature like an ox, the third living creature with a face like a human face, and the fourth living creature like a flying eagle. (Rev. 4:6–7)

Irenaeus argues that the Gospel of Matthew focuses on Jesus' humanity and therefore is symbolized by the human face, whereas Mark begins his Gospel with reference to an Old Testament prophecy, so that Gospel is symbolized by the soaring image of the eagle. Luke, he says, focuses on the sacrificial ministry of Jesus and is thereby symbolized by the calf (or ox), whereas John focuses on the deity of Jesus, resulting in the royal symbol of the lion.[1]

Down through the centuries others have disagreed with Irenaeus's reasoning and have changed the symbols to reflect which one they believe applies to each Gospel, but to this day in Christian art the images of a man, an ox, a lion, and an eagle are frequently assigned to the Gospels. The reasons given may be fanciful at times, but they reveal a consistent recognition that the four biblical accounts of Jesus' life are distinct.[2] Augustine

Use of B.C.E. and C.E. in Modern Scholarship
Increasingly, as Christian scholars interact with people from other religious backgrounds, the abbreviations B.C.E. (= before the common era) and C.E. (= common era) are used instead of B.C. (= before Christ) and A.D. (= anno Domini, Latin for "in the year of the Lord"). Jewish scholars, for example, do not wish to specify a year with reference to Jesus, whom they do not recognize as Messiah. So, to foster harmony, the abbreviation C.E. is now used to designate the same year as A.D. (e.g., A.D. 180 = 180 C.E.). Similarly, 44 B.C.E. designates the same year as 44 B.C. The dates are the same; only the way of abbreviating them is different.

5

(354–430 C.E.), for example, after summarizing his understanding of the intent of Matthew, Mark, and Luke, says:

> John, on the other hand, had in view that true divinity of the Lord in which He is the Father's equal, and directed his efforts above all to the setting forth of the divine nature in his Gospel in such a way as he believed to be adequate to men's needs and notions. Therefore he is borne to loftier heights, in which he leaves the other three [Gospels] far behind him; so that, while in them you see men who have their conversation in a certain manner with the man Christ on earth, in him you perceive one who has passed beyond the cloud in which the whole earth is wrapped, and who has reached the liquid heaven from which, with clearest and steadiest mental eye, he is able to look upon God the Word, who was in the beginning with God, and by whom all things were made. (*Harmony of the Gospels* 1.3.7)

Augustine proceeds to quote distinctive passages from John that focus on the deity of Christ, clearly revealing his detailed grasp of the many differences between the Gospel accounts. The way in which he explains this material differs substantially from interpretations provided by modern scholars, but his work is evidence of a great mind.

Thus, the existence of four canonical Gospels poses both a wonderful challenge and a complicated problem for studying the life of Jesus. On the one hand, these four, distinct witnesses contribute more to our knowledge of Jesus than any one of them could alone. On the other hand, the fact that Matthew, Mark, Luke, and John give uniquely different portraits of Jesus provides the basis for endless speculation on what he actually said and did.

For some Christians the diversity of the Gospel witnesses to Jesus brings stress, because for faith reasons they believe it to be important that there be a unitary presentation of the truth. This unfortunate mentality leads some to employ what I call the "blender method" of studying the Gospels. When they dump them all into a blender, so to speak, and hit the start button, an amorphous glop emerges, called a harmony of the Gospels. In the name of glorifying the Bible, they tragically destroy the carefully crafted contributions of the four Evangelists. While modern biblical scholars analyze the distinctions among the Gospels and seek to understand their overall messages, blender-method Christians employ severely outdated, naive methodologies designed to show how all the stories are really the same. After using this book to work through the Gospels, you will see with great clarity why the blender approach is completely out of touch with reality.

The Rewards of Inductive Study of the Gospels

You will learn to look for and appreciate the distinctive com-positional styles and theological perspectives of Matthew, Mark, Luke, and John. After some experience with studying the Gospels inductively, you will begin to nod knowingly as you see the telltale signs of the styles and content of the four authors. Rather than viewing these differences as a threat to faith, you will start to anticipate and enjoy seeing the distinctive portraits of Jesus unfold.

2

Mark the Evangelist

SECTION ONE:
MARK AND ORAL PROCLAMATION

For centuries, Christian teachers largely ignored the Gospel of Mark because they viewed it as a shortened version of Matthew.[1] After the intense literary and historical investigations conducted during the nineteenth and twentieth centuries, however, most biblical scholars now believe that Mark is the earliest New Testament Gospel. This assessment of historical priority has brought it greater attention, and today we have a far more positive evaluation of Mark's content, structure, and theology.

Mark's Gospel apparently represents the earliest extant written account of the career of Jesus. Prior to its composition, there may have been only smaller collections of written material to accompany the oral *preaching* of the good news. The early Christians had no New Testament as we know it. When they referred to the "scriptures," they meant what Christians today call the Old Testament. Except for those who were eyewitnesses to Jesus' ministry, most people's knowledge of him consisted only of what they *heard* in stories from Christian preachers who proclaimed the good news (= gospel) about salvation in Christ, the anointed of God. There were no books to read about Jesus, only stories testifying to the central work God accomplished through sending his Son. "Faith comes from what is *heard,* and what is heard comes through the word [preaching] of Christ" (Rom. 10:17; emphasis mine).

Mark's writing style provides a fine example of "oral litera-ture," stories that took shape as missionaries and teachers told and retold the good news about Jesus, patterning their message for the needs of their audiences. For example, Mark often tells his stories using present-tense verbs (such as "And he *says* to them . . . "), although most English translations obscure this char-acteristic in order to produce greater readability ("And he *said* to them . . . "). In Mark, one *hears* the sounds of stories proclaimed to listening audiences. If you have ever been in a group of peo-ple intently listening to a master storyteller who captures your imagination as he or she describes some event, you can better un-derstand the manner in which Mark composed his Gospel.

The modern practice of private, individual reading differs from most reading in antiquity. All ancient authors wrote their lit-erature to be heard. People spoke the written words out loud as they read from a scroll, even when reading alone. And for prac-tical reasons, a great amount of reading was performed before groups of people. Prior to the invention of movable type by Jo-hannes Gutenberg around 1450 C.E., producing books was a slow and expensive process. This severely limited the number of avail-able copies of any particular document, and the most efficient means of communicating the contents of a book was through public reading. Even if manuscripts had been more numerous, most people in antiquity could not read, so they depended on the educated for information obtained from books.

PRIMARY ORALITY

First-century Christians lived in predominantly oral cultures, and their primary access to information about Jesus was through storytelling.[2] Scholarly investigations of the ways in which people living in predominantly oral cultures think and express them-selves have illuminated the conceptual differences between peo-ple living in primarily literate and primarily oral cultures. This knowledge helps clarify the manner in which the New Testament authors composed their works.

Although early Christians did not live in completely oral soci-eties, the ways in which they functioned on a day-to-day basis, ed-ucated the new converts, and so forth probably shared much in common with oral patterns of remembering information. Today, with reference books readily available, we often do not bother to expend effort in memorizing information unless we need to know it for our work. In oral societies, however, the combined knowl-edge of the entire group is stored in the individual memories of its members. If they all forget something, they cannot run to a bookshelf and look it up in an encyclopedia; the information is lost. So developing their ability to remember material important for the group is a vital part of the oral society. Knowledge is difficult to obtain, so memorizing it and passing it on to future generations assumes paramount importance. Consequently, the older members of the group play a vital role in the educational process. And much of the knowledge they pass on comes in the form of stories, for people remember things more easily when they hear them in story form.

Scholars who study oral cultures have noted that abstract thinking is relatively foreign to members of these societies. If asked to identify a round shape drawn on paper, for example, such people call the object an apple or some other concrete object familiar to them. They do not call it a circle, for such abstract thinking is primarily associated with literacy. This also holds true with abstract theological concepts. Asking most first-century Christians to define the technical, theological terms explained in modern systematic theology textbooks would elicit puzzled stares. But these same illiterate believers would readily tell stories about Jesus that would practically illustrate issues of faith.

Stories place us in contact with the concrete (not abstract) world of people and events. Few early Christians would have thought to *define* theological terms; they *recounted* how Jesus addressed particular issues. They lived in a world of stories, not in an environment of written data. Consequently, they greatly respected the value of oral proclamation, expressing higher regard for hearing a person speak about a particular event than for reading an account of the same. The living voice carried greater authority than symbols written on paper, as the following quote of the elder Papias clearly indicates. Writing early in the second century C.E., he described his approach to learning about Jesus:

> And whenever anyone came who had been a follower of the presbyters [= elders], I inquired into the words of the presbyters, what Andrew or Peter had said, or Philip or Thomas or James or John or Matthew, or any other disciple of the Lord, and what Aristion and the presbyter John, disciples of the Lord, were still saying. For I did not imagine that things out of books would help me as much as the utterances of a living and abiding voice.[3]

Another important factor in predominantly oral cultures is that the needs of the community frequently dictate what is remembered by group members. People remember things because they are useful. Early Christians quite likely remembered and passed along many of the stories we now have recorded about Jesus because these readily addressed situations in the life of the Christian community. This obviously does not account for all the Gospel narratives, but many reflect practical concerns, ranging from missionary proclamation of salvation to instructing believers on dealing with conflicts in the local assemblies. When, for example, a nonbeliever questioned Jesus' identity as the Son of God, missionaries could tell stories of the virgin birth, miracles, resurrection, and so on. When a Christian asked what to do about conflicts between members of the church, teachers could tell stories such as the one in which Jesus instructs Peter to forgive "seventy times seven times."

Early Christianity was primarily an oral movement. Decades elapsed before Christians began seriously engaging in the literary enterprise. Mark probably wrote about 65 C.E., which means that our first New Testament Gospel was produced after more than thirty years of primarily oral development of the gospel message. The earliest Christian documents we have are Paul's missionary correspondence to churches located in present-day Greece and Turkey. And Paul wrote these letters because he could not be there to deliver his message orally, in person.

One reason Christians did not begin writing books about Jesus earlier was that they did not believe the world was going to last very much longer. Paul, for example, says in 1 Corinthians 7:29, 31, "the appointed time has grown short. . . . For the present form of this world is passing away." In 1 Corinthians 10:11 he adds, concerning Old Testament stories, "These things . . . were written down to instruct us, on whom the ends of the ages have come." Elsewhere Paul expresses the firm belief that Jesus Christ will return for the final judgment during Paul's lifetime: "And the dead in Christ will rise first. Then *we who are alive, who are left,* will be caught up in the clouds together with them to meet the Lord in the air" (1 Thess. 4:16–17; emphasis mine; see also 1 Cor. 15:51–52). Statements by Jesus such as "Truly I tell you, there are some standing here who will not taste death until they see that the kingdom of God has come with power" (Mark 9:1) contributed greatly to this expectation.

The realization that Jesus' return would not happen as soon as they expected served as one impetus to produce literary works. The apostles were dying, and Christians needed some means of preserving the stories of Jesus. This need probably contributed substantially to the birth of the written Gospel. And the written Gospel retains much of the flavor of the oral preaching and teaching out of which it grew. Each of the four Evangelists wrote his story of Jesus to address the needs of a particular audience and intended his words to be read out loud to them.

LOOKING AHEAD

Comparing the four Gospels is extremely productive, as long as we are careful not to destroy the distinct literary creation of each. Mark's portrait of Jesus differs from those presented in Matthew, Luke, and John, for his purpose in writing differs from theirs. The more we understand and appreciate the diversity presented in the Gospels, the more clearly we see the intent of the biblical authors. Especially if Mark wrote first, we should not appeal to Matthew or to Luke to explain what Mark meant in any given passage. We need to grapple with Mark on his own terms, appreciating his portrait of Jesus: the powerful but secret and suffering Messiah.

As you read this Gospel, you will see that most of Jesus' ministry occurs in and around Galilee, yet a third of the book deals with the last week of Jesus' life during his one, momentous journey to Jerusalem. In Mark's story, Jesus is an authoritative teacher and miracle worker who is shrouded in mystery. Both his disciples and his opponents misunderstand him, for he does not conform to their messianic expectations. People in his hometown do not believe in him, and his own family questions his sanity. As Mark's fast-paced narrative pushes events toward the crucifixion and the enigmatic conclusion, you will see far more clearly the significance of Jesus' ministry than do the characters in the story. Be alert to what causes their confusion, as well as to the way in which Mark develops his portrait of Jesus.

SECTION TWO: MARK 1:1–2:12: THE BEGINNING OF THE GOSPEL

Begin by reading through this series of stories, preferably out loud, imagining that you are listening to a storyteller. Notice the continuity of events and be aware of Mark's style of storytelling, from the types of things he chooses to report to the manner in which he composes his sentences. When you have finished, interact with the following questions.

1. Imagine that you are about to write a biography. What basic components of a person's life would you be sure to include?
2. Which of these basic biographical components are missing from Mark's account, showing that he is not writing a biography of Jesus?
3. What distinctive characteristics do you see in Mark's writing style

in 1:1–2:12? Note, for example, the repeated use of "and immediately" in 1:10, 18, 20, 21, 23, 28, 29, 30, 42, 43; 2:8, 12. (Your translation might modify the wording of some of these in order to produce more variety of expression.) How does this style affect the sense of speed with which the events occur in the narrative?

Now go back and analyze each paragraph carefully:

Mark 1:1–13: "The beginning of the good news of Jesus Christ"

The Gospel is anonymous; the title "The Gospel according to Mark" across the top of the page in your Bible was added by scribes at some later time. The author begins his story with a verbless clause: "The beginning of the good news of Jesus Christ, the Son of God" (his title?). In this identifying line, "Jesus" is the Greek form of the Hebrew name Joshua, whereas "Christ" is not a name but a title, meaning "the anointed One."

Many Jews of Jesus' time thought that the messiah would appear first in the wilderness because of the statement in Isaiah 40:3–5:

> A voice cries out: "In the wilderness prepare the way of the LORD, make straight in the desert a highway for our God. Every valley shall be lifted up, and every mountain and hill be made low; the uneven ground shall become level, and the rough places a plain. Then the glory of the LORD shall be revealed, and all people shall see it together, for the mouth of the LORD has spoken."

On the basis of this expectation, some religiously fervent Jews went out into the wilderness to purify themselves in preparation for the coming of the messiah. Among these was a community of men, whose writings an Arab shepherd accidentally discovered in 1947 in a cave near Qumran on the western shore of the Dead Sea. These scrolls provide considerable insight into a particular Jewish sectarian community that was eschatological in orientation (*eschaton* is Greek for "last"; hence, eschatology is the study of "last things").

The Dead Sea Scroll community at Qumran prepared themselves with great seriousness for the coming of God's military messiah. (They also seem to have expected a priestly messiah who would teach them and lead their religious ceremonies.) Some of their writings present an extremely rigorous regimen for remaining pure from all worldly defilement. They believed that when the messiah came they would be his primary army, driving the wicked out of the land and establishing an eternal rule of peace and righteousness. Like other eschatological Jews, they thought they were living in the last times, just before the day when God's anointed leader would bring an end to the present age of evil and usher in the glorious age to come.

Other eschatologically oriented Jewish groups differed theologically from the Qumran sect but nevertheless agreed that the messiah would rid Judea of all foreign oppressors. Most of these people in first-century Judaism seemed to have shared some form of the concept of the *two ages*. They believed God would abolish the *present evil age*, the one dominated by sin and death, which began with the sin of Adam and Eve, and then usher in the *age to come*, the age of peace under the direct rule of God through his messiah. Many New Testament passages assume this belief, and some refer to it explicitly (e.g., Gal. 1:4; Eph. 1:21). A nice description appears in the Old Testament Apocrypha, in a document probably written during the first century:

> This present world is not the end; the full glory does not remain in it. . . . But the day of judgment will be the end of this age and the beginning of the immortal age to come, in which corruption has passed away, sinful indulgence has come to an end, unbelief has been cut off, and righteousness has increased. (2 Esd. 7:112–14)

The following diagram, in a rather simplistic way, shows visually what they expected:

Present Evil Age	Coming of Messiah	Age to Come
(pain, sickness, death, evil, and oppression)		(no more pain, death, or evil; righteousness and peace the norm)

The coming of the messiah was to be one of the major events of history, obliterating evil and its effects and ushering in the eternal rule of God.

When John the Baptist appeared in the desert, powerfully proclaiming repentance, he generated considerable excitement and speculation. John sought to prepare the people for the end-time events that he believed God was about to perform.

1. What does Mark emphasize about John the Baptist, and what significance does his baptizing have concerning Jesus' ministry?
2. Is the descent of the Spirit on Jesus seen by the crowd or by Jesus alone?

Your conclusion will be enhanced by noting several details. "You" in 1:11 is singular in the Greek text, and Mark's description of the heavens splitting open was at that time used for heavenly visions. For example, in Ezekiel 1:1 the prophet says, "As I was among the exiles by the river Chebar, the heavens were opened, and I saw visions of God." Similarly, a passage in the Old Testament Pseudepigrapha, *Testament of Levi* 2:6, recounts a vision by beginning, "Sleep fell upon me, and I beheld a high mountain, and I was on it. And behold, the heavens were opened, and an angel of the Lord spoke to me." Later in the same text the author says, "At this moment the angel opened for me the gates of heaven and I saw the Most High sitting on the throne" (*T. Levi* 5:1).[4]

Mediterranean Overstatement

To emphasize John's popularity, Mark uses a type of overstatement that is common in the Bible (for example, Exod. 8:17: "All the dust of the earth turned into gnats throughout the whole land of Egypt"). When Mark states, "And there went out to him all the country of Judea and all the people of Jerusalem . . . ," he means "a lot of people went out." A modern analogy is a sports reporter who describes the victorious return of a championship team to their hometown by saying, "The entire city turned out to greet the team as they stepped off their charter jet."

Mark 1:14–34: "He taught them as one having authority"

1. Jesus' ministry does not begin until John is removed from the scene. How does the message Jesus proclaims (1:15) compare with that preached by John (1:4–8)?
2. How does the response of the men to Jesus' call in 1:16–20 emphasize his authority?
3. How does 1:21–28 further emphasize Jesus' authority? How does this passage relate to and help us understand the significance of 1:12–13?

Matthew and Luke contain longer accounts of Jesus' ordeal in the wilderness for forty days, including his temptation by Satan. Although Mark's version is very brief by comparison, 1:21–28 reveals that Jesus was victorious in the wilderness over Satan. When he begins his ministry, he has power over the domain of the great deceiver.

4. What further area of Jesus' authority does 1:29–34 emphasize? (Note that he refuses to allow the demons to proclaim his identity.)

Each *Sabbath*, Jews gathered for worship, prayer, singing, and learning in *synagogues*.[5] The elders of the Jewish community taught the scriptures in these assemblies; but priests did not sacrifice animals in the synagogue, since that aspect of worship was limited to the temple in Jerusalem.

The Jewish day extends from sundown to sundown, so the Sabbath begins at sunset Friday and continues until sunset Saturday. Since the law of Moses forbids work to be done on the Sabbath, and since healing was considered work, the people in Mark 1:32 show religious piety by waiting until after sunset on the Sabbath (see 1:21, 29) to bring their sick and demon-possessed to Jesus.

Mark 1:35–45: "If you choose, you can make me clean"

The hectic nature of Jesus' life, caused by his rapidly increasing popularity as described in 1:33, causes him to seek a place of solitude to pray. (Mark mentions Jesus praying only three times: 1:35; 6:46; 14:32–34. Each time he is alone and seeking guidance from God.)

Leprosy in Jesus' time was dreaded much as AIDS was in the 1980s. People did not know its cause, so they restricted lepers from associating with healthy people. The following Old Testament law provides a graphic description of their ostracism:

> The person who has the leprous disease shall wear torn clothes and let the hair of his head be disheveled; and he shall cover his upper lip and cry, "Unclean, unclean." . . . He is unclean. He shall live alone; his dwelling shall be outside the camp. (Lev. 13:45–46)

Living outside of town, often in colonies, people with true leprosy—not one of the various skin diseases sometimes mistakenly diagnosed as leprosy—faced a hideous degeneration of skin and nerves that led to certain death. They had no hope.

1. What risks does the leper take by approaching Jesus?
2. What risks does Jesus take in touching the leper?
3. Why does Jesus send him to the priest? (Leviticus 14:1–32 gives the procedure accomplished by the priest.)

By disobeying Jesus' command of silence (1:44–45), the leper negatively affects Jesus' ministry. The result is like a reversal of roles between the two. Whereas prior to his healing the leper was forced to remain outside populated areas, his proclamation of the healing results in Jesus being forced to remain out in the country.

Mark 2:1–12: "Son, your sins are forgiven"

After leaving Capernaum (1:21, 35–39), Jesus returns in 2:1 and again attracts a large crowd. The Greek text of 2:1 reads, "He is in the house," perhaps indicating the house of Simon and Andrew, since Jesus' prior ministry took place there. Many Galilean homes had an outside access to the roof, where family members dried food in the sun and slept during hot weather. Roof construction generally consisted of thick clay on reed mats and branches supported by ceiling beams.

1. In musical terms, how does 2:1–12 function like a crescendo to the emphasis on Jesus' authority that Mark presents throughout 1:16–2:12?
2. How does this revelation of Jesus' authority bring him into conflict with the scribes?

SCRIBES, AUTHORITY, AND THE SON OF MAN

Scribes in first-century Judea played an important role in Jewish theological matters. Historically, the importance of scribes as theologians dates back to the Babylonian exile (597–539 B.C.E.), when an increased emphasis on studying written texts made desirable the development of a scholar class of men devoted to teaching the law of Moses. Ezra (ca. 458 B.C.E.), who was both a priest and a highly educated scribe, was one of the main figures in the genesis of this scholar class, whose members increasingly gained a high degree of respectability in Jewish society. Since the law of Moses addresses matters pertaining to many areas of life, scribes were called on to decide on everyday issues as well as more overtly theological matters. People gave them considerable respect, as may be seen, for example, in ref-

Personal Reflection
Imagine being banned from everything normally associated with giving meaning to a person's life: family, friends, work, society as a whole. You must wear ragged clothes and sloppy hair, and every time healthy people approach, you must warn them that you are unclean. What effect would this have on you? What kind of self-image might a leper have? What possible evidence of this do you see in the leper's statement to Jesus in 1:40?

Houses beside the ruins of ancient Jericho. Note the flat rooftops and simple construction.

erences to their having seats of honor at banquets (Mark 12:38–39). This probably explains why the scribes are "seated" in 2:6.

To become a scribe, one had to undergo a lengthy educational process involving extensive study under a particular teacher. When the pupil learned his master's teaching, the teacher would lay hands on him and ordain him for his career. At this point he was deemed worthy to discuss Mosaic law on his own and was called a scribe, a title of respect. Because a variety of Jewish groups existed in the first century, scribes represented different theological positions (Pharisees, Sadducees, and so forth). But on some things they would all agree, and one of these was the belief that God alone had authority to forgive sins. Hence, the scribes in Mark 2:6–7 are understandably shocked and offended when Jesus forgives the sins of the paralytic.

Jesus uses the situation to prove that he has authority to forgive sins, referring to himself as the "Son of Man" (2:10). This is the first occurrence of "Son of Man" in Mark's Gospel, and without exception this title is used only by Jesus himself. The history of the use of this title has instigated considerable scholarly investigation, with an impressive number of pages written on it.[6] Prior to Jesus' time, in Jewish literature the title "son of man" occurs in an eschatological context only in Daniel 7; 4 Ezra 13:1–4; and *1 Enoch* 37—71.[7] At other times in the Old Testament, especially in Ezekiel, the expression "son of man" is merely an alternate way of saying "human being." Therefore, the title has sufficient ambiguity to allow for different interpretations when used by Jesus. People could wonder if he was using a humble expression equivalent to "human being" or an exalted title indicating a heavenly figure of great power and authority.

In Mark 2:10, "Son of Man" seems to have an eschatological meaning, for in the preceding narrative Jesus is the Son of God (1:1), whom his prophetic forerunner, John the Baptist, proclaimed would be the mighty one who comes to baptize with the Holy Spirit (1:8). Also, that Jesus connects "Son of Man" with authority to forgive sins seems to indicate he is using the phrase as more than a mere designation of his humanity. In a veiled way that fits with the secret messiah concept in the Gospel of Mark, documented in 1901 by W. Wrede,[8] Jesus reveals his splendor without making an overt claim to be Messiah.

For those who want to see Jesus' messianic identity, the grandeur associated with the title "Son of Man" is available from the Jewish apocalyptic tradition, even though no one understanding of this title dominated in apocalyptic literature.[9] Jesus' claim to have authority "on earth" to forgive sins suggests an authoritative role for the Son of Man that fits nicely with the imagery used in Daniel 7 and *1 Enoch* 37—71 of the Son of Man as a glorious figure associated with activities in the heavens. Mark 2:1–12 connects the heavenly Son of Man tradition with Jesus, claiming for him the right to forgive sins.

SUMMARY

This section of Mark's Gospel emphasizes Jesus' power and authority in a variety of realms: calling disciples, teaching, casting out demons, healing, and forgiving sins. Yet it presents a strong theme of secret identity, as Jesus orders the demons not to speak about him, commands the leper not to speak about the cleansing, and so on. Mark's writing style creates the feeling of a sequence of events happening in rapid succession by beginning nearly every sentence with "and," repeatedly implementing the phrase "and immediately," and using many present-tense verbs in the narration. Jesus suddenly appears on the scene, quickly reveals his tremendous authority, and soon comes into opposition with the religious leaders of his people. This opposition rapidly accelerates in the next series of stories.

SECTION THREE: MARK 2:13–3:6: RISING TIDE OF OPPOSITION

Each story in this section focuses on the escalating conflict between Jesus and the Jewish religious leaders, producing an obviously topical arrangement to the material. Note the vague time references at the beginning of each passage:

> "He went out again beside the sea . . . " (2:13)
> "Now John's disciples and the Pharisees were fasting . . . " (2:18)
> "One sabbath he was going through the grainfields . . . " (2:23)
> "Again he entered the synagogue . . . " (3:1)

Mark ordered his narrative not out of precise chronological considerations but in order to draw together a group of conflict stories. In so doing, he was following the lead of other Christian teachers.

We have testimony dating back to the early days of the church that Peter arranged his stories about Jesus in various ways to facilitate the communication of specific points. Papias, a bishop of Hierapolis in Asia Minor from about 125 to 150 C.E., was quite possibly a student of the apostle John when a youth in the first

Putting Yourself in the Story
Although Mark does not comment on the feelings of anyone in the story, our reading of the passage may be enriched by imaginatively placing ourselves into the picture. Implementation of such an approach may cause us to focus on dimensions outside the main intent of the author, so we should use it with care. But often it can bring about a personal dimension that enriches our reading of the text. Consider, for example, the following questions: What word best describes the four men who bring the paralytic to Jesus? What fears would a paralytic face in being hauled up onto the roof? In being lowered before Jesus? (Try to imagine what you would feel if you were the paralytic.) How would you have felt about this interruption if you were in Jesus' place, preaching to an attentive audience? If you were the owner of the house?

Questions like these focus our attention on matters outside Mark's central emphasis on Jesus' authority, but they enable us to identify with the mostly nameless characters in the narrative, such as the leper and the paralytic.

century. Only fragments remain of his five-volume work, *Explanation of the Sayings of the Lord;* but Eusebius, who in 325 C.E. finished the first great history of the church, quotes him:

> This, too, the presbyter [= elder] used to say. "Mark, who had been Peter's interpreter, wrote down carefully, but not in order, all that he remembered of the Lord's sayings and doings. For he had not heard the Lord or been one of His followers, but later, as I said, one of Peter's. Peter used to adapt his teaching to the occasion, without making a systematic arrangement of the Lord's sayings, so that Mark was quite justified in writing down some things just as he remembered them."[10]

The accuracy of Papias's claims is a matter of debate, but he does provide an interesting and early witness to the manner in which Peter and other Christian missionaries adapted the way they told the story of Jesus to fit the needs of their particular audiences. Effective communication requires that speakers consider the situation of their audience before explaining something.

Mark wrote what he deemed important for his audience to hear; and he was apparently a pioneer in blazing a path from the oral to the written gospel. He did not write a biography of Jesus, nor did he arrange his material according to chronological considerations. Exactly when the stories in 2:13–3:6 occurred is not important to him. Mark arranged them topically so that they all address the same issue: the rising tide of opposition from the Pharisees.

Mark 2:13–17: "Why does he eat with tax collectors and sinners?"

In first-century Mediterranean cultures, people normally ate only with others belonging to the same social group. Meals therefore reflected one's social standing, and most people were concerned with the identity of those with whom they shared table fellowship. Few would have looked upon tax collectors as honorable members of society. Men like Levi in 2:14 worked for the hated Roman overlords, collecting tolls on goods being transported through their areas. "In the process, the toll collector would collect as much as he could squeeze from the people over and above what the Romans demanded, then pay his share to the Romans and pocket the rest (Luke 3:13; 19:1–9)."[11]

1. According to Mark 1:16–20 and 2:13–15, Jesus relates socially with fishermen, as well as with tax collectors and other questionable people simply designated "sinners." What problems does this pose for the Pharisees?

Personal Reflection
*Would you invite folks like Levi
and his tax-collecting friends to
your home? What would your
friends and neighbors think if
they saw you going to the house
of a tax collector for dinner?*

In recent decades, both Jewish and Christian scholars have devoted considerable effort to studying the origin and beliefs of the *Pharisees.* A much broader picture of the Pharisees emerges when we do not limit our studies to the predominantly negative portrait of this group presented in the Gospels. In the Gospels, the Pharisees are opponents of Jesus, so naturally the stories do not focus on admirable characteristics of this Jewish movement. The positive aspects come into focus primarily as we investigate the writings of the rabbis, who were the successors of the Pharisees.

The Mishnah, the compiled traditions of Pharisaic teachers, edited into final form around 200 C.E. by Rabbi Judah, contains some stories about Pharisees of Jesus' time. Jacob Neusner has led the way in subjecting these stories to critical scrutiny, but even he allows that some of them reflect first-century Pharisaism. The Pharisees in these accounts are the heroes, not the villains as they usually are in the Gospels. In addition, the Jewish historian Josephus, who late in life claimed to belong to the Pharisees, records valuable information about them.[12]

Although scholars continue to debate over many details, there is widespread agreement on the following description of the Pharisees of Jesus' time. Most likely the name Pharisees comes from the Hebrew word *perushim,* which means "separated ones." This title quite probably came initially from their opponents, who called them "separatists," but by Jesus' time the name was accepted as the common designation for the group. In an attempt to remain in a constant state of purity before God, they sought to apply to everyday life the Mosaic laws pertaining to the cleansing ceremonies that priests performed prior to offering sacrifices to the Lord. The Pharisees were very concerned with proper religious observance in matters of fasting (Mark 2:18), Sabbath observance (2:23–3:6), and purity regulations, extending to the way in which food was prepared and eaten (7:1–13). They were careful to tithe all their food, even down to their table spices (Matt. 23:23).

Not wanting to risk incurring God's displeasure by eating untithed or improperly purified food, members of this movement avoided eating with non-Pharisees. Consequently, tension existed between many in the Pharisaic movement and those who chose not to maintain all the purity laws the Pharisees practiced. Some Pharisees looked with disdain on such people, calling them *'am ha-aretz,* a Hebrew expression meaning "people of the land." Later rabbinic literature reveals substantial tension between such common people and the successors of the Pharisees:

> R. Hillel said, "No *'am ha-aretz* is religious." R. Akiba [ca. 132 C.E.] said, "When I was an *'am ha-aretz* I used to say, 'If I could get hold of one of the scholars I would bite him like an ass.' 'You mean, like a dog,' said his disciples. 'No,' said Akiba, 'an ass's bite breaks bones.' "[13]

Anyone who has spent time around livestock on a farm or ranch readily understands Akiba's reference to a donkey's bite. This humorous comment helps clarify some of the seriousness of the situation described in Mark 2:13–17. Jesus ignores the Pharisaic practice of segregated table fellowship. He eats with impure people who refuse to regulate their lives according to the standards of the Pharisees.[14] Indeed, Jesus shares a meal with people despised even by most *'am ha-aretz:* the tax collectors.

1. How does Jesus' agenda for ministry in 2:17 differ fundamentally from that of the Pharisees?

The careful composition of Mark's Gospel becomes apparent when we compare 2:13–17 with 2:1–12. In 2:5, Jesus says to a man who is obviously sick, "Your sins are forgiven," so one might think a connection exists between the man's paralysis and his sinfulness. In 2:13–17, however, when Jesus eats with people who are extremely sinful but not physically ill ("tax collectors and sinners"), he calls them sick and refers to himself as a doctor (2:17). We may diagram it as follows:

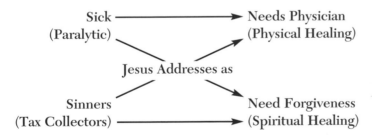

Mark apparently arranged these two stories so as to demonstrate Jesus' authority in both the physical realm, over sickness, and the spiritual realm, over sin. His power to heal physical infirmity becomes a validation of his power to heal those paralyzed by sin. The sequence of events is striking: Jesus cleanses the leper (1:40–45); then he heals the paralytic and forgives his sins (2:1–12); and then he associates with sinners to cleanse them and bring spiritual wholeness (2:13–17).

Mark 2:18–22: New Wine Needs New Wineskins

1. The Pharisees regularly fasted on Monday and Thursday (Didache 8:1),[15] and evidently John the Baptist and his followers also fasted as a religious discipline. The fact that Jesus and his disciples did not fast would certainly raise questions. What does Jesus' answer in 2:19–22 reveal about how he views his ministry over against that of the Pharisees?

Mark 2:23–27: Lord of the Sabbath

The intensity of the Pharisees' accusations increases in this passage, as the focus of controversy centers on *Sabbath observance.* Exodus 20:8–11; 31:12–17 and Numbers 15:32–36 vividly reveal the seriousness of breaking the Sabbath, yet Deuteronomy 23:24–25 shows that eating fruit or grain from a neighbor's field was acceptable behavior. The late-second-century Mishnah *Shabbath* 7.2 lists thirty-nine activities considered to be work and therefore illegal to perform on the Sabbath. Among these are "sowing, ploughing, reaping, . . . grinding, sifting, baking, . . . writing two letters, . . . lighting a fire. . . . "[16] And a much later commentary on this law specifies picking grain as reaping (Jerusalem Talmud, *Shabbath* 7.2, 9c). Given the Pharisees' question in Mark 2:24, it is probable that they held a similar view of "reaping" during the first century.

1. In your opinion, were Jesus' disciples doing something illegal according to Mosaic law (Exod. 31:12–17) or simply illegal according to the Pharisees' oral tradition?
2. To answer their question, Jesus refers to the story of David in 1 Samuel 21:1–6. What main point does Jesus make by using this story?[17]

Mark 3:1–6: "Is it lawful to do good . . . on the sabbath?"

1. How would you contrast Jesus' attitude toward the handicapped man with the Pharisees' attitude?

Mishnah *Yoma* 8.6 specifies concerning *medical attention on the Sabbath:* "If a man has a pain in his throat they may drop medicine into his mouth on the Sabbath, since there is doubt whether life is in danger, and whenever there is doubt whether life is in danger this overrides the Sabbath."[18] Evidently the Pharisees in Mark 3:1–6 held a similar view that medical attention on the Sabbath for illness other than life-threatening situations was illegal. The man's shriveled hand posed no danger to life; Jesus could have waited until the next day to heal it.

2. The Herodians were people who backed the political endeavors of Herod Antipas, and Mark 12:13 shows that they were loyal to the Roman Empire that stood behind Herod's power. The Pharisees detested Herod, who was an agent of Rome, and would not generally associate with his supporters. What does the Pharisees' action in 3:6 reveal about their true answer to Jesus' question in 3:4?

3. How does 3:1–6 bring to a conclusion the series of stories beginning with 2:1–12? What is the central point of this section?

Retrospect on the Meaning of Living for God

1. Summarize the main areas of conflict between Jesus and the Pharisees according to this section in Mark's Gospel.

2. Fundamentally, how does Jesus' approach to living for God seem to differ from theirs? On what premises is each approach based?

SECTION FOUR: MARK 3:7–4:34: SPEAKING IN PARABLES

Mark 3:7–12: "You are the Son of God!"

Note on a map the different locations from which people come to listen to Jesus (3:8). His popularity continues to grow in spite of his ongoing commands for secrecy (3:12).

1. How does the need for having a boat ready (3:9) compare with conditions faced by rock musicians in a crowd of fans at a concert?

Mark 3:13–19: He Gave Them Authority

1. How do the tasks Jesus gives to his chosen disciples compare with his own ministry?

2. What possible reason might he have had for choosing twelve, the number of the tribes of Israel? (Cf. 2:19–22.)

Mark 3:20–35: Blasphemy against the Holy Spirit

1. What different evaluations of Jesus do people make in this passage?

2. Why do Jesus' family members react as they do?

The official delegation of scribes sent from Jerusalem to investigate this popular Galilean miracle worker concludes that Jesus is leading the people astray, for he represents Satan, not God. Satan (3:23) is synonymous with Beelzebul (3:22). The reading Beelzebub, found in some ancient manuscripts, probably resulted from Christian scribes assimilating this text to 2 Kings 1:2, where Baal-zebub meant "lord of flies," a derogatory reference to the god Baalzebul, whose name probably meant

Personal Reflection

How would you respond if your family concluded that your religious zeal was a sign of insanity? How would you respond if you had a famous son whose religious zeal caused him to associate with questionable people, break social codes, and be so busy with his ministry that sometimes it negatively affected his health?

Christians sometimes struggle with the meaning of the unforgivable sin of blasphemy *against the Holy Spirit (3:28–30). For some, the possibility that they have committed this sin produces turmoil and uncertainty. Practically speaking, this concern is unfortunate. If people are concerned, this is a sure sign that they need not worry. In the story, Jesus' opponents observe Jesus' miracles but refuse to believe that his power comes from God. They are mired in willful disbelief, attributing the works of God to Satan. Their assurance that they possess the correct beliefs about God closes them off to seeing God's work in the ministry of Jesus. This obstinate resistance is equated with blasphemy against the Holy Spirit.*

Jesus' assertion that they "can never have forgiveness" but are "guilty of an eternal sin" is somewhat like 9:47: "If your eye causes you to stumble, tear it out." Such strong, unequivocal statements are designed to stress the seriousness of the matter under consideration. They are not meant to be understood literally, *but they are to be taken seriously.*

"lord of heaven." Beelzebul does not appear in any other Jewish writings, but its meaning in this particular context seems clearly to be "ruler of the demons" (3:22).[19]

3. What does Jesus' response to the scribes in 3:23–29 reveal about how he views his ministry? What does his power to plunder Satan's house reveal about the encounter with the devil in 1:12–13?
4. Notice that Jesus uses family terms in 3:34–35 to describe the kingdom of God that he is establishing. What does this response to his family's request to see him (remember their earlier questioning of his sanity in 3:21) indicate about Jesus' understanding of his ministry?

Mark 4:1–20: Who Has Ears to Hear?

Jesus' tremendous popularity continues (compare the boat in 4:1 with the one reserved for emergency in 3:9). Imagine that you are part of the crowd. You have walked for two days to listen to this Galilean teacher who speaks and acts with great authority (pick a location from 3:8). You are sitting in the midst of a great crowd of people (visualize the setting by the lake, and imagine the sounds and smells). At last, Jesus begins to teach (how much volume would he need to be heard by everyone?).

He begins his words with "Listen!" and ends with "Let anyone with ears to hear listen!" Read what he says in 4:3–9 as if hearing it for the first time. Now sit back and ask yourself,

1. "What did I hear?
2. What different ways might people in that crowd respond to what they heard? Why?

The scene of 4:10–20 apparently takes place later on, when Jesus is out of the boat and in a different location. The ambiguity of his parable of the seed and sower causes some of his confused followers to approach him for an explanation. Unexpectedly, however, Jesus tells them in 4:11 that they already have the *secret of the kingdom of God.* The secret of the kingdom in this context seems to involve responding positively to Jesus, even when you cannot make complete sense out of his teaching.

By itself, the parable (4:3–8) has no discernible application, so the listeners face a decision: They can give it their own meaning; or they can conclude that walking all that way to listen to Jesus was a waste of time; or they can approach him and say something like "I do not understand what you mean, but I am convinced that your words are important; and so I trust you and want to know what you are teaching." Mark 4:11 says nothing to indicate that the secret of the kingdom involves understanding Jesus' teaching. And the answer to his question of how the disciples will "understand all the parables" (4:13) is simply this: Come to Jesus and ask.[20]

1. What does "kingdom of God" seem to mean in this context? (Cf. 1:15; 3:34–35.)
2. Jesus' adaptation of Isaiah 6:9–10 in Mark 4:12 seems to indicate that he does not want people to be forgiven, but this is another example of prophetic overstatement, as in 3:29. What does this comment reveal about Jesus' reason for teaching in parables, as presented in the Gospel of Mark?

Remember that the preceding stories in 3:1–35 involve conflict with those who misjudge Jesus and assert false things about him. These "outsiders" do not understand Jesus, nor do they respond to his message and repent. His parables, therefore, like the title "Son of Man," are ambiguous pointers to his secret identity. Only those who respond in faith are part of the kingdom.

3. What does Jesus' explanation in 4:14–20 reveal about the purpose of the parable?

Mark 4:21–34: What Is the Kingdom of God Like?

1. Lest we conclude from Mark 4:11–12 that Jesus does not want people to understand what he says, Mark adds the parable of the lamp in 4:21–22. What "light" does this parable shed on the problem of understanding Jesus' "dark" sayings? What is Jesus' reason for hiding things?
2. What further insight into the relationship between responding to Jesus and understanding his teaching does 4:24–25 give?
3. What is the point of 4:26–29 in this context? (The farmer does not understand the processes of seed growth. What is his job?)
4. What is the central focus of the parable in 4:30–32? Why is it significant in this context when considering Jesus' ministry and the growing kingdom of God?
5. Mark 4:33–34 shows that Mark was very selective in which parables he included in this section. What does this passage reveal about Jesus' method of teaching in parables and its effect on his audience? (Note: The Greek text of 4:33 reads "as they were able to hear" [*akouein,* as in the NRSV], not "understand" [as in the NIV].)

TOPICALLY ARRANGED MATERIALS

Notice that the time reference in 4:1 is again deliberately vague (compare 4:21, 26, 30). Mark carefully orders his narrative in a topical, not chronological, manner. One cannot tell from the story if the parables in 4:21–34 were spoken to the crowd or only

What Kind of Soil Are You?
The people in this story believe they are listening *to a parable when, in fact, they are the parable. Scattered over that hillside are various kinds of soil. The seed (word) judges the quality of each soil by the harvest it produces. People respond differently to the same seed and are judged by their response. Those who are the good soil respond in faith and come to seek more information from Jesus.*

With which kind of soil do you most identify? Since the goal of the parable is tied with getting people into the fruit-bearing category, what do you need to do to end up in the "hundredfold" group?

to the disciples who approach Jesus in 4:10 and privately hear 4:11–20. Mark communicates theologically important details about Jesus and his ministry (preaches to his readers) by arranging his material topically, in this case into a parable collection.[21]

Reflection on Terrifying Experiences

What is the most terrifying experience you have ever had? What was foremost in your mind during this experience? How has this experience changed the way you view the world? What did you learn about yourself as a result?

SECTION FIVE: MARK 4:35–6:29: MIRACLES AND FAITH

Mark 4:35–41: "Why are you afraid? Have you still no faith?"

1. What contrast does this story draw between Jesus' response to the crisis and the way his disciples react? Between fear and faith?
2. What does the disciples' amazed response in 4:41 indicate about their understanding of Jesus? (Remember that these men were among those whom Jesus said already possessed the secret of the kingdom, in 4:11.)

In this story Jesus treats the sea and the raging storm as a demonic force. After the disciples' accusation that he does not care about their lives, in 4:39 he *rebukes* the wind (the Greek verb *epitiman* is used elsewhere when Jesus rebukes demons: 1:25; 3:12; and 9:25) and says to the sea, "Be silent, be muzzled!" (*siopa, pephimoso,* 4:39; cf. 1:25). Interestingly, the next story concerns Jesus exercising power over demonic forces. He truly was victorious in Mark 1:13.[22]

Mark 5:1–20: "Howling and bruising himself with stones"

1. Once on the eastern side of the Sea of Galilee, Jesus encounters a man with amazing powers. What effects does demonic possession have on the wild man from the tombs?

Jews considered *tombs* to be defiling (Num. 9:6–7; 19:11–16), so this adds to the bleakness of the portrait. Romans, however, viewed a *necropolis* (= graveyard or "city of the dead"; *necros* means "dead," *polis* means "city") as a sacred place. On special occasions, Roman families would hold banquets by the tombs of their ancestors as a way of honoring them. They customarily left food for their dead, and some of their tombs actually have food tubes going down into them from the ground surface. The Gentiles listening to Mark's Gospel would probably think the demoniac lived among the tombs because he could readily find food there.

2. What similarities are there between the way Jesus addresses the demons in this story and the way he stilled the storm in 4:35–41?[23]
3. Thus far in Mark, who recognizes Jesus' identity as Son of God?

28

Jews view the *pig* as an unclean animal, for Leviticus 11:7 forbids the eating of pork. Consequently, pigs became a symbol of something low and despicable in Jewish society, although Greeks and Romans considered them a good food source. Jews listening to the story would think it only fitting that the unclean demons would seek to go into the unclean swine. But the loss of two thousand pigs would seriously degrade the local economy of this section of the Decapolis, a predominantly Gentile region.

4. How do the local people respond to Jesus when they see that the wild man is liberated from the demonic chains that bound him and made him a menace to society?

Notice that instead of commanding silence, as he did after healing people in Galilee, Jesus tells the demoniac to proclaim what has happened to him, and the man declares it throughout the Decapolis (5:19–20). This striking reversal is not without effect in Mark's narrative. When Jesus returns to the east side of the Sea of Galilee later on (7:31–37), his reception differs substantially from the way in which the residents now want to get rid of him as a menace to their economy.

Mark 5:21–43: "Do not fear, only believe"

This passage clearly illustrates one of Mark's narrative techniques: *intercalation* (the inclusion of a parallel story within another story). Through this method, Mark reveals similarities between two events and often uses one as a commentary on the other.

1. Here we have the stories of two women. What similarities do you find between these two? What are some striking differences?
2. How do the helpless situations the women face resemble what the demoniac endured in the previous passage?
3. Compared with previous miracles, what is unique about the way in which the woman is healed in 5:25–34?
4. Although Mark does not comment on this, how might Jairus have felt while the events of 5:25–35 transpired? (Especially note 5:33, " . . . told him the whole truth.") How might Jairus have felt toward the woman and the crowd when the news of his daughter's death came in 5:35?
5. Remember the juxtaposition of "fear" and "faith" in 4:40: "Why are you afraid? Have you still no faith?" How are fear and faith once again contrasted in 5:32–36?

Note that, after commanding the demoniac to proclaim his deliverance in 5:19–20, Jesus now returns to his insistence on secrecy in 5:37–43.

"My name is Legion; for we are many"
Consider the pathetic condition of the demoniac (5:2–5). Note that the man does not even have a name—he is merely Legion, controlled by hostile forces. He has no sense of personal identity. What powers today enslave people and obliterate their humanity?

Picture yourself in a situation like that of the people in 5:14–17, where your possessions are in conflict with the well-being of a single human being. Which do you value the most? Why?

29

Mark 6:1–6: "Is not this the carpenter?"

1. Why do people in Jesus' hometown have difficulty with him?
2. What effect does their lack of faith have on his ability to do miracles?

In Mark's Gospel, there is a relationship between having faith and seeing Jesus do signs of the kingdom of God. Those who have faith see the miraculous; those who do not believe are "outsiders" and do not experience Jesus' power.

Although Mark mentions Jesus' mother, brothers, and sisters, he says nothing of his father, Joseph. This could be either an indication that Joseph was not living at this time or Mark's way of saying that Jesus had no earthly father. But the major point of the narrative remains clear: People in his hometown do not recognize his accomplishments. To say "son of Mary" (6:3) instead of "son of Joseph" indeed may have been a derogatory statement; Jews normally indicated a man's identity with reference to his father, even after the father was dead. This may be, therefore, a veiled reference to a belief that Jesus was illegitimate.[24]

Mark 6:7–13: Take Nothing Except a Staff

Having appointed his twelve apostles in 3:13–15, Jesus now sends them out in pairs to perform some of the same types of ministry he has been conducting. The account of the sending out of the apostles on their mission (6:7–13) and their return (6:30–44) is interrupted by the story of John the Baptist's death (6:14–29). This is yet another instance of intercalation whose significance we will consider.

1. Note carefully Jesus' instructions to the Twelve in 6:7–11. How will following these directions give them an opportunity to apply what they have been learning about faith?
2. "Staff" (Greek, *rhabdon*) in 6:8 may refer either to a walking stick or to a staff used by shepherds to tend their sheep. If Mark means for us to understand *rhabdon* as a shepherd's staff, why would Jesus give such an implement to fishermen and tax collectors? (Note Jesus' response in 6:34: "He had compassion on them, because they were like sheep without a shepherd.")[25]

Pharisaic scribes considered the dust of foreign lands defiling, so they and their followers carefully removed such dust before returning home. For the Twelve to shake dust off their feet was to pronounce judgment on those who refused to heed their

Hometown Identity

Whereas crowds of people elsewhere flock to hear him, residents of Nazareth cannot accept the change. Perhaps you have experienced something like this when you return to your parents' home for vacations or holidays. How do you feel when people in your hometown are seemingly oblivious to your adult accomplishments?

proclamation. It was equivalent to pronouncing these people unclean and rejected.

Mark 6:14–29: "He . . . brought his head on a platter"

Jesus' popularity made him known to *Herod Antipas,* tetrarch of Galilee from 4 B.C.E. to 39 C.E. According to Josephus, Herod built a city for himself by the Sea of Galilee and named it Tiberias, to honor the Roman emperor Tiberias. Since the site of the city included an old graveyard and tombs had to be removed during the construction, Jewish people faithful to the law of Moses refused to live there, lest they be rendered unclean according to Numbers 19:11 (Josephus, *Antiquities* 18.2.3 [§§36–38]). Herod's wife, Herodias, relentlessly urged him to seek the title "king," although Augustus Caesar had formerly refused to grant him this honor. Against his better judgment, he finally requested the title again, which resulted in his dismissal from office and exile from the country (*Antiquities* 18.7.1–2 [§§240–56]). Mark's use of "king" in 6:14 may therefore be sarcastic (cf. Matt. 14:1 and Luke 3:19, where the correct title "tetrarch" is used).

1. What do the speculations on the identity of Jesus put forward by people in 6:14–15 reveal about their understandings of the significance of his ministry?
2. Herod experiences ambivalent feelings toward John. On the one hand, he arrests John for criticizing his actions; on the other hand, he listens intently to the Baptist and protects him from death. What is the real reason Herod finally executes John?
3. What does the story reveal about Herod's character as a leader (ethics versus expedience)?
4. Given the circumstances surrounding John's death, what psychological factor might have caused Herod to conclude that Jesus was John the Baptist resurrected?

In Mark's Gospel, some aspects of Jesus' ministry parallel John's. His message of repentance (1:15) reflects John's preaching (1:4), and his execution at the hands of a Roman official who knew he was innocent (15:10, 14–15) resembles John's execution by Herod (6:20, 26–28). Thus it appears that Mark places the story of John's death between the sending out of the apostles and their triumphant return in order to foreshadow the coming death of Jesus and its implications for discipleship. Like Jesus, the Twelve exercise power over the domain of Satan (6:13), but behind the scenes stands the specter of death. Discipleship in this world involves suffering and death. It is not all victory, even for God's own Son.

A Different Account of John's Death

Josephus also comments on the death of John the Baptist. In a description of how the army of Herod the Tetrarch suffered defeat he says:

> Now, some of the Jews thought that the destruction of Herod's army came from God, and that very justly, as a punishment of what he did against John, that was called the Baptist; for Herod slew him, who was a good man, and commanded the Jews to exercise virtue, both as to righteousness towards one another, and piety towards God, and so to come to baptism; for that the washing [with water] would be acceptable to him, if they made use of it, not in order to the putting away [or the remission] of some sins [only], but for the purification of the body; supposing still that the soul was thoroughly purified beforehand by righteousness. Now, when [many] others came to crowd about him, for they were greatly moved [or pleased] by hearing his words, Herod, who feared lest the great influence John had over the people might put it into his power an inclination to raise a rebellion (for they seemed ready to do anything he should advise), thought it best, by putting him to death, to prevent any mischief he might cause, and not bring himself into difficulties, by sparing a man who might make him repent of it when it should be too late. Accordingly he was sent a prisoner, out of Herod's suspicious temper, to Macherus, the castle I before mentioned, and was there put to death. Now the Jews had an opinion that the destruction of this army was sent as a punishment upon Herod, and a mark of God's displeasure against him. (*Antiquities* 18.5.2 [§§116–19])

1. What are the similarities and differences between this account of John's death and the one found in Mark 6:14–29?

SECTION SIX: MARK 6:30–8:21: THE SCOPE OF THE KINGDOM WIDENS
Mark 6:30–44: "Like sheep without a shepherd"

When the apostles return,[26] Jesus compassionately seeks to take them away so that they can rest, but a persistent crowd thwarts the plan (cf. 6:31 and 3:20 with respect to inability to eat because of the people).

1. How does the apostles' perception of how to meet the needs of these people differ from Jesus'?
2. The command in 6:37, "You give them something to eat," seems audacious. Yet remember that understanding Jesus is not as im-

Fear and Faith

A substantial emphasis on faith exists in the stories comprising this section. To experience the power of Jesus and appreciate his greatness, one must respond in faith to him and to his message. Failure to do so results in relegation to a position "outside" the kingdom of God that Jesus proclaims.

With whom in this section do you most identify? Why?

portant sometimes as taking him seriously and seeking more information, as his followers did after the parable of the sower in 4:10–11. In light of 6:7, 12–13, how should they have responded?
3. What does this story reveal about Jesus' attitude toward people?

The reference in 6:34, "they were like sheep without a shepherd," may allude to Numbers 27:17, which describes the appointment of Joshua as leader to replace Moses, "that the congregation of the LORD may not be like sheep without a shepherd." There may also be an allusion to Ezekiel 34:1–7, a condemnation of evil shepherds of Israel (= the rulers of the people) who feed themselves but do not take care of the sheep (general Jewish populace): "Ah, you shepherds of Israel who have been feeding yourselves! Should not shepherds feed the sheep?" (Ezek. 34:2). To be good shepherds (Mark 6:8, 34), the apostles need to place the needs of people above their own.

Mark 6:45–52: "He intended to pass them by"

1. After the hectic events of this day, what would be the physical and emotional condition of the Twelve when Jesus comes walking on the water? (The "fourth watch of the night" [6:48] was just prior to dawn; hence the NRSV's "early in the morning." Mark 13:35 lists the four Roman watches: evening, midnight, cockcrow, and dawn. See H. Kosmala, "The Time of the Cock-Crow," *Annual of the Swedish Theological Institute* 2, 1963, 118–20. The fourth watch is from 3:00 to 6:00 A.M.)
2. Evidently to reveal further his power, Jesus means to walk past them (6:48). But the exhausted disciples think he is a ghost. How do his words of assurance in 6:50 reflect the theme of fear and faith we have seen in previous stories?
3. The concluding statement of this story, "for they did not understand about the loaves, but their hearts were hardened" (6:52), is very puzzling. Cover up verse 52 for a moment and read the story to that point. What would you anticipate that Mark would say in this concluding, explanatory statement?

The apostles' failure to recognize Jesus is connected to their failure to understand the loaves, and Mark asserts that their hearts were hardened. He evidently wants us to see that the Twelve should have been expecting the miraculous by now, and their failure to respond appropriately resulted in a condition of hardened heart.

4. When Jesus told the Twelve to feed the five thousand, instead of responding sarcastically, what response should they have given to Jesus?

Fighting Fatigue
Put yourself in the place of the apostles, returning weary from a journey filled with ministry to needy people, only to have your planned rest thwarted by the presence of a hungry crowd. How might you react?

Mark 6:53–56: Weren't They Headed for Bethsaida?

Although the disciples set out for Bethsaida (6:45), they end up in Gennesaret (6:53).[27] The overwhelmingly positive response of the townspeople there differs greatly from that which Jesus received in his hometown.

1. What does this story reveal about the role of faith in the success of Jesus' work? (Cf. 6:56 with 6:5.)

Mark 7:1–23: The Traditions of the Elders

The scribes from Jerusalem probably comprise an official delegation sent to examine Jesus for heresy (cf. 3:22).

1. What does Mark's editorial comment in 7:3–4 reveal about the practices of the Pharisees concerning ritual purity?
2. If Mark believes his readers need this information to understand the significance of the Pharisees' accusation, what does this indicate about who comprises his audience?
3. How does Jesus' accusation against the Pharisees differ from theirs against his disciples?

Corban means "a gift devoted to God." Although Deuteronomy 21:18–21 specifies the death penalty for rebellious sons who refuse to obey and thereby dishonor their parents (see also Deut. 27:16), the oral tradition of the Pharisees provided a loophole for getting around caring for one's parents. Placing a gift under corban devoted it to God and removed it from secular use by anyone else.

The Meaning of Sin
When you think of sinfulness, is your concept one of internal defilement, or is it one of external defilement by contact with unclean things?
What effect does your concept of sin have on the way you approach living for God?

In the hypothetical situation proposed by Jesus, if the son declared his property *qorban* to his parents, he neither promised it to the Temple nor prohibited its use to himself, but he legally excluded his parents from the right of benefit. Should the son regret his action and seek to alleviate the harsh vow which would deprive his parents of all of the help they might normally expect from him, he would be told by the scribes to whose arbitration the case was submitted that his vow was valid and must be honored.[28]

4. How does Jesus' understanding of "uncleanness" in 7:15–23 contrast with the Pharisees' view?[29]

Mark 7:24–30: "It is not fair to take the children's food and throw it to the dogs"

Jesus travels to Tyre, seemingly to escape the demands placed on him by the crowds of people. But he cannot remain hidden. A woman, who Mark 7:26 stresses was a Gentile, finds him and begs him to heal her daughter. You should know that the term *dogs* in 7:27 means "little dogs" (*kunarioi*) and probably refers to household dogs that were allowed around the table to eat scraps. These differed from the semiwild dogs that scavenged around the walls of a city.

1. What is unusual about Jesus' response to the woman's request?
2. How does she respond to his harsh-sounding comment about Gentiles?
3. How does her response to Jesus differ from that of the religious leaders in the previous story? From that of the disciples in 7:17–18?

This story of an understanding Gentile woman plays an important transitional role between the two miraculous feedings in Mark's narrative.

4. After the feeding of the five thousand (6:30–44), the Pharisees reject Jesus in a dispute over purification laws (7:1–23). How does the editorial comment in 7:19, "Thus he declared all foods clean," prepare the way for the story of the Syrophoenician woman, whose daughter Jesus cleanses from an unclean spirit?
5. When chided about taking food from the children, the woman's answer might (in Mark's narrative) hark back to the crumbs gathered after the feeding of the five thousand. If the children (Jews) have been fed and baskets of crumbs were left over, what is Mark saying about the Gentiles?

Mark 7:31–37: "He spat and touched his tongue"

On a map, trace Jesus' journey on the circuitous route north from Tyre to Sidon, east and then south along the east side of the Sea of Galilee, until he reached the Decapolis, where he previously healed the Gerasene demoniac (see 5:1, 20).

1. How does his reception this time differ from the one he received when he was last in this region? (Yet notice that, unlike 5:19–20, Jesus here returns to his normal policy of secrecy [7:33, 36].)
2. Compared to previous miracles in Mark, what is different about Jesus' method of healing the man in this story?

Mark 8:1–10: Seven Baskets Full of Leftovers

1. How is this miraculous feeding similar to the previous one in 6:34–44?
2. List the ways in which the two feedings are different.
3. How is the response by the Twelve in 8:4–5 different from that in 6:37–38?

One clue as to the significance of the differences between the feedings lies in the two words employed for the "baskets" used to collect the leftovers. In 6:43 the disciples use *kophinoi,* small Jewish traveling baskets used to carry personal provisions. They were so commonly carried by Jews that Gentiles associated Jews and their baskets (Juvenal, *Satires* 3.14; 6.542). In Mark 8:8, however, the type of basket used for gathering the leftovers is a *spuris,* a large Gentile basket of the type later used to lower Paul over the wall of Damascus (Acts 9:25). The geographical change from Galilee to the Decapolis for the second feeding is matched by changes in detail in the second account: bare ground instead of green grass, and no small companies.

4. In Mark's account it appears that Jesus fed the Jews (6:34–44), and crumbs were gathered from the surplus (6:43), and the Gentile woman requested crumbs (7:28). What is Mark saying about Jesus' ministry?

Mark 8:11–21: "Do you not yet understand?"

The Pharisees' request for a sign in 8:11 may seem ridiculous, coming immediately after the miraculous feeding of four thousand people; but they are seeking a sign from heaven that will show conclusively that Jesus' powers truly come from God. Jesus' refusal to do a sign for those who exhibit no faith is consistent with the narrative so far.

1. While the disciples discuss the fact that they forgot to bring bread (8:14, 16; as if this should be a problem with Jesus on board!), Jesus directs their attention to issues of faith and life. What things about the Pharisees and Herodians does he want them to avoid?
2. How does the assessment of the disciples' condition in 8:17–18 compare with what you have seen in the previous stories?
3. If there is "one loaf" in the boat (8:14), why does 8:16 say they had "no bread"? Is this Mark's way of saying that Jesus is the one loaf that feeds all, or does he just mean that they did not have enough bread for all of them to eat?
4. By focusing on the number of baskets full of leftover crumbs they collected after each feeding (8:19–21), what does Jesus want the disciples to understand?

SECTION SEVEN: MARK 8:22–10:52: GLORY AND SUFFERING

After the confusion over Jesus' identity in the previous section, in the next passages the disciples finally understand who he is.

But their pre-understanding of "messiah" comes continually into conflict with Jesus' agenda. They understand, but they do not understand.

Mark 8:22–30: The Second Touch

Although the disciples set out for Bethsaida in 6:45, after feeding the five thousand they landed in Gennesaret (6:53). Now, after feeding the four thousand, they finally arrive in Bethsaida in 8:22. The healing of the blind man here is similar to the healing of the deaf and dumb man in 7:32–35, for in both cases Jesus performs physical gestures during the healing.

1. What is unusual about the duration needed for the healing of the blind man (8:23–25)?
2. How does the list of possible identities of Jesus in 8:28 compare with that given in 6:14–16?
3. Reflect on the disciples' understanding of Jesus in the previous stories. Now look at Peter's momentous confession in 8:29. How might the healing of the blind man in 8:22–26 serve as a symbolic representation of Peter? Why does he need a second touch to see clearly?

Peter's confession in 8:29 is an important turning point in the Gospel. After the disciples' clearer insight into Jesus' identity, the scope of his ministry begins to change, and the narrative account rapidly progresses toward his final week in Jerusalem.

Mark 8:31–9:1: "Get behind me, Satan!"

Peter's brief moment of glory, as he understands that Jesus is the Christ (8:29 = Son of Man, 8:31), quickly degenerates into conflict with the one he just proclaimed Messiah.

1. How does Jesus' teaching in 8:31 compare with the disciples' expectations, and how does Peter respond?
2. How does Jesus' explanation of what it means to follow him radically differ from what the disciples would have expected, from both their previous beliefs about the messiah and their previous experiences with Jesus?
3. What does Jesus' statement in 9:1 indicate about the amount of time left in the "present evil age"?

Mark 9:2–13: "This is my beloved Son, listen to him!"

According to tradition, the transfiguration occurred on Mount Tabor; but in Mark's account, Jesus has been in the area of Caesarea Philippi (8:27), which is near Mount Hermon. This

Mount Tabor, traditional site of the transfiguration.

ninety-one-hundred-foot peak is the highest in the vicinity of Palestine, and historically, it is a better choice for the location of the event.

1. How might the transfiguration reinforce the disciples' view of Messiah?
2. How much of the significance of the transfiguration event do they understand?
3. How much do they understand Jesus' words pertaining to his coming death and resurrection? (Note the continuation of the secrecy motif by Jesus in 9:9.)

Peter, James, and John (the same three whom Jesus took with him in 5:37) ask about the scribes' teaching that Elijah must come before the advent of the messiah (9:11–13; see Mal. 4:4–6 and Deut. 18:15–22). Jesus indicates that Elijah has already come.

4. Who was this Elijah who had come?

Mark 9:14–29: "I believe; help my unbelief!"

While Jesus, Peter, James, and John have a "mountaintop experience," the other disciples suffer difficulty below. What they were able to do previously (6:7–13) does not work now. In addition, they are probably no match for the highly educated scribes who have come to debate with them.

1. How does the result of demon possession in the little boy compare with that seen in the account of Legion in 5:1–20?
2. What does 9:22–23 teach about the nature and necessity of faith?

Mark 9:30–37: Who Is the Greatest?

1. Why is the discussion in 9:33–34 so ironic in light of 9:30–32?
2. Why are the disciples hesitant to answer Jesus' question in 9:33–34?
3. How does Jesus redefine for them the meaning of "greatness"?

Mark 9:38–50: "If your eye causes you to stumble, tear it out"

1. Why might John and the others have felt the need to silence the man in 9:38? (Remember 9:18 and 9:33–34.)

Personal Reflection
Have you ever experienced a situation in which you could relate with the tortured cry of the father in 9:24, struggling with the difficulty of believing in spite of a desire to believe?

2. How does Jesus' attitude toward the man differ from John's?

The "little ones" who believe in Jesus (9:42) seem to include the man mentioned in 9:38. Therefore, the warning in 9:42–50 applies directly to Jesus' disciples, for they sought to hinder the man. Growth of the kingdom of God far exceeds in importance the insecure feelings of people seeking to defend the privileged position of their particular group. To eliminate the sin of stifling others' growth, violent measures must be taken (here compared with mutilation of the body). Entering into *life* (9:44, 45) is equivalent to entering into the *kingdom of God* (9:47). Compared with entry into the kingdom, everything else, including physical wholeness, pales by comparison. Jesus' followers must be purified ("salted with fire") of those things that separate them into factions. They need to judge themselves so that they can have peace with one another (9:50).

The disciples are competing with each other for greatness in the kingdom (9:33–34). They do not realize that greatness in the kingdom as Jesus understands it involves humility and service (9:35–37), not competition for status. They must terminate their quests for notoriety if they will be great in the kingdom; but as the next narrative reveals, they do not understand this.

Feeling Secure in an Insecure World
What is your source of security as a person? Do the successes of others threaten you, or do you feel joy over their accomplishments?

Mark 10:1–12: "Because of your hardness of heart he wrote this commandment"

1. The issue of divorce carries the problem of division between people (9:38) to a deeper level. Why do the Pharisees ask Jesus about it?

As in almost any religious group, there were various schools of thought among the Pharisees. The Mishnah indicates that the schools of Shammai and Hillel differed in their interpretations on a number of topics, and among these was the issue of divorce:

> The School of Shammai say: A man may not divorce his wife unless he has found unchastity in her, for it is written, *Because he hath found in her indecency in anything* [Deut. 24:1]. And the School of Hillel say: [He may divorce her] even if she spoiled a dish for him, for it is written, *Because he hath found in her indecency in anything*. R. Akiba says: Even if he found another fairer than she, for it is written, *And it shall be if she find no favour in his eyes* . . . [Deut. 24:1].[30]

2. With which school of thought does Jesus more closely agree: Hillel, who taught that a man had the right to divorce his wife if she spoiled his supper, and Akiba, who said a man had the right if he

found another woman more beautiful, who pleased him more? Or Shammai, who said a man should divorce his wife only if she was guilty of some moral sin?

3. Although the Pharisees ask him what is legal, on what does Jesus focus in his reply? Instead of appealing to Deuteronomy 24:1–4, to what scriptural passage does Jesus look for his view of marriage?

4. What does Jesus imply about some Old Testament laws through his assertion in 10:5?

Charting Your Course in Life
Do you tend to orient your life by doing what you believe to be the best course of action ("What is the best thing to do in this situation?")? Or do you tend to strive only to be legal ("How far can I go without actually breaking the law?")? Why?

Notice from 10:1 that this event occurs to the east of the Jordan River, a region ruled by Herod Antipas, the one who executed John the Baptist for criticizing his divorce and remarriage (see 6:14–29). The Pharisees' test question therefore posed potential peril for Jesus.

Mark 10:13–16: You Must Receive the Kingdom of God Like a Little Child

1. How does this story illustrate again the difference between Jesus and his disciples with respect to their views of greatness in the kingdom of God and, in general, of what indicates a person's worth?

Mark 10:17–31: "What must I do to inherit eternal life?"

After Jesus' assertion that becoming like a child is necessary to enter the kingdom (10:15), someone at the opposite end of the social ladder from children comes to Jesus, asking about eternal life. (Remember the teaching in 9:42–50 on entering the kingdom of God.)

1. What tensions does this story illustrate between worldly affluence and power on the one hand and participation in the kingdom of God on the other? Between keeping the Old Testament commands and entry into the kingdom? (Remember the new wine/old wineskin teaching in 2:18–20.)

2. In 10:26, why are the disciples so amazed at Jesus' words about the kingdom?

3. How does Jesus' description of the kingdom of God in family terms in 10:29–30 compare with 3:34–35?

The disciples' shock at Jesus' statement "It is easier for a camel to go through the eye of a needle . . . " indicates that they understood the comment literally, to mean the impossibility of the event. Jesus' words are strong, deliberately contrasting the largeness of the camel with the tiny hole through a needle. To paraphrase the disciples' reaction: "If a righteous rich man, whose wealth must surely result from God's favor, cannot enter the

40

kingdom, who can be saved? If an *important* man, powerful in this world and careful to obey the commandments, cannot enter, what about fishermen and tax collectors?"

The often-repeated explanation that the "needle's eye" was a gate in Jerusalem through which camels could go only by kneeling is a fanciful notion for which there is no historical evidence. An eleventh-century commentator named Theophylact first put forward this idea, probably because he also had difficulty with Jesus' statement. But Jesus did not say it is "hard"; he said it is "impossible." Nothing short of a miracle of God is needed. "For mortals it is impossible, but not for God; for God all things are possible" (Mark 10:27).

Mark 10:32–45: "We want you to do for us whatever we ask"

1. Why is the request of James and John in 10:35–37 ironic in light of 10:32–34?
2. How do the other disciples respond when they learn of this request? Why?
3. Compare these events with Mark 9:30–41. What misconception lies at the bottom of the disciples' inappropriate behavior in both stories?
4. To what is Jesus referring when he speaks of his cup and baptism in 10:38?
5. In 10:45, what significance does Jesus place on his coming death, which he has now predicted three times?

Mark 10:46–52: A Blind Beggar Announces the King

1. Perhaps tellingly, Bartimaeus means "son of honor." Why do you think the people in the crowd respond as they do to Bartimaeus's pleas?
2. "Son of David" is a messianic title, and blind Bartimaeus is the first to use it in Mark's Gospel. How are faith and understanding again connected in this story? (Cf. 7:24–30.)

The mantle or cloak mentioned in 10:50 was Bartimaeus's outer garment (a coat), which beggars would spread out in front of themselves. People passing by would throw coins onto the mantle; thus, it was his means of getting money to live. Note that he throws it aside.

SECTION EIGHT: MARK 11—13: ENTRY INTO JERUSALEM

We now enter the last week of Jesus' life, an intense sequence of events in Jerusalem culminating with his death and resurrection. The fact that the description of Jesus' last week comprises

Who Is the Greatest?
You have probably encountered a blind or otherwise handicapped person on a city street begging for money. Such people do not rank high on society's ladder of social worth. Imagine for a moment that you are with a political figure of great importance, and a beggar begins to accost you for something. How would you feel in such a situation? Why? How do you define greatness, and whom do you view as the "important" people in the world? How does your definition of greatness affect the way you live? How does it affect the way you relate with others?

41

one-third of the Gospel indicates its great importance to Mark. So striking is the amount of space devoted to this time that Martin Kähler in 1896 first called the Gospels "passion narratives with extended introductions."[31] Although somewhat simplistic and failing to appreciate the literary complexity of Mark that you have been seeing, Kähler's comment shows an awareness of the great importance placed on the death of Jesus.

Jesus came to Jerusalem for the Passover, one of the yearly feasts that many Jews traveled to the holy city to observe. During the Passover celebration, the normal population of Jerusalem would quadruple. Roman authorities tended to be nervous during such times, for messianic hopes and political unrest could easily erupt.

Mark 11:1–11: Riding into Town on a Donkey

1. How does Jesus' triumphant entry into Jerusalem build on the messianic title "Son of David," used by Bartimaeus in the previous story?
2. What are the people affirming about Jesus by their actions and proclamations in 11:8–10? What might they be expecting to happen?

Hosanna means something like "Save, we beseech you!" or "Save us!" This expression comes from the quotation of Psalm 118:25–26, a psalm written to express thanks to God for helping an Israelite king win a battle. Although "Hosanna" on some occasions may have been merely a polite form of greeting, it seems to have messianic significance in Mark's account. Note that Jesus inspects the temple before going back to Bethany to spend the night. Carefully peruse a map of Jerusalem in preparation for studying the next narrative.

Scale model of the first-century temple and surrounding courtyard. The scholars who created this large model of Jerusalem went to considerable care to try to reconstruct it as accurately as possible. On the hillside in the background are numerous modern homes made of the same white stone.

WHAT A MAGNIFICENT BUILDING!

Josephus explains in detail how Herod the Great, who had quite a reputation for his building projects, elaborately reconstructed the Jerusalem temple. To keep from offending the Jews, he specially trained one thousand priests in the arts of stonecutting and carpentry (*Antiquities* 15.11.2 [§390]). He used one thousand wagons to bring massive stones to the temple site, and the magnificence of the work far surpassed the former temple. "Now the temple was built of stones that were white and strong, and each of their length was twenty-five cubits, their height was eight, and their breadth about twelve; and the whole structure . . . [was] visible to those that dwelt in the country for many furlongs" (*Antiquities* 15.11.3 [§§392–93]). A cubit is approximately eighteen inches, so according to Josephus, a single stone measured thirty-seven by twelve by eighteen feet.

Josephus describes the magnitude of the temple grounds and the massive energy and expense required to construct the entire edifice, with its immense columns and intricate carvings (*Antiquities* 15.11.2–7 [§§388–425]). Gentiles could enter only the outer court, called the Court of Gentiles. Beyond that, they dared not go past the wall that separated this area from those inside. At each gate through this wall of partition was a sign "with an inscription which forbade any foreigner to go in under pain of death" (*Antiquities* 15.11.5 [§417]). Or, as Josephus says in *Jewish War* 5.5.2 (§§193–94),

> When you go through these [first] cloisters, unto the second [court of the] temple, there was a partition made of stone all around, whose height was three cubits [= 4½ feet]: its construction was very elegant; upon it stood pillars at equal distances from one another, declaring the law of purity, some in Greek, and some in Roman letters, that "no foreigner should go within the sanctuary."

In *Jewish War* 5.5.1–8 (§§184–247), Josephus elaborates further on the temple grounds, explaining that the area at first was a mountaintop barely big enough for a sanctuary, but Solomon's workers transformed it into a large plain by hauling untold tons of rock. Herod's project further enlarged the temple grounds on a grand scale. Each level toward the central sanctuary was higher than the one before and was ascended by steps. The temple proper was not a large meeting place for the people as a whole but an operational center for priestly activities. Its beauty was exquisite:

> Now the outward face of the temple in its front wanted nothing that was likely to surprise either men's minds or their eyes: for it was covered all over with plates of gold of great weight, and, at the first rising of the sun, reflected back a very fiery splendour, and made those who forced themselves to look upon it to turn their eyes away, just as they would have done at the sun's own rays. But this temple appeared to strangers, when they were at a distance, like a mountain covered with snow; for, as to those parts of it that were not gilt, they were exceeding white. On its top it had spikes with sharp points, to prevent any pollution of

it by birds sitting upon it. Of its stones, some of them were forty-five cubits in length, five in height, and six in breadth. (*War* 5.5.6 [§§222–24])

According to the standards of the disciples, the temple in Jerusalem met all criteria of greatness. It was an impressive structure, whose west wall measured 1,590 feet, the north wall 1,035 feet, the east wall 1,536 feet, and the south wall 912 feet. By way of comparison, this is more than five football fields in length and more than three football fields in width.

During Passover, Jerusalem bustled with activity, especially in the temple courtyard. To get an idea of the crowded nature of the temple precincts, think about what you experience in shopping malls the month before Christmas. The temple building proper, which might be compared with an extremely ornate church, occupied only a small portion of the total space of the temple area. The exchanging of currency and selling of sacrificial animals to those pilgrims who had come to Jerusalem from all over the Mediterranean region took place in the large outer courtyard called the Court of the Gentiles. Because bringing animals from distant lands would have posed many difficulties, pilgrims bought their sacrificial offerings from local businesspeople. Selling livestock in the temple precincts, however, was apparently a recently initiated practice that was the object of considerable debate among the Jews of this time.[32]

The Western Wall in Jerusalem, an important place of Jewish prayer today. The large stones at the right are part of the first-century wall that surrounded Herod's temple complex.

To return to the shopping-mall comparison, consider which people would be most upset if someone did something to shut down business at the mall for an afternoon before Christmas.

Mark 11:12–26: "It was not the season for figs"

The stories in this passage form another instance of intercalation. Notice how Mark associates the condition of the fig tree with the temple.

1. When Jesus brings things to a grinding halt, how does the crowd's response differ from that of the temple authorities?

2. How are the condition and fate of the fig tree symbolic of the condition and fate of the temple?
3. What are the disciples to learn from these events (11:20–26)?

Mark 11:27–33: "By what authority are you doing these things?"

In Mark's chronology, this is Jesus' third day in Jerusalem (see 11:1, 12, 20, 27),[33] and this passage begins a series of topically arranged controversy stories that extend from 11:27 to 12:40. The men who approach Jesus to ask about his radical behavior—the chief priests, scribes, and elders—are members of the *Sanhedrin* (a ruling council led by the high priest that consisted of seventy-one members, mostly from the ranks of aristocratic priests and Pharisaic scribes). Representing the highest Jewish authority, they come to question Jesus' authority.

1. Why will the Sanhedrin members not answer Jesus' question about the baptism of John?
2. How is their leadership like that of Herod in 6:14–28?

Mark 12:1–12: "This is the heir; come, let us kill him"

Vineyards sometimes had stone walls or hedges of thorny plants around them to protect the fruit from animals or thieves. The tower was built as an elevated place for a guard to stay in and keep watch for intruders. Workers picked the grapes and placed them in a large receptacle called a winepress. Then they stomped on the grapes with their bare feet to squeeze out the juice, which came out a pipe in the bottom of the press and emptied into a container.

1. What image of Jewish religious leaders does Jesus present in this parable, and how do they respond to this allegory?

Tied at Halftime
Imagine for a moment that you are at the Rose Bowl to watch your team play their last postseason football game. You have gone to considerable expense to fly down for the game, rent a hotel room, and pay for all the other activities you enjoy during such a trip. The game is terrific, and at halftime the score is tied. While anxiously awaiting the beginning of the second half, you suddenly hear the clanking sounds of a large bulldozer echoing across the stadium. To your horror, the driver begins digging up the playing field. How might the Rose Bowl officials, not to mention the crowd, react to this disruption? What parallels do you see between this situation and that described in Mark 11:15–18?

Ancient Egyptian tomb painting depicting men harvesting grapes (right) *and stomping them to make grape juice* (left). *Note the dangling vines that the men hold as they stomp the grapes (to keep from slipping and falling) and the grape juice coming out of the pipe to be collected and stored in containers to ferment and become wine.*

Mark 12:13–17: "Is it lawful to pay taxes to the emperor?"

1. Remember that it is unusual for the Herodians to join forces with the Pharisees (see under Mark 3:6). Why is the question posed to Jesus a "setup" that discredits him with the Jewish people if he answers yes and places him in danger with the Romans if he answers no?

2. How does Jesus' response show that he does not seek to over-throw the Roman government?
3. The coin shown to Jesus in 12:16 had the image of Caesar stamped on it, along with the statement "Tiberius Caesar Augustus, son of the divine Augustus." (Adolf Deissmann, *Light from the Ancient East* [London: Hodder & Stoughton, 1927; reprint, Baker Book House, 1978], 252.) How does Jesus' statement in 12:17 show that he does not consider Caesar to be divine?

Mark 12:18–27: "Whose wife will she be?"

The *Sadducees,* a priestly aristocracy, dominated the upper echelons of Jewish society because of their wealth and power. Their name means "sons of Zadok" and stems from their claim to be descendants of David's priest who backed Solomon as king (see 1 Kings 1—2). They accepted only the books of Moses, the Pentateuch, as inspired and authoritative, and they rejected the Pharisees' oral traditions as having no binding authority. Therefore, they did not believe in the resurrection of the dead, angels and demons, or other doctrines held by the Pharisees.

1. What tactic do the Sadducees employ in their effort to discredit Jesus?
2. What does Jesus' caustic reply reveal about human social relations in the afterlife?
3. Why does Jesus quote from Exodus 3:6 instead of a later document, such as Daniel 12:2, when responding to their question?

Mark 12:28–34: "You are not far from the kingdom of God"

1. How is Jesus' encounter with this scribe unlike his previous encounters with religious leaders in Mark's Gospel?

Jesus' response to the man's question comes straight from the Shema, a confession made daily by pious Jews. *Shĕma'* in Hebrew means "hear," and this is the first word of the confession found in Deuteronomy 6:4–5: "Hear, O Israel: The LORD is our God, the LORD alone. You shall love the LORD your God with all your heart, and with all your soul, and with all your might." The second command Jesus cites is from Leviticus 19:18: "You shall love your neighbor as yourself." Living for God is based on the double command of love: Love God with all your being; love your neighbor as yourself. All religious observance must be based on this to meet Jesus' standards, and the failure of Pharisees and Sadducees to realize this brings his criticism against them. Yet the anonymous scribe in this story appreciates Jesus' teaching, and his affirmation, like Jesus' triumph over opponents in previous stories, serves to establish Jesus' authority in the narrative.

Mark 12:35–44: "Beware of the scribes"

1. What vivid contrast does Mark show between the poor widow in 12:41–43 and the scribes in 12:38–40? (Mark provides an equivalent value in Roman terms for the two copper coins in 12:42. What does this tell you about his audience?)
2. How does the widow illustrate Jesus' teaching to his disciples on the meaning of greatness in the kingdom of God?

Mark 13:1–37: The End of the Present Evil Age

1. How is the disciples' misunderstanding of the meaning of greatness again reflected in their comment in 13:1?

The disciples interpret Jesus' prediction of the temple's destruction as a sign of the end of the age (13:3–4; remember the fig tree in 11:12–21). So Jesus explains what will happen before the end. (Remember 9:1: "Truly I tell you, there are some standing here who will not taste death until they see that the kingdom of God has come with power.") In Jewish apocalyptic documents of this general time period, the standard expectation was for a time of unparalleled stress prior to the end of the present evil age, just before the messiah would come to straighten out everything. They called the terrible suffering to be endured during this time *the woes of the messiah*. Like a woman in labor undergoing horrible birth pangs (13:8), the world (especially the righteous) would writhe in pain before the birth of the age to come.

2. What does Jesus indicate his followers will have to endure before the end comes?
3. For what reason and for whose sake will this intense time of trouble be "cut short"?

The suffering ends when the Son of Man comes with great power and glory to gather his people (13:26–27). So, in the midst of persecution, they can look expectantly for Jesus' return, because these terrible events indicate that his return is very close (13:28–30).

4. How long might the disciples reasonably expect to wait before these terrible events begin? (Note especially 13:30.)
5. What does Jesus indicate about his own knowledge of exactly when the end will come?
6. This discourse about the end of the age does not merely

Social Standing and Human Worth
Those who stand on the lower rungs of the ladder of Jewish society become important figures in Mark's story of Jesus. The Syrophoenician woman's persistence makes an important transition between the feeding of the Jews and the feeding of Gentiles; children provide models for members of the kingdom of God; a blind beggar announces the kingly Son of David; and a poor widow shows what true obedience to God is like. How is your perception of people's worth affected by their societal standing?

function to give interesting predictions to those who follow Jesus. According to 13:32–37, how should Christians use this information?

SECTION NINE: MARK 14—16:
THE PASSION NARRATIVE

The account of Jesus' arrest, suffering, and death is called the *passion narrative*. In its stories, all disputing with religious authorities ceases. Now events rush toward the death that the Pharisees began plotting back in 3:6, and that Jesus predicted to his disciples in 8:31; 9:9–13, 31; 10:33–34. The threatened religious leaders wait until the opportune moment to strike—away from the observing eyes of the crowd they fear to offend (11:18; 12:12; 14:1–2).

Mark 14:1–11: "Why was the ointment wasted?"

After all the earlier indications that power and prestige impress the disciples, now, ironically, they get angry over this woman "wasting" money on Jesus. The expensive nature of the perfume becomes obvious in 14:5: Three hundred denarii was almost a year's wages for a laborer. Although it is the disciples who now are worrying about social concerns, Jesus has been the one throughout who championed compassion for the poor, sometimes in spite of their opposition.

On Receiving Love
Are you able to receive love when it is expressed lavishly, or does such generosity make you self-conscious and nervous? Explain why, in either case.

1. Why does Jesus now accept such an expensive gift?
2. What does the fact that Jesus defends the woman's action add to Mark's portrait of him?
3. Compare 14:4–5 with 14:10–11. What does this show about Judas?

Mark 14:12–31: "Take; this is my body"

Since women normally carried water jars, the unusual sight of a man carrying water (14:13) would be a good signal, especially if Jesus arranged in advance for using the home. Jews had to eat the Passover meal inside Jerusalem's city walls, so Jesus returned there from Bethany (14:3) after dark to avoid detection.

Jews normally sacrificed their lambs on the fourteenth of Nisan (the first month of the Jewish year, which corresponds with our March–April) and ate an extended Passover meal that evening which continued on into the night. Preparation for Passover included taking one's lamb to the temple and standing in line until a priest could assist with the sacrifice. Later, the family roasted their lamb and followed a set ritual for this important meal.

1. Jesus applies the symbolism of the Passover liturgy to himself, pointing to his own death. What meaning does this give to his crucifixion? (See Exod. 24:6–8 and Jer. 31:31–33.)
2. When Jesus first predicted his death in 8:31, Peter rebuked him, trying to convince him of the error of his view of Messiah. Now Jesus tells his disciples they will all forsake him. What does their response reveal about them?

Mark 14:32–52:
"I am deeply grieved, even to death"

1. What does this story reveal about Jesus' emotions as he faces his death?
2. What does it show about the struggle Jesus endures as he wrestles with knowing the will of God?
3. How does the passage portray the disciples?

One of the ancient olive trees in the garden of Gethsemane.

The enigmatic story of the young man in 14:51–52 seems to make a symbolic statement about the condition of the disciples. Their flight into the darkness, after their brave words of 14:31, resembles the escape of the young man, who flees naked to avoid capture. All their dreams of sharing a glorious position of power with the Messiah are dashed; and except for the account of Peter's denial of Jesus in 14:66–72, the disciples disappear from the narrative. They flee into the night, stripped of their hopes and aspirations.[34]

Mark 14:53–72: Trial and Denial

Mark describes a nocturnal trial before the Sanhedrin that is extremely illegal. Having already passed their verdict, Jesus' accusers seek only some pretense for sentencing him to death. This reveals again their lack of ethics. (Jesus calls them sinners in 14:41.) Their own scriptures clearly warn against giving false witness (read Exod. 23:1–2, 6–8; Deut. 17:6–7; 19:15–17), saying that the false witness must receive the penalty he tried to gain for the innocent party.

1. Why does the Sanhedrin have difficulty obtaining a guilty verdict?
2. During this "trial," what claim does Jesus make for himself that he kept secret for most of the Gospel? (Read Daniel 7:13.)

"Right hand of the Power" in 14:62 is a circumlocution for "right hand of God." Jewish people, as a way of showing reverence, commonly use such indirect references to avoid use of the divine name.

3. How does the last picture of Peter in the Gospel (14:66–72) compare with his brave words in 14:31?
4. Overall, how does Mark portray the disciples?

Mark 15:1–20: "Why, what evil has he done?"

As a people subjugated to Roman rule, the Jews apparently did not have the power to execute people.[35] So the Sanhedrin took Jesus to the procurator, Pilate.

1. How does the charge they level against Jesus before Pilate differ from their charge of the night before?
2. If Pilate believes Jesus is innocent, why does he crucify him? How does his leadership compare with Herod's (6:21–28)?
3. When the Son of David finally receives official recognition as "King of the Jews," in what form does it come?

The name Barabbas means "son of the father" in Aramaic, and Mark may intend it to have symbolic meaning in this context. On occasion, Jesus describes the kingdom of God in family terms (for example, 3:33–35; 10:29–30), and now this convicted criminal obtains his freedom because the innocent Jesus dies in his place. "Son of the father" is set free because of the sacrificial death of Jesus, who gives his life as a ransom for many (10:45).[36]

Mark 15:21–41: "My God, my God, why have you forsaken me?"

Crucifixion was such a brutal form of execution that Roman citizens were exempt from it. On a charge of high treason, Jesus suffered the worst set of punishments. The initial scourging alone was enough to kill him.

> A Roman scourging was a terrifying punishment. The delinquent was stripped, bound to a post or pillar, or sometimes simply thrown to ground, and was beaten by a number of guards until his flesh hung in bleeding shreds. The instrument indicated by the Marcan text, the dreaded *flagellum*, was a scourge consisting of leather thongs plaited with several pieces of bone or lead so as to form a chain. No maximum number of strokes was prescribed by Roman law, and men condemned to flagellation frequently collapsed and died from the flogging. Josephus records that he himself had some of his opponents in Galilee scourged until their entrails were visible (*War* II. xxi. 5), while the procurator Albinus had the prophet Jesus bar Hanan scourged until his bones lay visible (*War* VI. v. 3). Although scourging was a customary preliminary to execution after a capital sentence (e.g., Josephus, *War* II. xiv. 9; V. xi. 1; VII. vi. 4; Livy XXXIII. 36), it was also inflicted as an independent punishment.[37]

50

Mark the Evangelist

Prior to crucifixion, the accused normally carried the cross beam to the execution site. In his weakened state, Jesus could not manage this, so one of the Jews who came to Jerusalem for the Passover, Simon of Cyrene, was forced to carry it. (Since by Mark's time Simon and his sons were evidently widely known, Mark mentions them by name for his readers in 15:21. Cyrene was in northern Africa, located in present-day Libya.) Once at Golgotha, the Roman soldiers nailed Jesus' wrists to the cross beam and his feet to the upright beam. To prevent his weight from tearing the flesh away from the nails and also to prevent suffocation, there was a knob on the upright beam underneath his crotch to support his body. This ensured a more protracted and painful death. A man could hang on a cross for two or three days before finally dying. During that time he was prey to insects, and sometimes wild dogs were allowed to chew on his legs at night.

In Mark's account, Jesus hangs dejected on a cross. The thronging crowds shouting "Hosanna" are gone; his closest friends, the disciples, have fled; opponents mock him while he suffers on the cross; and finally, Jesus in an anguished cry asks, "My God, my God, why have you forsaken me?" (15:34). He is a picture of absolute desolation.

1. When James and John asked, "Grant us to sit, one at your right hand and one at your left, in your glory" (10:37), Jesus pointed to his cup and his baptism. Who ends up at his right and left in 15:27?
2. What does the repeated use of "King of the Jews" in this story reveal about the meaning of Jesus' glory in the Gospel of Mark?
3. What cosmic signs show the astounding significance of this death on the cross? (Cf. 8:11.)
4. In light of Jesus' predictions concerning the temple in 13:2 and 11:12–21, of what significance is 15:38?

Note the irony in the fact that a Roman soldier is the one who makes the pronouncement "Truly this man was God's Son!" (15:39).

5. Although the apostles have fled, which disciples faithfully remain to watch their Lord? (15:40–41)

Mark 15:42–47: Buried in a Tomb Cut out of Rock

1. Jesus' relatively rapid death surprises Pilate. How does the procurator make sure the report is true before releasing the body?
2. Which disciples of Jesus follow to observe the cave where Joseph

of Arimathea (a member of the Sanhedrin) places his body?
3. Which disciples are absent whom one might expect to be there?

Mark 16:1–8: The Unending Ending

The best Greek manuscript evidence indicates either that Mark's Gospel ended with 16:8 or that the original ending is now lost. The various endings that have since been appended come from different hands than Mark's. Because the present version, ending with the women fleeing in fearful silence from the tomb, sounds anything but victorious, later scribes added what they believed to be more appropriate endings. But Mark's de-emphasis on glory in human terms makes it likely that he intended to end his Gospel at verse 8. We shall proceed with this assumption.

1. Jesus predicted his death and resurrection, beginning at 8:31; yet what practical matters do the women discuss as they go to the tomb?
2. When they discover the empty tomb, what assurance does the young man inside give to them? What command?

There is good evidence that women were not considered credible witnesses in first-century Jewish culture. Josephus, for example, asserts, "But let not the testimony of women be admitted, on account of the levity and boldness of their sex" (*Antiquities* 4.8.15 [§219]). Similarly, Mishnah *Rosh Ha-Shanah* 1.8, although second-century in composition, treats such disqualification of women as a commonly accepted fact.

3. Of what possible significance to Mark's story of Jesus is the fact that women are the first disciples to witness evidence for the resurrection, and that Peter and the other men must learn about it from them?
4. What seems surprising about how the women respond to the good news from the young man in white?

All of Jesus' predictions pertaining to his earthly life have been correct so far in Mark's account, and it is reasonable to assume that Mark intends for us to understand that Jesus will indeed meet his disciples in Galilee, even though Mark does not actually describe the meeting. If Mark deliberately left his ending "unended," he may well have had pastoral intentions in so doing. He has completed his story of Jesus, a story designed to communicate certain things about Jesus and the implications of following him. Now he calls on his readers to respond. Will they follow him in a life of suffering discipleship and leave behind their ideas of glory in human terms? Symbolically speaking, will they follow directions given to faithful but frightened women to go and meet him in Galilee?

SUMMARY QUESTIONS ON THE GOSPEL OF MARK

1. From reading the story, what do you conclude about the identity of the author? About his style of writing?
2. What sort of audience did the author write to address?
3. What does the author emphasize in his portrait of Jesus? (Do you find an emphasis more on Jesus' teachings or on his actions?)
4. What does Mark emphasize in his portrait of Jesus' disciples?
5. Why do the Jewish religious leaders reject Jesus as the promised messiah?
6. Why does Jesus judge the religious leaders as unfit for the kingdom of God?
7. If you had only Mark's Gospel to form an opinion, how much time would you estimate transpired from Jesus' baptism to his resurrection? Why?
8. What do you think was Mark's purpose in writing his Gospel?
9. Construct a brief, chronological outline of Jesus' movements in Mark, from his initial trip from Nazareth in Galilee to be baptized by John in the Jordan River just north of the Dead Sea, to his trip from Galilee to Jerusalem for his death. In other words, develop a sequential outline of where and in what order the events of Jesus' ministry occurred. This will prove helpful when comparing Mark's portrait of Jesus with that produced by the other Gospel writers.

FURTHER READING ON THE GOSPEL OF MARK

Achtemeier, Paul J. *Mark.* Proclamation Commentaries. Philadelphia: Fortress Press, 1975.

Best, Ernst. *Mark: The Gospel as Story.* Edinburgh: T. & T. Clark, 1983.

Cranfield, C. E. B. *The Gospel according to Saint Mark.* Cambridge Greek Testament. Cambridge: Cambridge University Press, 1963.

Fowler, Robert M. *Let the Reader Understand: Reader-Response Criticism and the Gospel of Mark.* Minneapolis: Fortress Press, 1991.

————. *Loaves and Fishes: The Function of the Feeding Stories in the Gospel of Mark.* Chico, Calif.: Scholars Press, 1981.

France, R. T. *The Gospel of Mark.* Doubleday Bible Commentary. New York: Doubleday, 1998.

Guelich, Robert A. *Mark 1–8:26.* Word Biblical Commentary. Dallas: Word Books, 1989.

Gundry, Robert H. *Mark.* Grand Rapids: Wm. B. Eerdmans Publishing Co., 1993.

Hooker, Morna D. *The Gospel According to Saint Mark.* Peabody, Mass.: Hendrickson, 1991.

Kee, Howard Clark. *Community of the New Age: Studies in Mark's Gospel.* Philadelphia: Westminster Press, 1977.

Kelber, Werner. *The Oral and the Written Gospel: The Hermeneutics of Speaking and Writing in the Synoptic Tradition, Mark, Paul, and Q.* Philadelphia: Fortress Press, 1983.

Lane, William L. *The Gospel according to Mark.* New International Commentary on the New Testament. Grand Rapids: Wm. B. Eerdmans Publishing Co., 1974.

Mann, C. S. *Mark.* Anchor Bible 27. Garden City, N.Y.: Doubleday & Co. 1986.

Schweizer, Eduard. *The Good News according to Mark.* Richmond: John Knox Press, 1970.

3

Luke's Jesus

Reversing Social Expectations

As with Mark, the Gospel of Luke is anonymous. One of the earliest ascriptions of authorship to Luke is found in a list of books called the Muratorian Canon, written about 170 C.E.: "The third Gospel book, that according to Luke. This physician Luke after Christ's ascension, since Paul had taken him with him as an expert in the way (of the teaching), composed it in his own name according to (his) thinking."[1] We can only speculate on when this Gospel was first attributed to Luke. On the basis of the available evidence, we cannot positively ascribe authorship of the Gospel to a particular person, but we can make many significant observations of how he constructed his Gospel. For convenience, we will simply call the author Luke.[2]

Luke's writing style differs strikingly from that of Mark. Mark's prose bursts with action, stringing together sentence after sentence through the use of "and" to create a feeling of rapid movement and connection of events. His frequent use of present-tense verbs causes his stories to simulate the informal, oral form from which they sprang. Luke, by contrast, writes in a more formal style. A well-educated man, he comfortably uses the literary conventions of his day to communicate his story of Jesus.

Luke moves easily from a highly refined style, such as in the prologue to his Gospel (1:1–4), to a very Semitic Greek that sounds like a literal translation of Aramaic or Hebrew.[3] The latter style resembles the syntax commonly found in the *Septuagint*, a Greek translation of the Hebrew scriptures (Old Testament) made in Alexandria, Egypt, beginning in the third century B.C.E. Because most of the Jews in Alexandria by that time had lost the ability to speak and read Hebrew, scribes translated the scriptures into Greek. In the Pentateuch especially, most of the Hebrew syntax in the Septuagint is preserved in translation, producing very Hebraic-sounding Greek.

When Luke describes events occurring in Jewish settings, such as in the Jerusalem temple in Luke 1, his language resembles Septuagintal Greek. When, by contrast, he describes events in Gentile settings, such as Paul's speeches toward the end of Acts, his language is refined and highly rhetorical. In patterning the language for the occasion, Luke follows an ancient tradition of the Greco-Roman world that one may trace back to the famous historian Thucydides (ca. 472–395 B.C.E.). In his *History of the Peloponnesian War* 1.22.1, Thucydides describes what is often called the *historical speech,* a literary device widely implemented by ancient authors; he explains his method as follows:

> As to the speeches that were made by different men, either when they were about to begin the war or when they were already engaged therein, it has been difficult to recall with strict accuracy the words actually spoken, both for me as regards that which I myself heard, and for those who from various other sources have brought me reports. Therefore the speeches are given in the language in which, as it seemed to me, the several speakers would express, on the subjects under consideration, the sentiments most befitting the occasion, though at the same time I have adhered as closely as possible to the general sense of what was actually said. (In Loeb Classical Library [LCL])

Similarly, in the second century C.E., Lucian comments in his *How to Write History* 58: "If a person has to be introduced to make a speech, above all let his language suit his person and his subject" (LCL). Thus, ancient authors used the practice of placing speeches at key points in their narratives to set before their readers important matters that the authors sought to communicate about the events described. On the one hand, the person giving the speech in the narrative served as the author's mouthpiece, stating clearly what the author needed to relate at that point in the story. On the other hand, authors tried to recount what they thought particular speakers would have said on the occasions under consideration, even though the authors usually would not have been there to hear the actual speeches being delivered.

Ancient biographers as well as historians used the historical speech in their works, and understanding the difference between ancient biography and historiography is important in studying the Gospels. The following quotation from the famous biographer Plutarch (ca. 46–120 C.E.) clearly reveals the different approaches taken when writing these kinds of literature.

> For it is not Histories that I am writing, but Lives; and in the most illustrious deeds there is not always a manifestation of virtue or vice, nay, a slight thing like a phrase or a jest often makes a greater revelation of character than battles where thousands fall. . . . Accordingly, just as painters get the likeness of their portraits from the face and the expression of the eyes, wherein the character shows itself, but make very little account of the other parts of the body, so I must be permitted to devote myself rather to the signs of the soul in men, and by means of these to portray the life of each, leaving to others the descriptions of their great contests. (*Life of Alexander* 1.2–3; LCL)

Because ancient biographies focused on portraying the character of the individual under consideration, their contents were only loosely chronological in nature. Stories about the subject's birth and death were obviously placed first and last, but the biographer felt no constraint to organize all the stories about the person's life chronologically. Topical arrangements often accomplished the biographer's purposes much more effectively.

Comparing the Gospels with ancient biographies and histories, therefore, helps us better understand their contents. Luke, for example, contains more material associated with biographies than does Mark, for the Lukan Gospel tells of the circumstances surrounding Jesus' birth and briefly recounts an incident from his childhood. Like Mark, Luke arranges much of his material topically, with little concern for precise chronological ordering of events. (For example, note the vague time references in 5:12, 17, 27; 6:1, 6, 12.) In these ways Luke writes like a biographer. Yet he shows a definite interest in locating events in the broader context of world events (for example, 2:1–2; 3:1); and the fact that Luke-Acts forms one large work shows that Luke deliberately intended to produce a kind of history of the early Christian movement. In short, Luke's Gospel does not conform exactly to either biography or history according to ancient parallels. He follows Mark's lead, but he goes beyond Mark's pattern in utilizing creatively the historical and biographical literary conventions of his day.[4]

The structure of Luke's Gospel differs substantially from Mark's, although they use many of the same stories. Unlike Mark, Luke begins with a birth narrative (Luke 1—2), gives an expanded version of John the Baptist's preaching (3:1–22), provides a genealogy for Jesus (3:23–37) and a longer account of Jesus' temptations in the wilderness (4:1–13), recounts a story in which Jesus announces the purpose of his ministry (4:14–30), and only then begins to use many of the stories from Mark's Gospel (4:31–9:50). Interspersed with these stories from Mark are a number of teaching passages that are found in modified form also in Matthew, and Luke leaves out significant portions of Mark's account as he develops his own portrait of Jesus. In this material, it becomes obvious that Luke is more generous in the way he portrays the apostles.

Then, in 9:51–19:27, Luke constructs a section called the *travel narrative* that is unique to his Gospel. Providing an extended amount of information about Jesus' journey to Jerusalem, much of the material in this section is found only in Luke and is central to his portrait of Jesus. From 19:28 on the narrative once again draws heavily from Mark, but with characteristic Lukan touches and additions. For example, Luke also places heavy emphasis on the events surrounding Jesus' death, yet his telling of the stories results in a different emphasis on the crucifixion. In addition, his conclusion is far more positive than Mark's mysterious ending.

Although Luke uses many of the same stories as Mark does, he often employs them for different purposes. We must therefore be careful not to interpret stories in Luke in light of Mark's use of them. Each Evangelist wrote for a different audience and had a different agenda in writing.

SECTION ONE: LUKE 1:1–4: PREFACE: LUKE'S QUALIFICATIONS AND PURPOSE

Carefully read 1:1–4. It reveals much about Luke and his intentions in telling the story of Jesus.

1. What does Luke say his goals are in writing this Gospel?
2. How did he gather his resources, and where did he get this material?
3. How does he evaluate previous attempts made by other Christians (like Mark) to tell the story of Jesus?
4. How far in time does Luke seem to be from the events he records?
5. Luke dedicates the Gospel to a man named Theophilus. Although we do not know the identity of this man, what does the prologue indicate that he knows about Jesus and the early church?
6. Compare Luke's prologue in Acts 1:1–2 with Luke 1:1–4. What details make it clear that these two documents, Luke and Acts, are parts of one large work?

7. Compare Luke's prologue with the opening statement of Mark's Gospel. What differences are there between their styles of beginning a Gospel?

Luke's prologues contain some of the most polished Greek in his two-volume work. Luke 1:1–4 is one long sentence, written in the elevated style of the better Greek and Roman authors of his day. Compare it with the following prologue from Josephus' *Jewish War:*

> Whereas the war which the Jews made with the Romans hath been the greatest of all those, not only that have been in our times, but, in a manner, of those that ever were heard of; both of those wherein cities have fought against cities, or nations against nations; while some men who were not concerned in the affairs themselves, have gotten together vain and contradictory stories by hearsay, and have written them down after a sophistical manner; and while those that were there present have given false accounts of things, and this either out of a humor of flattery to the Romans, or of hatred towards the Jews; and while their writings contain sometimes accusations, and sometimes encomiums, but nowhere, the accurate truth of the facts, I have proposed to myself, for the sake of such as live under the government of the Romans, to translate those books into the Greek tongue, which I formerly composed in the language of our country, and sent to the Upper Barbarians; I Joseph, the son of Matthias, by birth a Hebrew, a priest also, and one who at first fought against the Romans myself, and was forced to be present at what was done afterwards, [am the author of this work]. . . .
>
> It is true, these writers have the confidence to call their accounts histories; wherein yet they seem to me to fail of their own purpose, as well as to relate nothing that is sound; for they have a mind to demonstrate the greatness of the Romans, while they still diminish and lessen the actions of the Jews, as not discerning how it cannot be that those must appear to be great who have only conquered those that were little; nor are they ashamed to overlook the length of the war, the multitude of the Roman forces who so greatly suffered in it, or the might of the commanders, whose great labors about Jerusalem will be deemed inglorious, if what they achieved be reckoned but a small matter.
>
> However, I will not go to the other extreme, out of opposition to those men who extol the Romans, nor will I determine to raise the actions of my countrymen too high; but I will prosecute the actions of both parties with accuracy. (*Jewish War,* Preface 1, 3–4; LCL)

1. What similarities do you see between Luke 1:1–4 and this prologue?

Now compare Luke 1:1–4 with the prologue from Josephus' *Against Apion,* a document defending the Jewish people against accusations from Gentiles:

> I suppose that, by my books of the Antiquities of the Jews, most excellent Epaphroditus, I have made it evident to those who peruse them, that our Jewish nation is of very great antiquity, and had a distinct subsistence of its own originally; as also I have therein declared how we came to inhabit this country wherein we now live. Those Antiquities contain the history of five thousand years, and are taken out of our sacred books; but are translated by me into the Greek tongue. However, since I observe a considerable number of people giving ear to the reproaches that are laid against us by those who bear ill will to us, and will not believe what I have written concerning the antiquity of our nation, while they take it for a plain sign that our nation is of late date, because they are not so much as vouchsafed a bare mention by the most famous historiographers among the Grecians, I therefore have thought myself under obligation to write somewhat briefly about these subjects, in order to convict those that reproach us of spite and voluntary falsehood, and to correct the ignorance of others, and withal to instruct all those who are desirous of knowing the truth of what great antiquity we really are. As for the witnesses whom I shall produce for the proof of what I say, they shall be such as are esteemed to be of the greatest reputation for truth, and the most skillful in the knowledge of all antiquity, by the Greeks themselves. I will also show that those who have written so reproachfully and falsely about us are to be convicted by what they have written themselves to the contrary. I shall also endeavor to give an account of the reasons why it hath so happened, that there hath not been a great number of Greeks who have made mention of our nation in their histories. (*Against Apion,* Preface 1; LCL)

In their prologues, ancient authors often dedicated their books to a wealthy patron whose financial assistance made possible the time involved in research and writing. Notice how similar Josephus's "most excellent Epaphroditus" in *Against Apion,* Preface 1, is to Luke's "most excellent Theophilus" in Luke 1:3. It is also interesting that Josephus, in another work, commends Epaphroditus as "a lover of all kinds of learning," especially history (*Antiquities,* Preface 2; LCL).

The name Theophilus means "beloved of God," and this man was probably Luke's patron (the title "most excellent" in Luke-Acts also occurs in Acts 23:26; 24:3; 26:25). Apparently a Gentile convert to Christianity, he represented the more educated additions to the church who wanted a documented source on the history of the Christian movement. As Josephus commends Epaphroditus for his historical interest, so Luke commends Theophilus.

When Luke tells Theophilus that he has written an "orderly account" (1:3), however, this need not mean "strictly chronological." Suetonius, for example, says in his biography of Augustus Caesar, "I shall now take up its various phases one by one, not in chronological order, but by classes, to make the account clearer and more intelligible" (*Life of Augustus* 9). "Orderly" in a biography often indicates a carefully arranged, topical treatment placed within the general sequence of events in a person's life. This seems to match Luke's topical arrangement of parts of the narrative, indicating that he was not concerned so much to produce a strictly chronological account as to portray certain things about Jesus.

Notice also the similarities between Luke 1:1–4 and the prologue from Philo of Alexandria's biography of Moses:

> I have decided to write the life of Moses, whom Gentiles know to have been the lawgiver of the Jews while the Jews acknowledge him to be the interpreter of their sacred laws, a man in every respect the greatest and most perfect, to make him familiar to those who deserve not to remain ignorant of him. For even though the fame of the laws which he left behind has already gone out through the whole world, ranging even to the uttermost corners of the earth, what sort of man he himself really was is not known to many people since the historians among the Greeks did not consider him worth remembering, no doubt out of jealousy and because not a few of the commandments of the lawgivers of their cities are the opposite of his. Instead they waste the talents they have acquired through education in composing poems and long-winded narratives that are supposed to be funny, filled with voluptuous licentiousness, and notoriously shameful. Rather they should have used their natural abilities for the sake of the instruction to be gained from telling about good men and their lives, lest anything that is good whether ancient or recent, once it is consigned to silence, be deprived of the light it might give. If they had done this they would not seem so constantly to ignore noble things in order to turn our attention to things not worth hearing about, telling wicked stories elegantly just for the sake of revealing something disgusting.
>
> But I for one will ignore their insulting disregard of Moses and will myself make known the facts concerning the man, namely what I have learned both from the sacred books which he left behind as marvelous memorials of his wisdom and also from some of the elders of the Jewish people. By combining oral tradition with the written I think I know more accurately than others the facts concerning his life. (*Life of Moses,* Preface to book 1)

Portraits of Jesus

1. What common features do you see in all the prologues?
2. How does studying them help in understanding Luke's purpose in writing?

Writing Your Own Preface

Using the style of ancient prologues, write a prologue for your own eyewitness account of some event. In other words, write a preface as if you were Josephus or Luke, beginning your account of some public event (college homecoming, basketball tournament, important set of church meetings, military engagement, environmental activist confrontation with workers at a government installation, etc.), incorporating all the elements used by these ancient authors.

SECTION TWO: LUKE 1:5–2:52: THE BIRTH NARRATIVE
Luke 1:5–25: Zechariah and Elizabeth

Luke carefully places his story of Jesus in a particular historical setting, and we do well to understand this setting. Herod the Great ruled as king over Judea from 37 B.C.E. until his death in 4 B.C.E. For John and Jesus to have been born during his reign, therefore, they were born no later than 4 B.C.E. The Gregorian calendar most countries in the world use today is incorrect with respect to the date of Jesus' birth, and the mistake dates back to the sixth century. In 525 C.E., the Christian monk Dionysius Exiguus determined that Jesus was born in the Roman year 753. This calculation was introduced into historical writings in 731 C.E., when the Venerable Bede used Dionysius's chronology in his *Historia ecclesiastica gentis Anglorum* (Ecclesiastical history of the English people). Bede made Dionysius's determination of the date of Jesus' birth the basis for specifying the dates of events recorded in his history. Much later, the Gregorian calendar, sponsored by Pope Gregory XIII in 1582, continued the incorrect calculation of Dionysius, and we inherit it yet today.

Although Matthew's birth narrative includes a section on the actions of Herod the Great, Luke's account merely mentions this wicked king to inform the reader of the time in which John and Jesus were born. Luke focuses first on the priestly parents of John the Baptist, who lived outside Jerusalem (Luke 1:39). Only a fraction of the total number of Jewish priests actually lived in Jerusalem. Most lived in small towns dotting the countryside. Priests like Zechariah were placed into twenty-four "divisions," and each division came to Jerusalem for one week of temple duty twice a year. (See 1 Chron. 23:6; 24:7–18, for a listing of the divisions.)

62

They rotated among themselves the various priestly duties, and one of the most desirable tasks was to burn incense on the altar of incense in the temple. The rising smoke symbolized the prayers of the people ascending to God. On completing this task, the priest came out of the temple and pronounced a blessing on the people.

1. What was Elizabeth's "disgrace" (1:7, 25), and why would this be in tension with the description of her and her husband in 1:5–6?
2. How was Zechariah chosen to burn incense on the altar? (See Exod. 30:1–10 concerning the altar of incense.)
3. According to 1:14–17, what unique qualities will John have, and what role will he play in the history of salvation?

Luke 1:26–56: Don't Worry, Joseph. It's God's Baby!

Quite unlike present-day engagements, *betrothal* was a binding, legal contract that could be broken only by formal divorce proceedings. Typically, when a girl began to menstruate, about age twelve to thirteen, she was betrothed to the young man who her parents had decided would be her husband. It was not uncommon, however, for parents to negotiate marriage contracts even while their children were quite small. The betrothal period lasted approximately one year, after which a marriage celebration occurred and the couple began living together. At the time of marriage, the new husband was usually about eighteen and his wife about thirteen or fourteen.

1. How does Mary differ from Elizabeth with respect to her age, marital status, and where she lives?
2. How many months pregnant is Elizabeth when Mary comes to see her? When Mary returns home?

In Jesus' day, people calculated pregnancies using a lunar calendar, and they began their calculations from the time of the woman's last period. Consequently, they determined the gestation period to be ten months instead of nine (e.g., Wisd. Sol. 7:1–2 says, "In the womb of a mother I was molded into flesh, within the period of ten months").

3. Note the similarities between the way Mary acts when the angel greets her (1:26–29) and the way Zechariah acted (1:11–12). How does Mary's response to Gabriel's announcement (1:34) compare with Zechariah's response (1:18)? How do the consequences of their responses differ?
4. What does the angel's message in 1:32–33, 35 reveal about the person and work of Jesus?

5. What does Mary's song in 1:46–55 (called the Magnificat) say about the rich and the poor?
6. What similarities are there between 1:46–55 and the song of Hannah in 1 Samuel 2:1–10?

A variety of expectations concerning the messiah existed in the first century, but prior to Jesus' time there was no clear belief that the messiah would be born of a virgin. The Jewish writings before Jesus show no expressions of belief in a virgin birth. And when the early Christians began to proclaim this about Jesus, Jews as a whole rejected the argument, as may be seen in a second-century C.E. document by Justin Martyr. Trypho, the Jewish character in this dialogue, says:

> We all expect that Christ will be a man [born] of men, and Elijah when he comes will anoint him. (*Dialogue with Trypho* 49; Ante-Nicene Fathers [ANF])

> And Trypho answered, "The Scripture has not, 'Behold, the virgin shall conceive and bear a son,' but, 'Behold, the young woman shall conceive and bear a son' [Isa. 7:14] and so on, as you quoted. But the whole prophecy refers to Hezekiah, and it is proved that it was fulfilled in him, according to the terms of this prophecy. Moreover, in the fables of those who are called Greeks, it is written that Perseus was begotten of Danae, who was a virgin; he who was called among them Zeus having descended on her in the form of a golden shower. And you ought to feel ashamed when you make assertions similar to theirs, and rather [should] say that this Jesus was born man of men. And if you prove from the Scriptures that He is the Christ, and that on account of having led a life conformed to the law, and perfect, He deserved the honour of being elected to be Christ, [it is well]; but do not venture to tell monstrous phenomena, lest you be convicted of talking foolishly like the Greeks." (*Dialogue with Trypho* 67; ANF)

Contrary to many naive Christian claims, Mary could not have excitedly appealed to a widespread belief among the Jews when she told her parents and Joseph about her pregnancy. She could not have happily announced that she was the long-awaited virgin who would give birth to the messiah. They would have had no such expectation. Indeed, her announcement would have been contrary to their beliefs about the messiah and how he would come.

Luke 1:57–80: You're Going to Name Him What?

1. What does this passage reveal about Jewish customs in naming children?

Personal Reflection

Imagine that you are a young, engaged woman hearing an angel say that you will be pregnant by the Holy Spirit. How might you respond?

Now imagine that you are the fiancé of the young woman who turns up pregnant by the Holy Spirit. How might you feel about the situation? (Notice that, unlike Matt. 1:19, which says, "Joseph . . . planned to dismiss her quietly," Luke does not mention Joseph's response to learning of Mary's condition.)

Now consider what it might be like to be the parents of the pregnant girl. How might you explain the situation to your extended family and neighbors?

2. Zechariah's poetic prophecy in 1:68–79 is called the Benedictus for the first word in the Latin translation of it. What does 1:68–75 reveal about the role that the coming Messiah will play?
3. What does 1:76–79 reveal about John's role in the coming of the Messiah?
4. What are the meanings of redemption in 1:68 and salvation in 1:69? (Notice the nationalistic tone to Zechariah's prophecy.)

As we saw in chapter 2, on Mark, on the basis of Isaiah 40:3–5 many eschatologically oriented Jews believed that the messiah and his predecessor, Elijah, would appear in the wilderness. In line with this expectation, John, the one who will announce the Messiah, dwells in the wilderness (1:80).

EXPECTATIONS FOR THE COMING MESSIAH

Jesus lived in a world of turmoil. The Jewish people were subject to Roman overlords, and this indignity produced considerable theological debate over why God allowed foreigners to dominate his chosen people. Many Jews (although certainly not all) believed that God would send a great leader, his anointed one, the messiah, to liberate and establish them as the rulers of the world. Those who held such beliefs disagreed on many details, but on one thing they agreed: He would be a powerful ruler who would destroy foreign oppressors.

One excellent source of pre-Christian, Jewish messianic beliefs is the *Psalms of Solomon,* a collection of nonbiblical poetry apparently written by Pharisees between 60 and 30 B.C.E. *Psalm of Solomon* 17 gives an extended description of what they thought the messiah would be like:

> [21]See, Lord, and raise up for them their king, the son of David,
> to rule over your servant Israel in the time known to you, O God.
> [22]Undergird him with the strength to destroy the unrighteous rulers,
> to purge Jerusalem from gentiles who trample her to destruction;
> [23]in wisdom and in righteousness to drive out the sinners from the inheritance;
> to smash the arrogance of sinners like a potter's jar;
> [24]To shatter all their substance with an iron rod;
> to destroy the unlawful nations with the word of his mouth;
> [25]At his warning the nations will flee from his presence;
> and he will condemn sinners by the thoughts of their hearts.

[26]He will gather a holy people whom he will lead in
    righteousness;
      and he will judge the tribes of the people
      that have been made holy by the Lord their God.
[27]He will not tolerate unrighteousness (even) to pause
    among them,
      and any person who knows wickedness shall not live with
        them.
      For he shall know them that they are all children of their
        God.
[28]He will distribute them upon the land according to their
    tribes;
      the alien and the foreigner will no longer live near them.
[29]He will judge peoples and nations in the wisdom of his
    righteousness.
Pause.
[30]And he will have gentile nations serving him under his
    yoke,
      and he will glorify the Lord in (a place) prominent
        (above) the whole earth.
And he will purge Jerusalem (and make it) holy as it was
    even from the beginning,
[31](for) nations to come from the ends of the earth to see his
    glory,
      to bring as gifts her children who had been driven out,
      and to see the glory of the Lord with which God has
        glorified her.
[32]And he will be a righteous king over them, taught by God.
      There will be no unrighteousness among them in his days,
        for all shall be holy,
      and their king shall be the Lord Messiah.
[33](For) he will not rely on horse and rider and bow,
      nor will he collect gold and silver for war.
      Nor will he build up hope in a multitude for a day of war.
[34]The Lord himself is his king, the hope of the one who has a
    strong hope in God.
      He shall be compassionate to all the nations (who)
        reverently (stand) before him.
[35]He will strike the earth with the word of his mouth forever;
      he will bless the Lord's people with wisdom and
        happiness.
[36]And he himself (will be) free from sin, (in order) to rule a
    great people.
      He will expose officials and drive out sinners by the
        strength of his word.
[37]And he will not weaken in his days, (relying) upon his God,
    for God made him powerful in the holy spirit
      and wise in the counsel of understanding, with strength
        and righteousness.
[38]And the blessing of the Lord will be with him in strength,
    and he will not weaken;
[39]His hope (will be) in the Lord.

Then who will succeed against him,
[40]mighty in his actions and strong in the fear of God?
Faithfully and righteously shepherding the Lord's flock,
he will not let any of them stumble in their pasture.
[41]He will lead them all in holiness and there will be no
arrogance among them,
that any should be oppressed.
[42]This is the beauty of the king of Israel which God knew,
to raise him over the house of Israel to discipline it.
[43]His words will be purer than the finest gold, the best.
He will judge the peoples in the assemblies, the tribes of
the sanctified.
His words will be as the words of the holy ones, among
sanctified peoples.
[44]Blessed are those born in those days to see the good
fortune of Israel
which God will bring to pass in the assembly of the tribes.
[45]May God dispatch his mercy to Israel;
may he deliver us from the pollution of profane enemies;
[46]The Lord Himself is our king forevermore.

(Ps. Sol. 17:21–46)[5]

This expectation of a righteous, world-conquering hero was common in first-century Jewish messianic thought. Many of Jesus' early followers grew up hearing it at home and in their synagogues, and the concept is pervasive in the birth narrative of Luke 1—2 and in the message of John the Baptist in Luke 3.

1. List the similarities between the prophecy in Luke 1:67–75 of what the Messiah will accomplish and the predictions in *Psalm of Solomon* 17:23–51. (Remember that "redemption" in Luke 1:68 is the salvation of Israel from her enemies, 1:71.)

Luke 2:1–20: Our Nativity Set
Never Looked Like This!

Augustus Caesar ruled as emperor from 27 B.C.E. to 14 C.E., but no ancient Roman historian mentions an empire-wide census during the time that Herod the Great ruled over Palestine (37–4 B.C.E.). Augustus did conduct localized censuses of the Roman provinces, but these were done according to the needs of each area, and not all at once. According to Josephus, Quirinius journeyed to Judea in 6 or 7 C.E. to conduct a census of the people in Palestine and Syria for taxation purposes (*Antiquities* 18.1.1 [§§1–3]), a date supported by Cassius Dio (*Roman History* 55.27.6). This was ten to twelve years after the time listed by Luke 2:1–2, which places the birth of Jesus prior to 4 B.C.E., during the reign of Herod (Luke 1:5). Scholars have proposed a variety of explanations for the historical discrepancy between Luke 2:1–2 and the account provided by Josephus. For a good explanation of the complicated issues surrounding this historical problem, see the detailed investigation by Emil Schürer.[6]

1. Because Joseph had kinship ties with the inhabitants of Bethlehem (2:4), where would he and Mary most likely stay while there?

As the story of Jesus' birth was told and retold through the centuries, a number of details were added that have no basis in the biblical text. For example, the typical stories told about Joseph and Mary arriving in Bethlehem, desperately trying to find a room because she was going into labor, are dramatic but rather fanciful. To think that an honorable man would take his wife in an advanced state of pregnancy on a seventy-five-mile walk from Nazareth to Bethlehem is outlandish. There is no indication in the story that their situation was desperate. Luke 2:6 simply says, "*While they were there*, the time came for her to deliver her child (emphasis mine)."[7] This in no way indicates that they arrived at the last minute of her pregnancy. They could have been there for months. Furthermore, even the belief that she and Joseph were trying to rent a room is unfounded.

According to Luke 2:4, Joseph had kinfolk in Bethlehem; and Mediterranean norms of hospitality would ensure that he and Mary would be received by some of them. Also, it is very doubtful that a small town the size of Bethlehem, close to Jerusalem and with only around one hundred to two hundred residents, would even have a commercial inn. The term *kataluma* in 2:7, which is frequently translated "inn" because of the pressure of Christian tradition, should be translated "guest room." When Luke designates a commercial inn, he uses the term *pandocheion,* as in 10:34, to specify where the Good Samaritan takes the injured man to recover. When Luke uses *kataluma* he means "guest room," as in 22:11, where Jesus says, "Where is the guest room [*kataluma*], where I may eat the Passover with my disciples?" Commercial inns in Judea at that time were rather notorious for vice and not the sort of place an honorable man would take his wife.

Guest rooms, however, were built onto some homes in Palestine. Therefore, the comment in Luke 2:7 that the guest room was full probably indicates that someone else of higher status (i.e., older) already occupied it. So Jesus was born in a manger, which was, in fact, part of the furniture in peasant homes. The average peasant home was a kind of split-level arrangement, with one room occupying about 80 percent of the area. This space was used for cooking, eating, sleeping, and so forth. The remaining 20 percent was lower, reached by a few stairs, and that is where the few animals the family owned spent the night. Each morning the animals were taken outside, their space cleaned; then the other chores of the day began. Between the living area for the family and the bedding area for the animals was a feed box called the *manger*. Thus the manger was in the actual living space of the home, and it would provide a natural place for the women to assist Mary with the birth of her child.[8]

Yet, because Christians for so long have read the story of Jesus' birth in light of their own cultural assumption that a manger is located in a barn, the stable is a standard feature of nativity scenes. So is the unconcerned innkeeper who sends the desperate couple to the stable because there is no room in what is depicted as a cold and unfriendly town far away from home (quite the contrast to what we know of Jewish hospitality for kinfolk!). For that matter, the donkey that so much Christian art depicts Mary as riding is never mentioned in Luke's account. Some of the details that are commonly added to the Christmas story originate with a second-century document called *The Protevangelium of James*, a wildly fanciful account designed primarily to exalt Mary.

In this bizarre text, Joseph is an old widower who is supernaturally chosen to take Mary, who is described as the darling of all Israel and has grown up in the temple in Jerusalem. Joseph protests vigorously that he has grown children and that he will be a laughingstock for taking her. (Note how many nativity sets depict Joseph as an old, bald man.) When the time comes for Jesus to be born, Joseph is leading a donkey on which Mary is riding, and he takes her to a cave near Bethlehem and runs to seek a midwife. Joseph notices that suddenly everything on earth stops; even the birds hang motionless in midair. And then a blinding light appears in the cave, and there is Jesus by Mary, whose birth canal is unused. Ironically, further legends became attached to the story of Jesus' birth to such an extent that Christians today find it difficult not to see Mary on a donkey, almost bursting with child when she reaches Bethlehem, and giving birth in a stable because no one would provide room for her.[9]

2. Consider the conspicuous absence of any royal trappings in the conditions surrounding Jesus' birth (e.g., birth in a manger, shepherds chosen to come and adore him). How does his birth story compare with what one might expect from the descriptions in 1:46–55 and 1:68–75?
3. How does the shepherds' response to the angelic messengers compare with the reactions of Zechariah in 1:12 and Mary in 1:29–30?

Luke 2:21–40: Presenting Jesus in the Temple

1. Compare 2:21–24 and 1:59 with Leviticus 12:1–8 and Exodus 13:2, 12. What procedure did Jewish parents follow after the birth of their boys?
2. What do Luke 2:24 and Leviticus 12:8 tell you about the financial status of Mary and Joseph?
3. What do the testimonies of Simeon and Anna in 2:25–38 contribute to the expectation of what Jesus will accomplish?
4. How does the statement about Jesus in 2:40 compare with the description of John the Baptist in 1:80? With 1 Samuel 2:26?

Luke 2:41–52: The One Story of Jesus' Childhood

1. How could Jesus' parents have left him behind and not have realized it?
2. What does the story reveal about Jesus? About his relationship with his parents?

At thirteen years of age Jewish boys go through bar mitzvah, a ceremony by which they become part of adult society. *Bar mitzvah* means "son of the commandment," and in this initiation ritual the young men take on the weight of the law. Interestingly, the only story recorded in the Gospels about Jesus' childhood occurs during Jesus' twelfth year, showing him seated among the learned teachers, discussing theology in the same temple where he was circumcised as an infant. This not only reveals Jesus' depth of understanding at a young age but is also Luke's way of showing the piety of Jesus and his parents. They were faithful members of the Hebrew culture, obedient to the laws of Moses.

As such, they would not find it unusual to refer to *God as Father,* which Jesus does in 2:49. Although some scholars in the past argued that Jesus' reference to God as Father was unique in Jewish culture, recent studies have demolished this thesis.[10] The older view that Jesus used the Aramaic *Abba* in a unique way, to call God "Daddy," has simply not stood the test of careful examination. There are a number of instances in the Jewish literature of this time period in which characters in stories call God Abba. We should therefore be cautious of arguing on the basis of 2:49 that Jesus is claiming to be God's divine Son when he responds, to his mother's complaint, that she should have known he would be about his Father's business. To do so is to read too much into the statement. His words in the temple at age twelve could reveal a messianic awareness, but not necessarily so. They could also merely represent the intense piety of a young Jewish male who is extremely committed to God.

Reflection: "But I Thought He Was With You!"
Like Mark, Luke says little about the feelings of people in his stories. But ponder for a moment what it would be like to be Mary and Joseph in 2:41–51. What emotions might you experience?

SECTION THREE: LUKE 3—4: THE MINISTRY BEGINS

Luke 3:1–22: Prophetic Ministry of John the Baptist

Tiberius Caesar ruled the Roman Empire from 14 to 37 C.E.; Pontius Pilate governed Palestine from 26 to 36 C.E.; Herod Antipas was tetrarch of Galilee from 4 B.C.E. to 39 C.E.; and Philip was tetrarch from 4 B.C.E. to 34 C.E. The identity of Lysanias is uncertain. Annas was high priest from 6 to 15 C.E., and his son-in-law Caiaphas was high priest from 18 to 36 C.E. Luke speaks of both men being high priest in 3:2 because Annas continued to exert considerable influence (cf. John 18:13, 22).

1. According to Luke 3:1, therefore, in which year by our calendar did John the Baptist begin his ministry?

In contrast to Mark 1:1–8, Luke 3:1–20 omits the details of John's appearance and strange diet (Mark 1:6) and adds a substantial portion concerning John's preaching to various groups who came out to hear him (Luke 3:7–14). Luke 3:4–6 also eliminates the citation of Malachi 3:1 at the beginning of the scripture quotation in Mark 1:2 and extends Mark's quotation of Isaiah 40:3 to include Isaiah 40:3–5. Using Gospel parallels greatly facilitates noticing these differences.

The Jordan River with very high water. (Note the bird.)

2. How does John's ministry fulfill Isaiah 40:3–5 differently than the actual, physical highway envisioned in Isaiah?
3. What attitude toward others characterizes the actions John commands in 3:11–14?
4. John's powerful preaching in the wilderness causes some to wonder if he is the messiah (3:15). What portrait of the coming Messiah does he then paint in 3:16–17? How does this compare with 3:7–9?

Note that, unlike Mark's version, the account of John's arrest (Luke 3:19–20) occurs *prior to* any mention of Jesus' baptism (3:21–22). Luke does not even say that John baptized Jesus, although one can conclude from 3:21 that he did. Also, Luke's account of Jesus' baptism adds that Jesus was praying (3:21; cf. Mark 1:9–10). The theme of prayer plays an important role in Luke's Gospel.

Luke 3:23–38: Genealogy of the Son of God

According to Luke 1:26, 36, Jesus was six months younger than John the Baptist, and both were born before 4 B.C.E., during the rule of Herod the Great (1:6). Luke 3:1 specifies that John began his ministry "in the fifteenth year of the reign of Tiberius Caesar" (= 29 C.E.), and 3:23 states that Jesus was *about* thirty years old when he began his ministry. Exactly thirty years, however, would place Jesus' date of birth at 1 B.C.E., three years *after* the death of Herod. In Luke's chronology, therefore, Jesus was at least thirty-three years old when he was baptized by John in the Jordan River.

Luke places the genealogy of Jesus between the baptism and temptation stories. The resulting separation of these two events effectively diminishes the strong connection Mark gave them, further revealing that Luke pursues his own, distinct agenda. Later we will compare Luke's genealogy of Jesus with that given by Matthew, but notice one difference now. Matthew traces Jesus' ancestry back to Abraham (Matt. 1:2), whereas Luke traces it back to Adam (Luke 3:38).

1. God calls Jesus his beloved Son in 3:22, just before the genealogy; and Adam is called the son of God in 3:38, at the end of the genealogy. What insight does this give into Luke's reason for composing this genealogy of Jesus and placing it here in the narrative?
2. Jewish society in the first century was strongly patriarchal. Through whom does Luke trace Jesus' lineage: Joseph or Mary? Why does he qualify this in 3:23? (See also 4:22.)

ANTIQUITY OF THE CHRISTIAN FAITH IN LUKE-ACTS

The fact that the book of Acts traces the history of the Christian movement to Paul's imprisonment in Rome indicates that Luke wrote at least three decades after Jesus' crucifixion, and most biblical scholars believe he wrote several decades after that. Luke states in his prologue that he was not an eyewitness but collected and arranged stories others told him about Jesus (1:1–4). By the time he wrote his Gospel, some of the initial expectations for the imminent return of Jesus had faded, as Christians began to realize that they were going to be on the earth for some indeterminate time. Luke represents those Christians who had concluded that Jesus would not return soon, and his story of Jesus reflects this modified hope.

Luke begins by telling how the Christian movement fulfills some of the ancient promises God gave to Israel. This is partially to show that Christianity is not an upstart, new religion with no long history. In Roman thinking, the antiquity of a religion contributed substantially to its validity. Roman leaders tended to resist the mystery religions that sprang up and flourished during this time, with strange rites of initiation and bizarre rituals. As you recall from reading the preface to *Against Apion,* Josephus vehemently defended the antiquity of the Jewish religion against Gentile claims to the contrary:

> However, since I observe a considerable number of people giving ear to the reproaches that are laid against us by those who bear ill will to us, and will not believe what I have written concerning the antiquity of our nation, while they take it for a plain sign that our nation is of late date, . . . [I write] to correct the ignorance of others, and withal to instruct all those who are desirous of knowing the truth of what great antiquity we really are. (*Against Apion,* Preface 1; LCL)

Likewise, to show Romans that the Christian movement should not bear the reproach of a religion without antiquity, Luke indicates that Jesus came as a deliverer to fulfill the promises God made to the Patriarchs many centuries earlier. This theme of the fulfillment of Old Testament promises is highly visible in the hymnic portions of Luke's birth narrative (1:32–33, 54–55, 68–79). However, the following stories reveal that Jesus Messiah does not fulfill the promises in the ways the Jewish people expected. His actions largely turn upside down the standard messianic expectations of the day.

Luke 4:1–15:
"If you are the Son of God"

The initial story about Jesus' ministry involves his temptation by the devil. Jesus, full of the Holy Spirit (4:1), begins his ministry by enduring a series of tests.

1. How do the three areas in which Satan tempts Jesus challenge the heavenly pronouncement of 3:22?
2. What do Jesus' responses reveal about his desires for accomplishment in life?

Luke 4:16–30: Jesus Announces His Mission

Luke provides a much longer version of Jesus' return to Nazareth and places it earlier in the narrative than the version found in Mark 6:1–6. Whereas Mark uses the story to show the effects of lack of faith, Luke uses it as his first example of Jesus' public proclamation—as Messiah's declaration of the purpose of

Reflection on Jesus' Self-Understanding
If we consider these to be real temptations for Jesus, they might reveal some interesting things about his self-identity. Of central importance in the temptation story is the recurring challenge "If you are the Son of God . . ." What do you think Jesus understood about his identity at this point? If his experiences during childhood were somewhat typical, and he learned to walk and talk like others, when do you think he understood that he was the Son of God, the Messiah?

Jesus was praying when the Holy Spirit descended on him in 3:21, so his baptism might have played a significant role in understanding his identity and mission. We may only speculate. If we accept that the incarnation was not just a game, a mere act to make it look like Jesus was human, what might this indicate about the way in which Jesus came to know God's will?

his ministry. This passage is, therefore, extremely important in Luke's narrative.

Jesus goes to his hometown as one who has begun to gain a great deal of notoriety (4:14–15). The people there receive him warmly, but their welcome quickly degenerates into open hostility.

Remains of the synagogue at Capernaum.

Luke 4:1–16 takes place on the Sabbath in a synagogue. Within the synagogue, the most important articles were the scrolls of the scriptures, and the most sacred of these were the Torah scrolls. Each Sabbath someone stood behind a podium, facing the congregation, to *read* from the law of Moses and from one of the prophets. This was followed by a sermon on one or both of the chosen passages.

While *teaching*, however, the speaker sat down in a special chair. Thus, Jesus *stood up* to read from the Isaiah scroll (4:16), unrolled the scroll to find the desired passage from Isaiah 61:1–2 that summarized his mission, read it aloud, and then *sat down* to teach (4:20). At that time there were no verse markings as we now have in our Bibles, and finding something in a scroll was not nearly as convenient as turning pages.

1. What does the reading from Isaiah 61:1–2 indicate about the nature of Jesus' ministry?
2. Compare Luke 4:18–19 with Isaiah 61:1–2 (plus Isa. 58:6 for one phrase). How do the two differ? What parts of Isaiah 61:2 does Luke 4:18–19 omit? Why does Luke leave them out (especially the last phrase)?

Isaiah 61:1–2	**Luke 4:18–19**
The Spirit of the LORD GOD is upon me, because the LORD has anointed me; he has sent me to bring good news to the oppressed [or poor], to bind up the brokenhearted, to proclaim liberty to the captives, and release to the prisoners [or the opening of the eyes]; to proclaim the year of the LORD's favor, and the day of vengeance of our God. . . .	The Spirit of the Lord is upon me, because he has anointed me to bring good news to the poor. He has sent me to proclaim release to the captives and recovery of sight to the blind, to let the oppressed go free, to proclaim the year of the Lord's favor.

3. How does the congregation initially respond to his reading and teaching?
4. Why does his statement about Gentiles cause such a violent response?

Luke 4:31–44: Modifying Mark

At this point in the narrative we find the first clear indication that Luke used Mark's Gospel as one of his sources of information about Jesus. The four stories in verses 31–44 occur in the same order and contain much of the same wording as the parallel stories in Mark. Yet they contain alterations that attest to the way in which Luke modified them to fit his own purposes in telling the story of Jesus. Luke also rearranged Jesus' interaction with Peter, deleting the story of Mark 1:16–20 and deferring the story of his call until Luke 5:1–11. As we continue to read through Luke's Gospel, we will repeatedly see significant Lukan themes emerge as we observe the ways in which he modifies Markan material to fit his own efforts at portraying Jesus the Messiah. This kind of study is called *redaction criticism*.

1. In Mark, these stories function to illustrate Jesus' tremendous authority. While this is also true in Luke, how do they relate to Luke 4:18–19 and reveal the fulfillment of this passage?
2. Compare Luke 4:40–44 with Mark 1:32–39. In what ways does Luke change Mark's wording? How do these changes affect the meaning conveyed to the reader?
3. What does Luke primarily emphasize about Jesus' person and ministry in chapters 3—4?
4. How do the preaching of John in 3:7–17 and the proclamation of Jesus in 4:16–21 set the stage for future misunderstanding over the Messiah's role?[11]

EXCURSUS ON THE SYNOPTIC GOSPELS

Matthew, Mark, and Luke share in common a large number of stories about Jesus. This similarity distinguishes them from John, which recounts only a few of the stories that are found in the other three Gospels. The close relationship between Matthew, Mark, and Luke naturally brings about comparisons of the ways in which they tell the same stories. We have examples dating from the second century which show that Christians were greatly intrigued and puzzled by the similarities and differences among these three Gospels. Since the three books are so often compared with one another, they are called the *Synoptic Gospels*. This title comes from the Greek word *synoptikos: syn* means "with" and *optikos* means "vision," so the term means "viewed together" or "common view."

Although through most of the history of the church Christians commonly viewed Mark as an abbreviation of Matthew, most biblical scholars today believe that both Matthew and Luke used Mark's Gospel as a source of information about Jesus. Of the 609 verses that comprise Mark's Gospel, only about 20 appear in stories not found in either Matthew or Luke (Mark 3:20–21; 4:26–29; 7:31–37; 8:22–26; 9:49; 14:51–52). Matthew contains about 92 percent of the contents of Mark; and although the percentage is lower in Luke's Gospel, the "borrowings" are still substantial. At times the wording of material is identical in all three Gospels, and this high degree of verbal repetition indicates some sort of direct literary relationship between them (cf., for example, Matt. 21:23–27; Mark 11:27–33; Luke 20:1–8 and Matt. 24:4–8; Mark 13:5–8; Luke 21:8–11). The sequence of events in the Gospels also points to Mark as the common source of Matthew and Luke.

Sections of Matthew and Luke that contain material found in Mark also share the same sequence of events. In other words, when these Gospels employ stories found in Mark, they tend also to follow Mark's outline. However, when Matthew and Luke employ similar material that is not found in Mark, they differ substantially in where they place it in their narrative sequences. At times this material exhibits an almost word-for-word similarity (cf. Matt. 3:7–10 and Luke 3:7–9; Matt. 6:25–34 and Luke 12:22–31; Matt. 7:7–11 and Luke 11:9–13; Matt. 11:4–6 and Luke 7:22–23; Matt. 12:43–45 and Luke 11:24–26; Matt. 24:45–51 and Luke 12:42–46). Yet, in spite of the fact that Matthew and Luke frequently use the same non-Markan material, they often place it in very different positions in their Gospels. Matthew, for example, exhibits a tendency to gather together the teachings of Jesus into large blocks of discourse material (especially Matthew 5—7; 10; 13; 18; 23—25). Thus, the teachings that Matthew records in one section (for example, the Sermon on the Mount in chapters 5—7) are scattered over a much larger portion of Luke's Gospel.

Most of the non-Markan material contained in Matthew and Luke is discourse material, with very little narration of events. A plausible theory, therefore, is that Matthew and Luke both used a non-Markan source composed almost entirely of sayings, teachings, and parables. Scholars call this sayings source *Q* after the German word *Quelle*, which means "source"; and an archaeological discovery has added validity to the theory of its existence. In 1945, near Nag Hammadi, Egypt, two peasants quite by accident unearthed a jar containing a number of ancient Gnostic texts written on parchment. One of these documents, called the *Gospel of Thomas*, is a collection of sayings attributed to Jesus and has no narrative framework.[12] The existence of this sayings source adds credibility to the belief that both Matthew and Luke used an "orthodox" sayings source when composing their Gospels.

We may speculate, therefore, that Matthew and Luke had two common sources of information before them as they wrote their Gospels: Mark and Q. Further study, however, shows that Matthew also contains information not found in Mark or Luke, and likewise, Luke contains material not found in Mark or Matthew. Thus, both Gospels employ sources other than Mark and Q. The following diagram is often used to visualize the literary relationships among the Synoptic Gospels:

Four-Source Theory of Gospel Composition

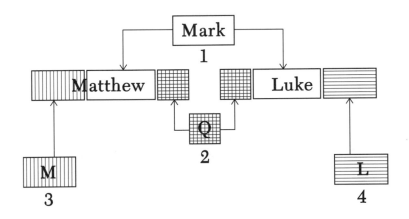

SECTION FOUR: LUKE 5—6: GREAT REVERSALS
Luke 5:1–11: What Does a Carpenter Know about Fishing?

Luke leaves out the story from Mark 1:16–20 about Jesus calling Peter, James, and John to follow him. Simon Peter merely appears in the narrative unannounced in Luke 4:38, and now, in 5:1–11, there is a longer story about his call by Jesus, who recruits him for help in a flourishing ministry. Thus, in Luke's account Peter follows Jesus only after he has seen him in action.

Personal Reflection
If you were trained in a particular occupation and someone trained in another skill told you how to do your work, how might you respond? Why?

Although Mark 1:16 designates the place where Jesus called the first disciples as the Sea of Galilee, Luke 5:1 calls it the *lake of Gennesaret,* a more proper title deriving from the heavily populated region west of the lake, called Gennesaret. Fishing on the lake was done with nets, primarily at night in shallow water (cf. John 21:3, 8).

Small boat on the Sea of Galilee (lake of Gennesaret).

1. What circumstances cause Jesus to speak from Peter's boat?
2. What dilemma does Peter, a professional fisherman, face when Jesus, a carpenter, commands him to row his boat into the deep water for a catch of fish?
3. Why does Peter respond as he does to the large catch of fish?

Luke 5:12–16: Eliminating Emotions

Luke's subtle modifications of this story from its wording in Mark 1:40–45 reveal some of the themes he emphasizes in his Gospel. Note that Luke 5:14 omits the mention of Jesus' sternness (Mark 1:43). Omissions of such indications of emotion on Jesus' part form a significant pattern in this Gospel, which was evidently written for a Roman audience that prized strength and bravery. Similarly, Luke's emphasis on prayer may be seen in the way in which he changes the ending of this story taken from Mark 1:40–45 to show that Jesus went off to pray. Luke 5:15 deletes the mention in Mark 1:45 of the cleansed leper proclaiming his healing, effectively changing Mark's conclusion on the effects of the man's disobedience into a statement on Jesus' practice of praying. We frequently see this type of redaction of Mark's stories in Luke's Gospel.

Luke 5:17–39: Healing, Blasphemy, and New Wine

In Rome, roof construction differed from that of Palestine. The average house in Rome had tiles on the roof instead of the clay construction implied by Mark. So instead of digging through the roof (Mark 2:4), the men remove roof tiles to let the paralytic down to Jesus (Luke 5:19). The following questions call your attention to a few more Lukan redactions, and you may also observe others.

1. In the story of the paralytic (5:17–26), how does Luke change (a) the description of who came to listen to Jesus (cf. Luke 5:17 with Mark 2:1); (b) what Jesus calls the paralyzed man (Luke 5:20; Mark 2:5); (c) who is questioning Jesus' actions (Luke 5:21; Mark 2:6); and (d) the crowd's expression of amazement (Luke 5:26; Mark 2:12)?
2. How does the small addition of "to repentance" (Luke 5:32) produce a significant qualification from the wording in Mark 2:17?
3. How does the end of the story with the wineskin analogy (5:39) differ from the conclusion in Mark 2:22? How does Luke's ending change the meaning of the Markan story?

Luke 6:1–11: Sabbath Controversies

Luke continues to modify his Markan source in these stories. For example, Luke 6:1 adds "rubbed them in their hands" (cf. Mark 2:23); Luke 6:2 reads "Why are *you* [plural] doing what is not lawful?" instead of "they" (Mark 2:24); Luke 6:4 deletes the problematic reference to Abiathar in Mark 2:26; and Luke 6:5 omits Jesus' reason for Sabbath law (cf. Mark 2:27).

1. What is the main point of the story in Luke 6:1–5?
2. Compare Luke 6:10 with Mark 3:5. What does Luke leave out of Mark's description of Jesus? Why? (Cf. with Luke 5:13.)
3. How does Luke 6:11 change the end of the story from Mark 3:6? Of what significance is this modification?
4. How do the stories in 5:1–6:11 conform to the agenda set forth by Jesus in 4:18–19?

Notice by the vague time references Luke uses to begin the stories in 5:12, 17, 27, 33; 6:1, 6 that, like Mark, he is not particularly concerned with chronological ordering but retains the sense of topical arrangement.

Luke 6:12–38: Happy Are the Poor, Hungry, and Miserable?

After spending all night in prayer (cf. 5:16), Jesus selects his twelve apostles while in the hills away from the crowd (6:12–13).[13] Then, descending with these men to a level plain, he teaches all the disciples, plus a mixed multitude of people from a large geographical area including both Jewish and Gentile regions (6:17). The power of the Spirit comes forth from him mightily (6:18–19; cf. 3:22; 4:1, 14), and Luke probably intends a connection between this display of power and the previous night spent in prayer.

On the plain, Jesus delivers a series of *beatitudes,* or congratulatory statements. In form they indicate that one is congratulated (or pronounced blessed) because of good fortune. Balancing these is a series of *woes,* a form of pronouncement common in the Old Testament prophetic works (for example, Amos 5:18; 6:1, 4; Nahum 3:1; Hab. 2:6, 9, 12, 15, 19; and Eccl. 10:16–17 contains a combination of congratulation and woe). In chapter 4, on Matthew, we will compare and contrast the Beatitudes and other parts of this *Sermon on the Plain* with the Sermon on the Mount in Matthew 5—7.

1. How do Jesus' beatitudes and woes reverse normal expectations?
2. What connection do the Beatitudes have with Jesus' pronounce-ment in 4:18–21? (Notice that the woes in 6:24–26, which are ab-sent from Matt. 5:3–12, form the reverse of the beatitudes in 6:20–23.)
3. How is Jesus' teaching in 6:27–31 a radical departure from the at-titude of most people?
4. What is Jesus' rationale for returning good in response to evil?
5. According to Jesus, how do God's attitudes and actions provide the foundational reason for loving one's enemies? What is the reward?
6. According to Jesus, how does our attitude toward other people determine God's actions toward us?
7. Why does Jesus' teaching go fundamentally against the way in which people normally function in society?

Luke 6:39–49: Why Do You Call Me Lord, but Ignore What I Say?

1. In 6:39–42, what role does self-analysis play? How does this teaching strike against common human tendencies?
2. How does 6:39–42 build on the previous teaching in 6:37–38?
3. How does the central message of 6:43–45 relate to 6:39–42?
4. How does the exhortation in 6:46–49 effectively conclude and ap-ply the Sermon on the Plain?

Personal Inventory
Which teaching in the Sermon on the Plain most challenges the way you live? How do you respond on a gut level to this teaching? What might keep you from taking it seriously in daily life?

SECTION FIVE: LUKE 7:1–9:50: MESSIAHSHIP AND DISCIPLESHIP

The stories in this section continue to illustrate Jesus' use of Isaiah 61:1–2 in his inaugural address in Luke 4:18–19, as he cares for the poor, the sick, and the physically disabled. The theme of discipleship also begins to play a major role, as those who follow Jesus begin to understand more about what he seeks to accomplish and what following him entails.

Luke 7:1–10: A Worthy Roman Military Commander

1. What is unusual about the attitude of the Jews in this story toward the Roman centurion? ("Centurion" is a Roman title for an offi-cer in charge of one hundred men.)

2. What words best describe the centurion?
3. What is so highly unusual about what this man says to Jesus?
4. The theme of salvation for all people is important in Luke. (Review, for example, the prophecy in 2:31–32; the genealogy of Jesus in 3:34–38; Jesus' words in 4:24–29.) How does the story in 7:1–10 fit this theme?

Luke 7:11–17: Help for a Desperate Widow

This healing miracle is somewhat unusual, because Jesus takes the initiative instead of healing someone who comes and asks for it. Expressing compassion for the widow and her son (7:13), he raises the dead youth to life. In ancient times, a widow without a son could suffer serious financial problems. (For a poignant example, see the story of Ruth and her mother-in-law, Naomi, in the Old Testament book of Ruth.)

1. What conclusion about Jesus' identity does the crowd reach after they observe the miracle?[14]

Luke 7:18–35: The Dilemma of Doubt

1. In 7:18–19, why would John the Baptist doubt Jesus' identity as God's Messiah after hearing that Jesus heals the sick and raises the dead? (Cf. 3:7–9, 16–17.)
2. What connection does Jesus' answer in 7:22 have with Luke 4:18–19?
3. What message should John receive from 4:23?
4. How does Jesus evaluate John and his ministry? (Note that the quotation of Mal. 3:1 in Luke 7:27 affirms Jesus' own identity as Messiah.)
5. According to 7:31–35, how does Jesus' approach to life and ministry differ from John's? (Be sure to connect the dancing and wailing in 7:32 to the drinking and asceticism in 7:33–34.)
6. Which previous stories in Luke illustrate Jesus' lifestyle, which the people slander in 7:34?

Although the majority of the crowd receive Jesus' words with joy (7:29), the Pharisees and lawyers reject both Jesus and John the Baptist (7:30; "lawyer" in 7:30 is *nomikos*, one learned in the law [*nomos*], and is synonymous with "scribe"). Jesus compares these men with disagreeable children who want to play neither wedding nor funeral. They cannot be satisfied; all they want to do is criticize. John the Baptist practiced great austerity and forcefully proclaimed repentance to all, including the Pharisees and lawyers. But they did not like his difficult game and refused to play. Jesus, by contrast, acts as if he is at a wedding, spending joyful time with questionable elements of society. This offends the religious sensibilities of the Pharisees and lawyers, and they pronounce him to be

Reflection on False Perceptions

A common saying is "You can tell what a person is like by the friends that person keeps." Luke's Gospel seriously calls this maxim into question, although 7:34 shows that the Pharisees applied it to Jesus. Perhaps a contemporary example will help us understand why they did so.

Imagine for a moment that you are an extremely moral pastor of a local congregation, and you are quite outspoken against vice in your community. This is an important time for you, because a famous evangelist is coming to hold a weeklong crusade in your area, and you have the good fortune of hosting a dinner for him in your home tonight. At lunchtime you leave your office and head for home to make sure everything is just right. You are enjoying the thought of spending a stimulating evening with your famous guest and selected pastors from the community.

While walking home, as you go past a rather questionable little restaurant, you glance through the window at those seated around the tables. To your shock, there is the famous evangelist having lunch with the most crooked used-car salesman in town. What might you think?

That evening, the dinner conversation is wonderful (very intellectual, very abstract— very male!). Suddenly, to your amazement and extreme embarrassment, a streetwalker strides into the room unannounced—and certainly uninvited. Everyone can easily see that she is a prostitute by the

a partying drunkard. Their form of piety prevents them from participating in the kingdom of God.

Luke 7:36–50: A Shocking Dinner Party

While reading this story, keep in mind Luke 7:29–30, and recall the material from Mark 7:1–23 on the Pharisees' purification practices for meals and their avoidance of the *'am ha-aretz* (people who did not follow the Pharisees' purity laws). The designation "a woman in the city, who was a sinner" (7:37) means "a prostitute," and the alabaster flask of ointment (7:38) was extremely expensive (see Mark 14:3). Most likely the woman earned the money to buy this ointment through the sale of her body.

1. What elements of this story make it shocking?
2. What might the Pharisees be thinking as they see the prostitute touching Jesus?
3. Contrast Jesus' approach to living for God with that of these Pharisees.
4. Contrast Jesus' attitude toward the less-desirable elements of society with that of these Pharisees? What is Jesus affirming about the value of people—all people?
5. Jesus' preaching of moral purity and repentance may well have brought the woman to a place of repentance. What was it that restored her as a person? How does this relate to 7:35? To 5:27–32?

Luke 8:1–3: These Women Are Doing What?

Jewish women frequently supported rabbis with money or food, but for a woman to travel with a rabbi, leaving her home and family, would be seen as simply outrageous and scandalous. Therefore, the account in 8:1–3 fits nicely with the previous story in 7:36–50.

1. What kinds of women travel with Jesus?
2. What financial relationship do they have with his ministry?
3. What might opponents of Jesus say about this?

Luke 8:4–18: Understanding the Secrets

1. Luke removes Mark's material about Jesus delivering this parable from a boat (Mark 4:1). How else does he shorten the parable from Mark 4:1–9?
2. Compare Luke 8:9–11 with Mark 4:10–13. How has Luke changed these verses?
3. How do these changes modify Mark's portrait of the disciples' lack of knowledge?
4. How do these changes alter Mark's view of the secret of the kingdom of God?

Luke's Jesus

The rhetorical question of Mark 4:21 becomes a straightforward assertion in Luke 8:16; and the explanation in Mark 4:22, that Jesus deliberately hides things *so that* they will come to light (intentionality of secrecy), becomes in Luke 8:17 simply an assurance that the meaning of hidden sayings will be made known. Thus, for Luke, the disciples are those who "know the secrets [plural] of the kingdom" (Luke 8:10). By so modifying the stories he takes over from Mark's Gospel, Luke stresses the disciples' hearing, understanding, and maturing in both knowledge and actions.

Luke 8:19–21:
Reducing Family Resistance and Eliminating Parables

Mark places this story involving Jesus' mother and brothers immediately before the parable collection of Mark 4:1–32. Luke, however, moves the story to the end of the parable section and eliminates the parables found in Mark 4:26–34. In addition, Luke leaves out Mark's story in which Jesus' family questions his sanity (Mark 3:20–21), thereby softening the impact of the pronouncement in Luke 8:19–21. Thus, in Luke's narrative, 8:21 concludes the parables much as Luke 6:47–49 concludes the Sermon on the Plain, with an assertion to hear and do the word of God.

Luke 8:22–25: "Where is your faith?"

Luke effectively removes this story from its Markan context, where Jesus speaks parables from a boat, by changing the precise time reference of Mark 4:35, "On that day . . . ," to a vague "One day . . ." (Luke 8:22). This day, however, includes all the following four miracle stories (8:22–56) in Luke's narration of events. These stories form a prelude to Jesus' empowering and sending out the Twelve in 9:1–6 to perform miracles of healing.

1. Compare Luke 8:23–24 with Mark 4:37–38. (Note that Luke omits the part about Jesus being in the stern, asleep on a cushion.) How does Luke modify the disciples' accusation that Jesus does not care?

Luke 8:26–39: Deviled Ham

1. This is Jesus' only excursion into Gentile territory in Luke's Gospel. What does the story show about Jesus' power over satanic forces even in pagan lands? How does it reinforce Luke 8:22–25?
2. What assurance would it give to those readers who are Jewish-Christian missionaries in Gentile lands?

way she is dressed. She looks around quickly, and her gaze fixes on your famous guest. She walks straight toward him!

In the midst of irritated murmurs, she places a very expensive gift in his hands and begins rubbing his shoulders. Those defiled hands that have caressed the bodies of many men deliver a gift purchased with money earned from selling her body. And he does not shrink away from her touch! He smiles, pats her hand, and says, "Thank you." What would you think?

Luke 8:40–56: "Who touched me?"

1. What does this story, which is slightly abbreviated from Mark 5:21–43, contribute to the ongoing themes of Jesus' power as Messiah and the meaning of following him?

Luke 9:1–17: Modifying Mark

Luke continues to follow Mark's outline in these stories, with varying degrees of modification. In 9:1–6, Jesus allows the disciples to take *no* means of support for their mission, not even the staff mentioned in Mark 6:8, but the account largely coincides with Mark 6:6–13. Luke 9:7–9, however, substantially abbreviates the story of John the Baptist's death, eliminating entirely Mark 6:17–29.

1. How does Herod's response in 9:9 differ from his words in Mark 6:16?
2. Compare Mark 6:45 with Luke 9:10. How is Luke's account different concerning where the feeding of the five thousand occurs?

Note that Luke deletes Jesus' statement that the disciples need to escape the crowd and rest (Mark 6:31); Luke 9:11 removes the shepherd imagery from the account in Mark 6:34; and Luke 9:13 removes the disciples' sarcasm toward Jesus (Mark 6:37). Luke also moves back the concluding statement of the number of people (Mark 6:44) so that it follows immediately the disciples' question about feeding so many people. This helps justify the disciples' response and make them look better in Luke's account than in Mark's.

3. What role does the feeding of the five thousand apparently play in this narrative? (Note that there is only one miraculous feeding in Luke.)

Luke 9:18–27: Major Omission

Luke deletes all of Mark 6:45–8:26, skipping over the debates with the Pharisees, the story of the Syrophoenician woman, the second miraculous feeding, and so forth. This allows him to move quickly to the question of Jesus' identity.

1. The Lukan theme of prayer again appears in 9:18, to introduce Peter's important declaration that Jesus is the Messiah. Of what possible significance is the fact that the first prediction of Jesus' death is connected with time spent praying? (Cf. this with his choosing of the Twelve in 6:12–15.)
2. How does this passage answer the question posed by Herod in 9:9?

3. Luke omits the account of the confrontation between Jesus and Peter in Mark 8:32–33. How does this affect the portrait of Peter in Luke's narrative?
4. What does 9:23–27 add to Luke's depiction of discipleship? Of what significance is the addition of the word *daily* in 9:23?

Luke 9:28–36: The Transfiguration

1. Compare 9:28–29 with Mark 9:2. What important Lukan theme forms the background for this story? (Also note that Luke specifies "eight days" instead of "six.")
2. What does Luke's addition of 9:31–32 contribute to his portrayal of the disciples?

Luke 9:37–50: Demons, Determinism, and Distinction

In this account, Luke deletes from Mark 9:9–13 Jesus' command to secrecy and the disciples' confusion about Elijah and John the Baptist. He also places the story of the spirit-possessed boy on the day after the transfiguration experience, instead of on the same day as in Mark 9:14, as well as omitting the disciples' question from Mark 9:28–29 and substantially reducing the description of the demon-possessed boy from Mark 9:20–26.

1. How does Luke 9:45 exonerate the disciples for their inability to understand Jesus (cf. with 8:10)? How does this differ from Mark's reason for the lack of understanding by the Twelve?

Reflection on Luke 7:1–9:50

1. What different kinds of people does Jesus befriend? What do his associations reveal about the kingdom of God?
2. What aspects of Jesus' ministry does Luke emphasize in these passages?
3. What does Luke emphasize about discipleship?

SECTION SIX: LUKE 9:51–12:34: THE JOURNEY TOWARD JERUSALEM BEGINS

One very distinct aspect of Luke's Gospel is the *travel narrative in 9:51–19:27* (see 9:51; 10:38; 13:22, 33; 17:11; 18:31; 19:11, for references to the journey). Jesus has already stated that his "departure" will occur in Jerusalem (9:31), and his passion predictions set the stage for his journey there. The movement now is toward Jesus' destiny, toward Jerusalem.

Luke's journey motif is, however, more a literary form than an actual, linear description of a trip from Galilee to Jerusalem. Such a journey would take only three days, but the stories in 9:51–19:27 portray events occurring over a much greater time period. Indeed, within this series of stories Jesus sends out seventy disciples to go ahead of him on a preaching tour, and they return after some days to report their success (10:1–20). In 10:38, the village of Mary and Martha is Bethany (see John 11:1), located scarcely two miles from Jerusalem. In 17:11, Jesus travels from south to north instead of north to south. In short, Luke uses a journey motif as a literary backdrop for including a large portion of extremely important material, most of which is unique to his Gospel. This material is of great significance in understanding Luke's portrait of Jesus.

Luke 9:51–56: Hatred
between Jews and Samaritans

Jews and Samaritans mostly avoided contact with each other, due to conflicts that had started centuries earlier. Samaria fell to Assyria in 722 B.C.E., and the Assyrians deported many of its inhabitants to other regions of the empire. They also resettled people from other regions in Samaria. These people brought their religions with them, and some combined their religious expressions with worship of the God of Israel, whom they believed lived in that area (see 2 Kings 17:24–34). When the Hebrew exiles returned to Judea from Babylon in 539 B.C.E., they refused to allow Samaritans to help in rebuilding the temple at Jerusalem, because they viewed them as tainted by this syncretism with other religions (Ezra 4:1–3).

The actual history of the Samaritans is very obscure, but a few historical events help us understand the deep rift between them and Judea. One relates to their temple. In 331 B.C.E., the citizens of Samaria revolted against the rule of Alexander the Great and assassinated Andromachus, the governor. As a result, the Greek army destroyed the city of Samaria and resettled the area with people from other regions. Some of the dispersed citizens of Samaria evidently resettled at Shechem and built a temple on Mount Gerazim (see John 4:20). Later, during the Maccabean rebellion, the Jews in Jerusalem refused to obey Antiochus Epiphanes and dedicate their temple to Zeus, but the Samaritans complied with the edict. Hostilities developed between the Maccabean leaders and the Samaritans, and in 129 B.C.E., John Hyrcanus destroyed the temple on Mount Gerazim. Twenty years later, in 109 B.C.E., Hyrcanus also destroyed the city of Shechem, further embittering the Samaritans against Judea and its rulers.

Other incidents followed. For example, during a Passover somewhere between 6 and 9 C.E., Samaritans defiled the temple in Jerusalem by scattering bones in it. Such acts of hostility illustrate the deep animosity that existed between Judean Jews and Samaritans.

1. How does the reaction of James and John reveal the tensions between Jews and Samaritans?
2. What does Jesus' response to their question reveal about his view of such religious and cultural hatred?

Luke 9:57–62: Eager and Hesitant Disciples

1. What does this story reveal about the cost of discipleship?

The harsh command in 9:60 seems to mean "Let those who reject the call of the kingdom of God, and are thus spiritually dead, bury the physically dead. Your mission is too important to delay!" In 9:62, the imagery of the plow indicates that family relationships cause one to look back, distracting from the all-consuming present task of preaching the kingdom. When plowing a row in a field, one must look ahead at an object in the distance in order to plow straight. Looking back over one's shoulder results in a crooked row.

Luke 10:1–24: The Mission of the Seventy

1. How does the mission of the seventy compare with the mission of the Twelve in Luke 9:1–6? With Jesus' ministry as outlined in 4:18–19?
2. How do Jesus' instructions to the seventy build on the sense of urgency expressed in 9:57–62?
3. How do the ominous pronouncements of doom in 10:13–16 relate to the journey toward Jerusalem and the mission of the seventy?
4. What does the joyful return in 10:17–20 reveal about the battle between the satanic forces of evil and the forces of the kingdom of God at work through Jesus' ministry?
5. What does 10:21–24 indicate about discipleship? About Jesus? About the kingdom of God?[15]

Luke 10:25–37: Isn't "Good Samaritan" an Oxymoron?

The well-educated teacher of the law (or scribe) comes to test Jesus' theological understanding (10:25), but he finds himself forced into an uncomfortable situation of self-analysis. Knowing the identity of the people in Jesus' parable helps us appreciate more fully how the parable confronts the scribe's theological complacency.

The *Levites* comprised one of the twelve tribes of Israel, the tribe into which Moses was born (Exod. 2:1–2). Moses' brother, Aaron (Exod. 4:14), became the *high priest,* and his sons and their descendants were the *priests* for the Israelite people (Exod.

28:1). The other members of the tribe of Levi were merely designated Levites, and they functioned as helpers for the priestly sons of Aaron (see, for example, Num. 1:47–54; 3:11–13, for details on their various services). The Levites were to be supported by a portion of the tithes of the members of the other eleven tribes of Israel, so that they could carry out their services for the people as a whole.[16]

St. George's Monastery in the Wadi Qelt, on the way from Jerusalem to Jericho. The many caves in this rugged area provide places for robbers to hide.

Before telling the parable of the Good Samaritan, Jesus and the scribe have a brief interchange. Jesus throws the scribe's initial question back at him, asking what the law of Moses says one should do. This highly trained individual responds with the Shema, a basic statement of faith recited twice daily by all faithful Jews (Josephus, *Antiquities* 4.8.13 [§212]). Consisting of quotations from Deuteronomy 6:4–9; 11:13–21; and Numbers 15:37–40, this central affirmation of Jewish faith gets its name from the Hebrew word for "hear" (*shĕma‘*): "Hear, O Israel: The Lord our God, the Lord is one. . . . " But simplicity of recitation sometimes betrays difficulty of application, and the scribe is forced to reevaluate his understanding of what one must do to please God.

1. The scribe questions how far one must go in fulfilling the law of love. (How far should love extend?) What answer does Jesus' parable provide?
2. Why would Jesus' choice of hero for this parable be very obnoxious for a faithful Jew to hear? (See under Luke 9:51–56.)
3. If the scribe was a Sadducee, thus representing the priests, what would he have been thinking as Jesus spoke verses 31–32?
4. If, as is more likely, the scribe was a Pharisee and thus did not agree with the priests on many issues of belief, and probably did not particularly appreciate them either, what might he have thought as he heard verses 31–32?
5. Who would a Pharisaic scribe have expected Jesus to say came to the poor man's assistance in verse 33?
6. How would the parable thus confront a Pharisaic scribe with his prejudices, as well as with what it means to love people?

Luke 10:38–42: Sibling Rivalry and Cultural Norms

1. How does this story reverse normal expectations about the role of women in Jesus' culture?

Luke's Jesus

Following immediately after the conclusion of the parable of the Good Samaritan ("Go and do likewise"), this story affirms that discipleship is not just "doing." A disciple is one who is *with* Jesus, listening to him first and then going out in obedience to do what he or she hears.

Luke 11:1–13: Persistent Prayer

1. Summarize what Jesus teaches about prayer in vv. 2–4; in vv. 5–13.
2. What do vv. 9–13 teach about God?

Beware of trying to allegorize Jesus' parables, seeking a direct correspondence between each detail in the story and something outside the parable (as in the parable of the sower in Mark 4:1–9, 13–20). For example, if you apply Luke 11:7–8 to God, Jesus would be teaching that God is cantankerous and answers prayer begrudgingly, only because of the persistence of the one praying. This would, in fact, be the opposite of the intended message. Jesus' story is designed to make a strong point on persistence in prayer. His description of God occurs in 11:13.

Luke 11:14–28: Exorcism of Unclean Spirits

1. Note the different ways in which people respond to Jesus' miracle and how Jesus defends himself against the accusation that he is a representative of Satan. (See the section on Mark 3:20–29 for information on Beelzebul.) What does his response reveal about the kingdom of God (vv. 20–23)?
2. According to 11:24–26, what happens to a person who, after being freed from the demonic, fails to be caught up in the kingdom of God?
3. How does 11:27–28 reaffirm this lesson?

Luke 11:29–36: An Evil Generation

1. What connection is there between this story and 11:14–26?
2. Although Jesus refuses to give a heavenly sign to confirm his identity, what claims about himself does he make?

"This generation" in 11:29–32 seems to be Jesus' opponents, who call him a tool of Satan (11:15), seek a sign from heaven (11:16, 29), and do not repent at his teaching (11:32). Toward the end of his condemnation of the lawyers in 11:45–52, Jesus calls them "this generation" (11:51). They are those who reject Jesus and John the Baptist (7:30–34) and hinder others from responding (11:52).

3. Jesus seems to indicate in 11:33 that his works are not hidden and impossible to discern. How does the condition described in 11:34–35 show why those who seek a sign are blind to Jesus' significance?

Putting Yourself in the Story
Try to picture in your mind this rather embarrassing scene. How would you respond to Mary's behavior if you were in Martha's place? Would you feel justified in being angry with her? How would you feel if you heard Jesus say verses 41–42 to you? How would you feel if you were Mary and you heard your sister say verse 40? How would you have handled the situation of conflict if you were in Jesus' place?

Luke 11:37–54: Fools! Hypocrites!

Given the care that Pharisees took with maintaining purity in their table fellowship, the man in verse 37 must have considered Jesus to be a teacher who scrupulously kept the law. His astonishment in verse 38 seems to verify this assumption.

1. What does the Pharisee find offensive about Jesus?
2. What does Jesus condemn about the Pharisees? How do they fit the category of the spiritually blind in 11:34–35?
3. Jesus condemned the Pharisees and teachers of the law in 7:30–34 for refusing to respond to either John the Baptist or himself. Furthermore, he called them "this generation" in 7:31. How is his condemnation of the teachers of the law in 11:45–52 similar to that in 7:30–34?
4. What is the basic flaw that Jesus detests about these Pharisees and teachers of the law? (Note how these men respond to Jesus' criticism of them).

Luke 12:1–12: Whom to Fear

In spite of unbelief by some, the crowds following Jesus continue to grow larger (cf. 12:1 with 11:29). But popularity can lead to corruption.

1. How does Jesus motivate his audience to avoid the hypocrisy of appearing righteous when around others but being quite different when no one can see? (Cf. his criticism against the religious leaders in 11:43–46.)
2. How does 12:4–7 combine fear of God with great comfort in God? How will following Jesus substantially contribute to the individual's security before God?
3. How would 12:8–12 be reassuring to Luke's readers who are involved in evangelization?

Luke 12:13–34: The Meaning of True Riches

1. In Jesus' story in 12:16–21, how does the rich man's lack of an eternal perspective cause him to go astray in life, seeking only his own security? What is the result of a life devoted to fulfilling one's own desires?
2. What does 12:22–31 assert about values in life?
3. What does 12:22–31 reveal about replacing covetousness with peace?
4. How does almsgiving (giving aid to the poor) in 12:33–34 replace concern for self?

SECTION SEVEN: LUKE 12:35–15:32: THE KINGDOM OF GOD IN THE WORLD
Luke 12:35–40: Priorities

1. How do these instructions reinforce the previous passages on devoting one's life to building the kingdom of God on earth?

Reflection on Money and Security

Jesus' parable tells of a man who, although he already has plenty in life, is obsessed by a craving to hoard more and more. Explaining that life involves more than physical goods, Jesus indicates that misplaced priorities cause anxiety and failure to experience life as God's gift.

Upon what in life do you place the most emphasis? How does this affect the way you live day by day? How does it affect the way you set long-term goals? How does it affect the amount of anxiety you experience?

---

2. What might this paragraph indicate about Luke's understanding of when the Lord Jesus will return? (The second and third watches of the night [12:38] are between 9 P.M. and 3 A.M.)

Luke 12:41–48: Responsible Service

Jesus again stresses the necessity of integrity in a person's life. In 11:39–46 he attacked religious leaders for their hypocrisy, and in 12:1–3 he warned his disciples against such behavior. Now he warns against acting one way when one knows the master is present but quite another when the master is gone. The secret things of a person will be revealed and judged (12:1–3; note that the servant in 12:45 "says to himself," that is, in secret).

1. What message does this passage communicate to all of Jesus' followers?
2. How does this passage specifically address Christian leaders?
3. How does integrity in leadership relate to the severity of judgment experienced by those who do not accomplish God's will (12:47–48)?
4. In what way is judgment based on how much a person understands (12:48)?

Luke 12:49–53: "I came to bring fire to the earth"

1. Compare 12:49 with 3:16–17. Jews who had messianic hopes believed that the messiah would come bringing fiery judgment. But according to 12:50, what will happen to Jesus Messiah before this occurs?
2. Jesus taught his followers not to live in anxiety (12:22–34); but what does he now warn about the possible cost of living for him?

Luke 12:54–59: Interpreting the Signs of the Times

1. How does this teaching relate to 12:35–40? To 12:41–48?
2. The "present time" (12:56) refers to the events Jesus is accomplishing. How do people's responses to him reveal the ways in which they interpret the "signs"?

Luke 13:1–5: Divine Retribution

1. Many people tend to think that if life is going well, God is blessing, and if we experience tragedy, God is punishing us for something. How does Jesus evaluate this belief in 13:1–5?
2. How should these words speak to those who, although they hear Jesus teach about the kingdom of God, cannot get very excited about his radical call to discipleship because their lives are progressing so smoothly? (Cf. 12:16–21.)

Luke 13:6–9: What If Things Are Going Fine?

1. How does this passage relate to 13:1–5 in commenting on the idea that absence of judgment implies God's pleasure?
2. What does it say about God's patience?

Luke 13:10–21: "What is the kingdom of God like?"

This story reflects the high value that Jews faithful to the laws of Moses placed on observing the Sabbath. Some, like the Pharisees, would allow for the performance of limited activities on the Sabbath, such as those mentioned in 13:15. Members of the Dead Sea Scroll community, however, were extremely strict in the matter of Sabbath observance, as the following quotation reveals:

> No man shall walk abroad to do business on the Sabbath. He shall not walk more than one thousand cubits beyond his town.
> No man shall eat on the Sabbath day except that which is already prepared. . . .
> No man shall willingly mingle (with others) on the Sabbath.
> No man shall walk more than two thousand cubits after a beast to pasture it outside his town. He shall not raise his hand to strike it with his fist. If it is stubborn he shall not take it out of his house. (*Damascus Document* 10–11)[17]

Such passionate observance of the Sabbath helps us understand why Jesus' opponents thought that he was far too loose in what he did on this day.

1. What two approaches to religion clash in this story? Where does each place primary importance? With what result?
2. What do the parables of the expansion of the kingdom of God in 13:18–21 say about the nature of Jesus' ministry?

Luke 13:22–30: Enter by the Narrow Door

Luke continues the theme of the journey toward Jerusalem in 13:22, in the context of questions about who will enter the kingdom of God. Thus, Luke uses the journey toward Jerusalem as a means of commenting on the journey to the kingdom of God. (On the banquet mentioned in 13:29, see comments under 14:15–24.)

1. Why do verses 28–30 serve both as a warning to Jewish religious leaders, such as the scribes who are given places of honor in the synagogue (11:43), and as a word of encouragement to Gentiles?

Luke 13:31–35: Prophets Are Killed in Jerusalem

Herod was last mentioned in 9:7–9, where he heard about Jesus and sought to see him. "Fox" is an apt description for the cunning Herod Antipas, but he will not detain Jesus. No amount of human intervention can prevent Jesus from completing his God-ordained mission in Jerusalem.

Personal Reflection
By and large, people in the United States desire personal peace and affluence, and we believe that if we have these, we will be content. In your experience, how often do you hear people speak of Jesus as the one who comes to cast fire on the earth and bring division (12:49–53)? Why? Do you focus more on your own peace and security ("What is in it for me?") or on discerning the times by analyzing world events around you (12:54–56)?

1. According to this passage, what does Jesus desire for Jerusalem?
2. What do his words reveal about the responsiveness of Jerusalem, the center of Jewish religious life?

Luke 14:1–14: Choosing the Best Places

Some Pharisees helpfully warned Jesus of Herod in 13:31, and now some others invite him to a Sabbath meal. But they are carefully scrutinizing his actions (14:1), and when he heals the man with dropsy, they are apparently offended. *Dropsy* is an older term for edema, a condition in which fluid accumulates in the body, with resulting swelling. The man's life was not in danger; Jesus could have waited until the next day to heal him.

Conflicting views existed among the Jews on what was permissible on the Sabbath. Although the Pharisees were fairly pragmatic about such matters, allowing for "work" under extenuating circumstances, the Dead Sea Scroll sectarians were more strict. They would, for example, let an animal die before they would break the Sabbath rest:

> No man shall assist a beast to give birth on the Sabbath day. And if it should fall into a cistern or pit, he shall not lift it out on the Sabbath. (*Damascus Document* 11)[18]

Compare the following specification made later, by the rabbinic successors to the Pharisees, in Mishnah *Yoma* 8.6:

> If a man has a pain in his throat they may drop medicine into his mouth on the Sabbath, since there is doubt whether life is in danger, and whenever there is doubt whether life is in danger this overrides the Sabbath.[19]

1. Imagine the scene portrayed in Luke 14:1–14. How do you think the Pharisee who invited him would evaluate Jesus' behavior as a dinner guest?
2. This passage continues Luke's theme of Jesus' concern for the poor and oppressed (14:12–14). Given the purity practices of the Pharisees, how would you expect them to respond to Jesus' advice?
3. What does 14:12–14 communicate about motivation for hospitality?

Personal Reflection
Consider for a moment your own approach to attending and hosting social events. What motivates you in such circumstances? How would following Jesus' advice change your social life?

Luke 14:15–24: Who Will Come?

Pharisees, Essenes, and other Jews holding eschatological beliefs fondly looked forward to what was called the *messianic banquet*. They envisioned a time when the messiah would host a great banquet, to which he would invite the righteous to come and dine lavishly (see 13:29). This vision of blessed conditions in the future messianic kingdom lies behind the statement in 14:15, and when Pharisees gathered for meals like the one Jesus attended in this story, they considered the meal to be a kind of prelude to that great banquet to come. Jesus' vision of the kingdom of God and who will be part of it, however, differs substantially from theirs.

1. How does Jesus' parable serve as a warning to those who refuse to follow him yet think they will be part of the kingdom of God?
2. Compare 14:21–24 with 13:30 and 14:13–14. What Lukan theme does this story continue?

BANQUETS AMONG THE SOCIAL ELITE

Even by modern standards, the banquet described by Jesus in 14:16–24 seems bizarre. Among the social elite of Jesus' time, the action the offended rich man who hosted the banquet took would be absolutely outlandish. By its shocking nature, the parable focuses attention on the issue of who will attend the great messianic banquet. Those whom the Pharisees expected to attend—namely, themselves and others who carefully kept the purity laws and meticulously obeyed the laws of Moses—are among those who decline to come, largely because of social pressure.

Jesus describes a great banquet, such as could only be given by one of the social elite. Envisioned is a man who would occupy the top 2 percent of ancient Near Eastern society. He lives in a preindustrial city in a culture where social segregation is quite rigid: The wealthy elite inhabit a certain section of town, and the rest of the citizens live in other quarters, engaged in various kinds of crafts, manufacturing and selling goods in their homes. In the Jerusalem of Jesus' day, the Sadducees, Herodians, and other wealthy families formed the social elite.[20]

Members of the urban elite were the trendsetters in society, and they were quite concerned to make the right social moves to maintain their honor in the community. Attending and hosting proper banquets was part of this system; and of course, a man knew that he must invite only the proper people (i.e., social equals) to such functions. In Jesus' parable, it seems that the invited guests carefully observe that the eminent among the social elite decline to attend the banquet; so to save honor, the others also make excuses not to come, for they do not want to experience any social ostracism. Their excuses are lame and therefore signal their disapproval of the banquet. "No Middle Easterner would have bought either land or oxen without thorough inspection ahead of time."[21] The dishonored host then commits total social suicide, sending his slave out to invite those who have absolutely no business attending his party. The parable defies all expectations and virtually demands that the Pharisees reconsider their status in the kingdom of God.

Luke 14:25–35: The Cost of Discipleship

1. In spite of opposition from religious leaders, the crowd keeps getting bigger (14:25). But now, after proclaiming to the Pharisees the parable in which the lower classes of society are compelled to attend the banquet, what harsh message does Jesus proclaim to the masses of such people who follow him?
2. What do Jesus' examples emphasize about entering the kingdom of God?
3. How does the example of salt in 14:34–35 reinforce the point made in 14:26–33?

Luke 15:1–10: Seeking the Lost

1. According to Luke 15:1–3, what motivates Jesus to tell the parables in this chapter?
2. Luke 14:25–35 emphasizes the cost of discipleship. What does 15:1–10 emphasize?
3. What do these two parables affirm about God? About Jesus' ministry, which the Pharisees criticize? How does this compare with Jesus' self-description in 7:29–35?

Luke 15:11–32: The Return of the Wayward Son

1. Jesus' description of the prodigal son is graphic enough to offend deeply the sensibilities of pious Jews. In what different ways are the young man's actions offensive to Jewish expectations for a son?
2. With which character in Jesus' parable would one of the Pharisees from 15:2 most likely identify? Why?
3. With which character would one of the tax collectors most likely identify? Why?
4. With which character do you most identify? Why?
5. What does this parable affirm about God? About the kingdom of God?
6. What aspects of Jesus' teaching on the kingdom of God does Luke 12:35–15:32 most emphasize? What aspect did you personally find most challenging?

SECTION EIGHT: INTERPRETING THE PARABLES OF JESUS

Throughout much of the history of the church, parable interpretation predominantly involved allegory. This method of interpreting the details of a parable as referring to spiritual realities not readily apparent in the parable itself finds some justification in texts such as the parable of the sower and its interpretation in Mark 4:1–20; Matthew 13:1–23; and Luke 8:4–15. Here, Jesus explains to his disciples that the seed stands for the word of God; the soils represent different ways of responding to the word; and so forth.

But most of the parables are not allegories, and the endeavor to find numerous spiritual principles in them can lead to bizarre distortions of their content. The standard example of this is Augustine's interpretation of the parable of the Good Samaritan:

> *A certain man went down from Jerusalem to Jericho;* Adam himself is meant; *Jerusalem* is the heavenly city of peace, from whose blessedness Adam fell; *Jericho* means the moon, and signifies our mortality, because it is born, waxes, wanes, and dies. *Thieves* are the devil and his angels. *Who stripped him,* namely, of his immortality; *and beat him,* by persuading him to sin; *and left him half-dead,* because in so far as man can understand and know God, he lives, but in so far as he is wasted and oppressed by sin, he is dead; he is therefore called half-dead. The *priest* and *Levite* who saw him and passed by signify the priesthood and ministry of the Old Testament, which could profit nothing for salvation. *Samaritan* means Guardian, and therefore the Lord Himself is signified by this name. The *binding of the wounds* is the restraint of sin. *Oil* is the comfort of good hope; *wine* is the exhortation to work with fervent spirit. The *beast* is the flesh in which He deigned to come to us. The being *set upon the beast* is belief in the incarnation of Christ. The *inn* is the Church, where travelers returning to their heavenly country are refreshed after pilgrimage. The *morrow* is after the resurrection of the Lord. The *two pence* are either the two precepts of love, or the promise of this life and of that which is to come. The *innkeeper* is the Apostle (Paul). The supererogatory payment is either his counsel of celibacy, or the fact that he worked with his own hands lest he should be a burden to any of the weaker brethren when the Gospel was new, though it was lawful for him "to live by the Gospel." (*Quaestiones Evangeliorum* 2.19)

The excesses represented by this wholesale reading of Pauline theology into the parable may seem amusing, but many Christians through the ages have seen strong evidence of God's inspiration of the Bible in such imaginative reinterpretations. A valuable corrective came at the end of the nineteenth century.

One of the landmark books on parable interpretation is Adolf Jülicher's *Die Gleichnisreden Jesu* (The parables of Jesus), published in 1888. Jülicher argued that the parables are not allegories but merely seek to teach one main point, a general moral truth.

The main points that he believed the parables were designed to communicate, however, were the ideals of his own theological system, old-line liberalism, which emphasized such beliefs as the universal fatherhood of God and the brotherhood of man. Thus, for example, in the parable of the Good Samaritan, the details of the story (so important to Augustine) are insignificant. The main point of the parable is to show the need to be a good neighbor (help anyone in need).

Jülicher's major contribution was to show the inadequacy of allegorical interpretation, and for this reason his work is of great importance. The next major book on parables was *The Parables of the Kingdom* (1935), by C. H. Dodd, a British scholar. Dodd argued that we must seek to interpret the parables in light of what they would have meant in Jesus' own day. We must understand their meaning in the situations that elicited them during the life of Jesus, not in those of the early church that elicited the actual production of the Gospels (let alone our own, contemporary theological belief systems). The implications of this distinction are very important.

The life setting of Jesus differs from the life setting of the early church, and this needs to be taken seriously. By the time the Evangelists arranged the stories in their Gospels, they did not know the original situations in which Jesus delivered his parables. Followers of Jesus repeated his parables, but in the telling and retelling of them, the original contexts were lost. The Evangelists placed the parables in particular contexts in their Gospels, but the situations they have the parables address in their narratives do not necessarily coincide with the settings that elicited them during the life of Jesus. The Evangelists therefore actually interpreted the parables for us by placing them in their present settings.[22]

Dodd believed that in the life setting of Jesus, the parables assert what is called "realized eschatology." In the proclamation and ministry of Jesus, the powers of the age to come were breaking into the present age, meaning that the kingdom of God had come. The parables therefore reflect this, and if some of them now seem to speak of events after the lifetime of Jesus, they actually represent forceful ways of speaking of the crisis events that Jesus brought about (see, for example, Luke 11:20).

The next major work on parable interpretation was by Joachim Jeremias, *Die Gleichnesse Jesu* (English translation: *The Parables of Jesus*, 1954). Jeremias followed Dodd's lead in seeking the interpretation of the parables in the life setting of Jesus, but he did not agree with Dodd's view of realized eschatology. He saw the parables primarily as weapons of war that Jesus used against the Jewish religious leaders. Jeremias's book breathes excitement because, as he engages in the process of explaining what he believes to be the Aramaic substratum of the various parables, he truly believes he has found an avenue back to the historical Jesus.

Since Jeremias, a great deal of work has been done on parable interpretation, and doing justice to the rich variety of materials available lies beyond the scope of this book.[23] One area to which a number of scholars have devoted considerable effort is that of the story parables, such as the parable of the prodigal son in Luke 15:11–32. Contrary to Jülicher's approach of seeking one basic truth in such parables, biblical scholars today tend to appreciate the multivalent properties of these stories. When listening to the parable of the prodigal son, for example, different people legitimately hear different things. A Pharisee who has seriously attempted to live according to Mosaic law may well identify with the older brother in the parable and hear the story as a word of judgment against him. A tax collector or a prostitute, by contrast, may identify with the prodigal son and hear the parable as a word of grace, offering new hope in spite of a disappointing past.

In either case, the parable in Luke 15:11–32 turns normal expectations upside down, shattering the view of the world held by those who listen.[24] Gordon Fee perceptively compares the parables to jokes in the way in which they elicit a response from the hearer:

> It is this "call for response" nature of the parable that causes our great dilemma in interpreting them. For in some ways to interpret a parable is to destroy what it was originally. It is like interpreting a joke. The whole point of a joke and what makes it funny is that the hearer has an immediacy with it as it is being told. It is funny to the hearer precisely because he or she gets "caught," as it were. But it can only "catch" them if they understand the points of reference in the joke. If you have to interpret the joke by explaining the points of reference, it no longer catches the hearer and therefore usually fails to capture the same quality of laughter.[25]

Parables function to influence the listener in a way that is lost if one needs to hear an explanation of the meaning of the parable.

If speaking in parables were merely a folksy way of communicating certain truths, we could dispense with the parables themselves and simply assert the truths directly. There would be no reason to tell the story of the Good Samaritan; we could simply state that love should know no limits as we seek to be good neighbors to those in need. But in fact, when Jesus told the story, it functioned to shock and disturb the one to whom it was told, far more than merely stating a moral truth could do. A good story draws us into its narrative world, where we actively identify with the characters and the action. If the story suddenly turns our expectations upside down, like the punch line of a good joke, we experience laughter or anger or some other emotion. This participatory character of story cannot be replaced by explanation of the meaning of the story. You either get the joke or do not. If someone must explain it to you, the edge is gone; the experience of being "caught" evaporates, and along with it goes the impact of the story event. Story parables cannot be reduced to the "main point" without destroying their intended effect.

How we respond to a story reveals much about ourselves, and this dimension of response bears careful reflection. Instead of *interpreting* the parables, we actually find ourselves *being interpreted* by them. When, for example, you hear the parable about men who are hired throughout the day to work in a man's vineyard (Matt. 20:1–16), how do you respond to the ending? Some of the workers were hired at 6 A.M. and labored in the hot sun until 6 P.M.; others came to work at 5 P.M. and worked but one hour. At quitting time, the employer paid everyone the same wage, regardless of whether he worked one hour or twelve hours. When you hear this story, is your first reaction to think that the employer was unfair to those who had worked all day, even though they received the wage they agreed on that morning? Or do you think, "What incredibly good luck for those fellows who worked only one hour!"? How you respond—the person with whom you most identify in the story—tells much about where you are as a person. And interestingly, you may identify with one person in a parable today and a different person a year from now.

Not all Jesus' parables are story parables. Some are designed merely to communicate a simple truth, and their meaning is quite obvious. The meaning of the parable of the rich fool in Luke 12:16–21, at least in its present setting, is abundantly clear. The text even provides a moral in verse 21, so that no one will miss the point. Thus, there is no one rule that we can successfully apply in reading all the parables. We need to be sensitive to the character of each parable and read it in a way that is consistent with its composition. For a few, this will mean looking for allegorical intent; for others, it will involve understanding the one main point; and for others, it will mean imaginative participation in the story, perhaps by retelling the parable in contemporary terms so that we can relate to the situation described and perhaps feel the shattering of our expectations.

SECTION NINE: LUKE 16:1–19:27: THE KINGDOM OF GOD AND THE POOR

The major theme of Jesus' concern for the poor and outcast remains important in this last part of the travel narrative in Luke. Jesus' words also continue to present shocking reversals of expectations. Those whom people of his time would expect to be in good standing before God tend to oppose the advance of the kingdom of God in the person and ministry of Jesus. Those whom society would relegate as unfit for the kingdom forcibly enter into it.

Luke 16:1–15: Congratulations! You Were Magnificently Dishonest

The parable of the dishonest steward is notoriously difficult to interpret, and its conclusion shocks virtually all who read it. In light of the previous section, see how you respond.

1. What was your response to reading 16:1–9?
2. What point do you think Jesus seeks to communicate in this parable?
3. Does 16:10–13 seem to contradict or help us to understand 16:1–9? Why?
4. Luke 16:14 accuses the Pharisees of loving money, and 16:15 seems to indicate that they considered money to be a sign of God's blessing. Why does Jesus judge them unfit for the kingdom of God?
5. What does the Pharisees' response in 16:14 indicate about whether or not they were "caught" in the hearing of the parable in 16:1–9?

Imaginative interpretations abound for this parable. Perhaps it is meant to be humorous, a joke designed to shock the audience. (Note that the message of 16:10–13 directly contradicts the main point of 16:9.) Or perhaps it is a story taken from the world of the marketplace, where shrewd dealings won a certain kind of respect. Jesus might be instructing his followers to learn from unscrupulous businesspeople that shrewd use of money can be used effectively to build the kingdom of God. Some scholars believe that the dishonest steward put his master in a bind by forgiving extraordinarily large debts, sums substantial enough to represent the tax load of an entire village. If the villagers are already rejoicing at the magnanimity of the rich man, he will seriously lose face if he reverses the steward's actions. Thus, he chooses to retain the honor and suffer the financial loss.[26] A problem with this interpretation, however, is that the steward takes his action *so that* people will provide for *him* when he is kicked out, which implies that those who were given special deals knew the rich man was unaware of what was happening.

Luke 16:16–18: Forcefully Entering

1. During the ministry of Jesus, the kingdom of God advances (11:20). According to 16:16–18, how does the present reality of the kingdom affect Old Testament regulations, such as divorce?
2. What characterizes the people who are entering the kingdom?

Luke 16:19–31: Lazarus and What's-His-Name

1. What does this parable say to the belief that a person's status in earthly life is a barometer of his or her standing before God? How does this compare with 16:14–15?
2. How does the parable continue the Lukan motif of great reversals and the theme of God's concern for the poor?
3. What does 16:27–31 say about people who are so convinced they are right that they would refuse to change their minds even if someone came back from the dead to speak with them?

Reflection on the Value of Human Beings
On a gut level, how do a person's financial achievement and position within society affect the way in which you tend to evaluate his or her worth as a person? How does your attitude compare with Jesus'?

Luke 17:1–10: "Increase our faith!"

In Luke's narrative, Jesus moves from *confronting the Pharisees* with a story about a rich man who burns in Hades and a poor beggar whom God rewards in paradise (16:19–31) to *confronting his disciples* with the implications of what it means to serve (17:1–10). We have previously seen such reversals of emphasis in Luke 10, where Jesus stresses *doing* in 10:30–37 and then emphasizes *sitting* and *listening* in 10:38–42. Also, in 14:25–35, Jesus proclaims a hard line on the cost of discipleship, but in 15:1–32 his parables reveal God as actively seeking those who have gone astray and as throwing a party when they are found. Both aspects are true, and such juxtaposition makes Luke's narrative quite fascinating to read.

1. Forgiving a perennially offensive person can be extremely difficult. What guidelines does Jesus give for such relationships?
2. What seems odd about his disciples' response in 17:5?
3. Does the material beginning with 17:5 seem to be a random collection of sayings, or do you think that Luke intends us to see verse 5 as a response to verses 1–4, and verse 6 as an answer to how we are to accomplish verses 1–4?
4. What does 17:7–10 say about whether or not God is bound to reward people on earth for their righteousness? What does it say about a disciple's motivation for serving the Lord?

Luke 17:11–19: The Grateful Leper

1. How does the teaching about gratitude in this story compare with 17:7–10?
2. Compare this story with 10:30–37. Why would it be offensive to Jewish listeners?

Luke 17:20–37: The Kingdom of God and Vultures

1. How does Jesus' claim about the kingdom of God in 17:21 go against the expectations of most first-century Jewish people? Compare this with 11:20 and 13:18–21. What claim is Jesus making about his ministry?
2. What does 17:22–37 reveal about the second coming of Jesus Messiah? How is this different from what he says about the present situation of the kingdom of God on earth in 17:21?

Luke 17:23 warns Jesus' disciples not to run about checking to see if reports of his return are accurate. Evidently, in Luke's day there were problems with speculation about when Jesus would return, and this had upset the faith of some Christians. Luke 17:24 lets the reader know that Jesus' second coming will be a cosmic event visible to the entire world.

Luke 18:1–8: "I have no fear of God and no respect for anyone"

Jesus' parables abound with colorful characters. In this one he vividly portrays an unjust judge, who finally responds to a poor widow not out of concern but out of exasperation.

1. How does the message that this parable teaches about prayer compare with that presented in 11:5–13?
2. What comfort does this passage offer to those disciples of Jesus who are enduring persecution for the sake of the gospel?

Luke 18:9–14: Prayers That God Hears

1. What does this parable communicate about religious complacence?

Luke 18:15–17: Children and the Kingdom of God

1. How does the disciples' attitude toward children reflect some of the values held by Jesus' opponents?
2. How does the content of this passage compare with the message in 18:9–14?
3. How do both stories in 18:9–17 assert Luke's great-reversal theme?

Luke 18:18–30: The Eye of the Needle

This story continues Jesus' teaching on wealth, poverty, and the kingdom of God. The rich man's question in verse 18 is almost exactly what the lawyer asked in 10:25, but here Jesus responds differently. Instead of asking the man to rehearse theology, Jesus focuses on what is most important in his life.

1. What does the wealthy ruler learn about himself? What keeps him from eternal life? (See also 16:13.)
2. Why do those who listen show such surprise at Jesus' teaching in 18:26?

For people to leave their families and land (18:28–29; cf. 5:11) would place them in a precarious position, unless they became part of an alternative type of kinship group. To leave land and kinship connections was to leave an entire social network, involving one's ability to earn a living.

Personal Reflection
What fears would you have if you were asked to sever ties with your social network? What assurances would you want before doing so?

Luke 18:31–43: Three Kinds of Blindness

1. To what does Luke attribute the disciples' lack of understanding of Jesus' passion prediction?
2. How does Luke modify Mark's version (Mark 10:32–34) to produce this picture? (Note that Luke deletes Mark 10:35–45 about the disciples' argument over who is the greatest and transfers a shortened version of this event to Luke 22:24–27.)
3. What important Lukan theme does 18:35–43 again emphasize? (Notice that Jesus meets the blind man while approaching Jericho [18:35], whereas in Mark 10:46 the encounter occurs as Jesus leaves Jericho.)

Luke 19:1–10: Can You Believe He Is Going to Stay with That Scum?

In this story, Jesus deals not with a poor man but with a very rich one. Unlike the rich ruler in 18:18–23, however, this rich tax collector has gained his fortune through questionable means.

1. Why do the people in the crowd respond as they do when Jesus publicly announces that he is going to Zacchaeus's house for a meal?
2. How do the parables in Luke 15 provide valuable background information for answering the complaint in 19:7? (See also Luke 5:27–32.)
3. How is Zacchaeus's response to Jesus different from that of the rich ruler in 18:18–23?
4. What does this story reaffirm about how Jesus views people?

Luke 19:11–27: "Slaughter them in my presence"

Luke again mentions the mistaken belief that the kingdom of God would come with great signs when Jesus arrived at Jerusalem (19:11). This viewpoint, although commonly held, represented a misunderstanding of the kingdom.

The background for the parable in 19:12–27 may be the efforts of Herod's son Archelaus to rule after Herod's death. Archelaus journeyed to Rome to have Augustus Caesar confirm Herod's will, which named him as successor. But Archelaus was a brutal and tyrannical leader, whom the people hated. When he went to Rome to meet with Augustus, a delegation of Jews from Jerusalem followed him to protest his rule. Augustus decided to honor Herod's will, and Archelaus returned to rule over people who disliked him intensely (Josephus, *Antiquities* 17.9–11 [§§206–323]; *Jewish War* 2.1–6 [§§1–100]).

1. If this parable is allegorical of Jesus' own situation of conflict with religious authorities, and the servants who make ten and five pounds more are good models of discipleship, then what does the parable say about the role of taking risks to build the kingdom?
2. If, by contrast, this parable is a story against the rich who get more for themselves at the expense of the poor, which servant is the honorable one?

First-century Mediterranean societies did not function with the same presuppositions as does twentieth-century capitalism. Whether most people then would have viewed the "successful servants" in this parable as crooked or commendable is unclear. Perhaps the parable is a harsh condemnation against the unscrupulous practices of the foreign landowners, an example of how things work outside the kingdom of God.

One of the narrow streets in old Jerusalem.

Luke 19:13 states that ten servants each received ten pounds, yet only three are later called to give account of their efforts. In the similar parable of the "talents" in Matthew 25:14–30, three servants get differing amounts, and each is called to give account. (See the note under Matt. 25:14–30.)

3. What major themes does Luke relentlessly pursue in 16:1–19:27?

SECTION TEN:
LUKE 19:28–24:53: JESUS' HEROIC DEATH

The journey to Jerusalem ends. Jesus arrives at the city of his death. In the next stories, Luke largely follows Mark's outline when recounting the events of Jesus' final days; but he creatively orders the material to present his own perspective on the passion narrative and his own, distinct portrait of Jesus.

Luke 19:28–44: If You Only Knew What Brings Peace

Again, Luke shows that the common people proclaim Jesus king, but the Pharisees do not accept this and seek to have Jesus silence the crowd. Try to feel the excitement and drama in this story. Jerusalem is packed with pilgrims who have come with religious zeal to the central shrine of Israel. People are tense with expectancy over the pilgrimage, and suddenly the word spreads that the miracle worker, Jesus, is riding into town on a young donkey. A large crowd forms, and the mass of his followers proclaim him king. This excited proclamation poses a great threat to religious and political security. The theme of enthusiastic acceptance and bitter rejection of Jesus permeates the following narrative.

1. Whereas the story of Jesus' triumphal entry ends in Mark 11:10 with the shouts of the people, Luke adds verses 39–44 in chapter 19. Note the repetition of "peace" in verses 38 and 42. Why is this ironic?
2. Failure to acknowledge Jesus seals the fate of Jerusalem. What will happen to the city? (Compare 13:33–35.)

Luke 19:45–48: A Den of Robbers

In Mark's account, Jesus enters the temple to inspect it on one day (Mark 11:11) and returns the next day to drive out those involved in commerce on the temple grounds (Mark 11:15–19). The cursing of the fig tree and its subsequent withering form a framework around the temple-cleansing story and are symbolic for what happens to the temple. Luke, however, leaves the fig tree completely out of his story.

1. In Luke's account, on which day does Jesus cleanse the temple?
2. In what activity does Jesus primarily involve himself in the temple? (Cf. 2:46–49.)
3. What keeps the leaders from arresting Jesus?

Luke 20:1–19: "By what authority . . . ?"

As Jesus continues his teaching ministry in the temple (19:47; 20:1), the main leaders of the Jewish community come to question him about his seemingly subversive activities. The confrontation further intensifies their hostility toward him and their resolve to eliminate him.

1. Into what dilemma does Jesus' question about John the Baptist place these men?
2. Jesus' parable describes God's attempts to reach the Jewish leaders and their consistent rejection of God's messengers. To whom does Jesus say God will give the vineyard?
3. How does the response of the scribes and priests in 20:19 compare with 19:47–48?

Comparing God to a foreign landowner represents a surprising move in storytelling. A large percentage of the land on the northwest shores of the Sea of Galilee and in the Galilean uplands, not to mention virtually all of the upper Jordan valley, belonged to foreign landlords during the time of Jesus. The parable illustrates the attitude of many Galilean peasants toward these hated, wealthy, foreign landholders. Under the influence of the Zealots, such violence toward the messengers of these men is quite understandable. The killing of the only heir with the idea of gaining possession of the land seems to indicate that they believed the owner was dead and only his son remained alive to claim the land. Perhaps the tenants believed that under certain conditions the land would be viewed legally as ownerless property, which they could therefore claim on a first-come, first-served basis.[27]

Luke 20:20–26: "Is it lawful for us to pay taxes?"

As we saw in Mark 12:13–17, the scribes' question places Jesus into a "catch-22," for either a yes or a no answer poses a threat.

1. How does Luke's addition of verse 20 intensify the picture of evil intent seen in Mark 12:13?
2. How does Luke's addition of verse 26 intensify the picture of defeat given in Mark 12:17?

Luke 20:27–21:4: Children of the Resurrection

Belief in a limited resurrection was not uncommon among Jews of Jesus' time. For example, the *Psalms of Solomon*, written around 40 B.C.E., presumably by Pharisees, reveals a strong belief that only the righteous will be raised to life eternal. The wicked would experience total destruction, not eternal torment (see also Rev. 20:5–6, 11–15).

1. Note carefully how Luke 20:34–36 modifies Mark 12:23–25. Do these verses teach that only the righteous will rise from the dead? Why or why not?
2. Luke 21:1–4 continues the theme in this Gospel of the relationship between material wealth, pleasing God, and entering the kingdom of God. What connection does this have with the reason

the scribes receive a stricter judgment in 20:45–47? (Cf. 12:47–48 and 19:11–27.)

Luke 21:5–38: The End of the Age

Luke's wording of the *apocalyptic discourse* reveals his perspective, which we have seen before, that Jesus' return is not imminent. Carefully read and compare 21:8–9, 13–15, 20–22, 24 with the parallel material in Mark 13:6–7, 10–11, 14–16, 19–20.

1. What modifications does Luke make to emphasize that the end of the age will not be for a while?
2. Why might these Lukan modifications be seen as evidence that he wrote after the Romans destroyed Jerusalem in 70 C.E.?
3. How does the Lukan addition in 21:34–36 complement the central point of 21:29–33?

Luke 22:1–6: The Betrayal

Luke leaves out the story of the woman anointing Jesus with perfume at Bethany (cf. Mark 14:3–9), perhaps because it might give the reader an impression that Jesus was unconcerned for the poor. He also adds some details about Judas going to betray Jesus (cf. Mark 14:10–11).

1. To what does Luke attribute Judas' decision to betray Jesus?
2. How does this differ from the reason implied in Mark's account?

Luke 22:7–23: "The Son of Man is going as it has been determined"

The note of divine destiny once again rings in 22:21–23, a Lukan addition whose explanation of the betrayal echoes the same theological understanding as 22:3. A similar explanation occurs in Acts 2:22–24, this time in a sermon by Peter on the day of Pentecost.

1. Jesus says in 22:15 that he has greatly desired to eat this Passover meal with his disciples. Is there any indication in this passage that he ate the Passover meal?
2. Does Luke's account of the Last Supper give any indication that Jesus dreaded his coming death?

Luke earlier omitted Mark 10:45, where Jesus says, "The Son of Man came . . . to give his life a ransom for many," and this is consistent with his passion narrative. In Luke's account, Jesus does not describe his death as substitutionary atonement (giving his life in order to liberate others from the deadly effects of sin).

It seems to be more of a martyrdom, which functions as an example for his disciples to follow.

Luke 22:24–46: "You will sit on thrones"

Luke moved the story of the disciples' dispute over greatness (22:24–30) from Mark's context of Jesus' passion prediction at the beginning of his journey toward Jerusalem (Mark 10:42–45) to the context of the Last Supper (Luke 22:24–30).

1. Emphasizing again the reversal of normal expectations, what do verses 24–27 teach about greatness in the kingdom of God?
2. Luke adds the material in 22:28–30. What does this contribute to his portrait of Jesus' disciples?
3. Luke 22:31–33 is also unique to this Gospel, reemphasizing the familiar Lukan themes of divine sovereignty and prayer. How does 22:34 differ slightly from Mark 14:30?
4. Luke 22:35–38 again is found only in this Gospel. In what way does the contrast between the former days when Jesus sent his disciples out with no provisions (22:35) and the current situation of needing money and a sword for protection (22:36) reflect the Lukan perspective that the Lord will not come back very soon? What is the purpose of this material?
5. How many times does Jesus pray to God for guidance in Luke 22:39–46? How does this compare with Mark 14:32–42?

Note in your Bible the double brackets around Luke 22:43–44, which signal a potential problem with these verses. Luke 22:43–44 is quite dramatic, telling of Jesus' sweat falling like drops of blood. But the description contrasts sharply with the portrait of Jesus presented elsewhere in this Gospel. These verses were not originally in Luke's version of the story; they were added by a copyist later on. Good evidence of this may be seen in the considerable textual diversity among the Greek manuscripts of the Gospel. Some manuscripts contain verses 43–44 in this location, in the story of Jesus praying, whereas others place them after Matthew 26:39, and others omit them entirely. The substantial diversity among the Greek manuscripts and the fact that verses 43–44 do not fit Luke's theology demonstrate that we should not view them as authentically part of Luke's Gospel.

6. When 22:43–44 is removed from the text, how does the picture of Jesus' prayer in Gethsemane in Luke differ from that given in Mark 14:32–42?

Luke 22:47–53: Betrayal and Swordplay

The two swords mentioned in 22:38 now find use, albeit futile, as one of Jesus' followers cuts off the ear of the high priest's slave.

Whether or not the disciple meant to split the man's head and missed remains unstated, but the action brings Jesus' rebuke. Only Luke tells us that Jesus healed the man's ear (22:51).

1. In what ways does the story reveal that Jesus is in control of the situation?
2. What accusation does Jesus make to defend his innocence?

Luke 22:54–71: Denial and Trial

Luke modifies Mark's sequence somewhat, for in his account, the men who seized Jesus mock him during the night, but the actual assembly of the Sanhedrin does not occur at the same time. There are also differences from the trial account found in Mark 14:53–61.

1. Compare 22:54–62 with 22:31–34. How do these stories reinforce Luke's portrait of Jesus being calmly in control?
2. Compare 22:63–71 with Mark 14:53–61. How does Luke's account differ with respect to the time of day when the Sanhedrin gathers to conduct their trial? With respect to the false witnesses mentioned in Mark 14:55–59?
3. In 22:67–71, Luke culminates his account of the religious leaders rejecting Jesus. What does this trial scene establish about Jesus' identity?

Luke 23:1–25: "Are you the king of the Jews?"

The Jewish leaders convict Jesus and all go before Pilate to accuse him of misleading the Jewish people (23:1–2).

1. How do the accusations against Jesus that the Sanhedrin brings before Pilate compare with those made in their earlier, private trial?
3. What verdicts do Pilate and Herod Antipas reach concerning the guilt or innocence of Jesus? (Remember the warning delivered to Jesus about Herod in 13:31. Also note that the information in 23:4–16 is important for Luke's account; only he records this material.)
4. Why does Pilate finally condemn Jesus to death?

Throughout the Gospel, Jesus enjoys widespread popularity with the common people but is rejected by the religious leaders. Now, in the trial scene, Luke mentions no Jews other than the circle of the Sanhedrin as being there to condemn Jesus. In 23:1 the "assembly" designates all those who were involved in the arrest. This becomes clear in 23:13, where the same group is again mentioned. The leaders and their underlings alone are responsible for demanding the execution, as the next story clarifies. The common people were not even there to protest and are helpless to stop the Roman-imposed crucifixion.

Luke 23:26–49: "Today you will be with me in Paradise"

1. How do the majority of the people feel about Jesus' conviction?
2. In what ways does Luke demonstrate Jesus' bravery in this passage? (Note that 23:27–31 is found only in Luke.)
3. Which people silently observe the crucifixion? Which mock Jesus on the cross?
4. In spite of a wretched life, one thief confesses his sin and asks Jesus for mercy. How will his fate compare with that of the Jewish leaders? (Cf. 18:9–14.)

The concept of *paradise* first appears in Jewish literature after the time of the Jews' exile in Babylon. In Aramaic, the Babylonian language, "paradise" signified a luxurious royal garden with flowing water, green grass, and beautiful shrubs and trees. Jewish people adopted this picture into their thinking of the afterlife because of its vivid connotations of tranquillity and blissful living. In a similar way the name Gehenna, which signifies the eternal fires of hell, came from the trash dump outside of Jerusalem called Gehinnom, where fires continually burned the rubbish. Jesus' promise in Luke 23:43 indicates that the thief will enjoy the bliss of heaven that very day.

5. In the temptation story of 4:1–13, Satan tempted Jesus in three ways ("If you are the Son of God . . . "). How are the temptations on the cross (23:35, 37, 39) similar in composition to these?
6. Compare Jesus' words on the cross in Luke 23:34, 43, 46 with his words in Mark 15:34. What is the difference in emphasis?
7. How are Jesus' words from the cross in Luke's account consistent with his portrait of Jesus as having great strength and bravery? Of Jesus being in control of the situation?
8. How does Jesus' death vindicate his innocence?

Luke 23:50–24:12: "He is not here, but has risen"

In 23:50–54 we find that not all the Jewish leaders opposed Jesus. Joseph, "a good and righteous man," buries Jesus. He joins the women from Galilee (23:55), previously described in 8:1–3, in his devotion to the Lord. But there is no indication any of them expected Jesus to rise from the dead.

1. When do the women finally understand what Jesus had previously tried to explain about his death? (Cf. 24:6–8, a Lukan addition, with 18:31–34.)
2. How do the apostles initially respond to the women's story?

Luke's Jesus

Luke 24:13–35: The Walk to Emmaus

All the information from this point onward is found only in Luke's Gospel. In his story of Jesus, Luke begins and ends with his own special material.

1. How would you describe the mental and emotional state of the two disciples of Jesus as they walk toward Emmaus?
2. What do their words to Jesus reveal about their messianic expectations?
3. How do these men finally come to understand how the scriptures predict the suffering and death of the Messiah?

Luke 24:36–53: "A ghost does not have flesh and bones"

1. What reception does Jesus initially receive from his followers? Why?
2. How does he convince the disciples of his identity?

Jewish people believed that angels do not eat. For example, in the Apocrypha, in Tobit 12:15–22, the angel Raphael convinces Tobit that Raphael is an angel by saying, "Although you were watching me, I really did not eat or drink anything—but what you saw was a vision" (12:19).

3. How will the disciples be equipped to fulfill the mission proclaimed in 24:46–47?
4. How does the location of Jesus' ascension to heaven compare with that specified in Matthew 28:7, 10, 16–20? (Remember that in Mark 16:7, the messenger in the tomb tells the women that Jesus will meet the disciples in Galilee. Each Evangelist works on a unique agenda in the closing section of the Gospel.)

RETROSPECT ON JESUS' DEATH

Both Romans and Jews considered it noble to be willing to die for one's beliefs. Seeking martyrdom, however, was tantamount to desiring to die or to suicide. Plato records the poignant story of Socrates refusing to flee from Athens to preserve his life after his opponents accused him of corrupting the youth with his philosophy. Socrates died for his philosophy, and Greeks and Romans respected such courage. Similarly, Jewish martyrdom accounts glorify bravery that inspires men and women to suffer and die rather than deny their ancestral faith. (See, for example, in the apocryphal book 4 Maccabees, the graphic detail of the immense suffering endured by faithful Jews.)

Luke describes Jesus' death as a martyrdom. Jesus does not seek death: He asks God to avert it but fearlessly follows the will of God despite the consequences (22:41–46). Luke's account has no pained prayer in the garden of Gethsemane, no agonizing on the cross. Jesus' concern in the garden is for his disciples, that they not enter into temptation (22:40, 45–46). On the way to Golgotha, he shows no fear for himself but lectures the bystanders on how hard it will be for them in the future (23:28–31). On the cross he prays for others (23:34), talks to a thief about being in paradise that very day (23:43), and finally, with a note of triumph, commits his spirit to his Father (23:46). The dreadful loneliness a Jesus in agony expresses in Mark's account is entirely missing in Luke's. The Lukan Jesus knows his task and accepts it, as a model martyr. His followers can look to his example as they face the possibility of losing their own lives in missionary service.

Like Mark before him, Luke carefully designs his story of Jesus to communicate effectively to a chosen audience. He writes to persuade, to inspire people to action. And his story of Jesus is incomplete without the second half of his work, the book of Acts. In Acts, God's vindication of Jesus comes fully into focus. The church is God's creation. God unleashes a mighty force onto the world when the Spirit-empowered followers of Jesus proclaim his message of salvation, beginning at Jerusalem and ending up at Rome, the center of the Roman world. Luke tells the story of the church as one of triumph through suffering, and Jesus is the model for his followers as they face persecution by those who reject the message of the kingdom of God.

REVIEW OF LUKAN THEMES

1. What major themes does Luke develop in his Gospel?
2. What characteristics dominate in his portrait of Jesus?
3. How does Luke's portrait of Jesus compare with Mark's?
4. How does the chronology of Jesus' ministry in Luke compare with that found in Mark?

FURTHER READING ON THE GOSPEL OF LUKE

Bailey, Kenneth. *Through Peasant Eyes: More Lucan Parables, Their Culture and Style.* Grand Rapids: Wm. B. Eerdmans Publishing Co., 1980.

Brown, Raymond E. *The Birth of the Messiah: A Commentary on the Infancy Narratives in Matthew and Luke.* Garden City, N.Y.: Doubleday & Co., 1977.

Cadbury, Henry J. *The Making of Luke-Acts.* London: SPCK, 1958.

———. *The Style and Literary Method of Luke.* Cambridge, Mass.: Harvard University Press, 1920.

Caird, G. B. *The Gospel of St. Luke.* Baltimore: Penguin Books, 1963.

Conzelmann, Hans. *Die Mitte der Zeit*, 1953. ET: *The Theology of Saint Luke,* trans. G. Buswell. New York: Harper & Row, 1961.

Fitzmyer, Joseph A. *The Gospel according to Luke.* 3 vols. Anchor Bible. Garden City, N.Y.: Doubleday, 1981–1986.

Green, Joel B. *The Gospel of Luke.* New International Commentary on the New Testament. Grand Rapids: Wm. B. Eerdmans Publishing Co., 1997.

Herzog, William R. II, *Parables as Subversive Speech: Jesus as Pedagogue of the Oppressed.* Louisville, Ky.: Westminster John Knox Press, 1994.

Jervell, Jacob. *Luke and the People of God.* Minneapolis: Augsburg Publishing House, 1972.

Johnson, Luke T. *The Gospel of Luke.* Sacra Pagina. Collegeville, Minn.: Michael Glazier, 1991.

Juel, Donald. *Luke-Acts: The Promise of History.* Atlanta: John Knox Press, 1984.

Marshall, I. H. *The Gospel of Luke.* Grand Rapids: Wm. B. Eerdmans Publishing Co., 1987.

Nolland, John. *Luke.* 3 vols. Word Biblical Commentary, 35A–35C. Dallas: Word Books, 1989–1993.

Talbert, Charles H. *Literary Patterns, Theological Themes, and the Genre of Luke-Acts.* Missoula, Mont.: Scholars Press, 1974.

———. *Reading Luke: A Literary and Theological Commentary on the Third Gospel.* New York: Crossroad, 1982.

Tannehill, Robert C. *The Narrative Unity of Luke-Acts: A Literary Interpretation.* Philadelphia: Fortress Press, 1986.

4

Matthew's Jesus

Authoritative Interpreter of the Law

Unlike Mark and Luke, the Gospel of Matthew addresses a Jewish-Christian audience. For example, the author does not usually explain Jewish customs or interpret Aramaic expressions, as do Mark and Luke (cf. Matt. 15:1–2, 5 with Mark 7:1–5, 11). Matthew places a greater emphasis on the use of Old Testament quotations and allusions, most of which reveal how Jesus Messiah fulfills Old Testament prophecies.[1] Matthew typically uses Jewish circumlocutions for God so as not to speak the divine name directly. (For example, whereas Mark and Luke speak of the "kingdom of God," Matthew nearly always has "kingdom of heaven.") And Matthew devotes special material to addressing issues of extreme importance to Jewish people, such as the three pillars of Jewish piety in 6:1–18: almsgiving, prayer, and fasting.

In keeping with its Jewish setting, the Gospel of Matthew presents Jesus as the *authoritative interpreter and teacher of the Mosaic law.* Not only does this theme frequently appear, but the very structure of the Gospel reveals the serious pursuit of this subject. In contrast to Mark's action-packed narrative with few discourses, Matthew devotes a great deal of space to the words of Jesus, exhibiting a major concern to record his teaching. This may be seen most clearly in the way in which the Gospel contents are collected into large sections of discourse material, such as the Sermon on the Mount.

When Matthew uses the Gospel of Mark, he tends to reduce the descriptive elements of the stories and expand the amount of space devoted to Jesus' teaching. At times he reduces a contextual description to a mere question posed to Jesus, followed by Jesus' lengthy reply (cf., for example, Mark 9:33–50 and Matt. 18:1–9). Matthew's emphasis on the words of Jesus seems to lie behind the literary structure of the Gospel, an alternating sequence of six narrative and five discourse sections with the following arrangement:

First Narrative (1—4)
> First Discourse (5—7)

Second Narrative (8—9)
> Second Discourse (10)

Third Narrative (11—12)
> Third Discourse (13:1–52)

Fourth Narrative (13:53–17:27)
> Fourth Discourse (18)

Fifth Narrative (19—22)
> Fifth Discourse (23—25)

Sixth Narrative (26—28)

Matthew consistently ends his discourse sections with a formulaic expression: "When Jesus had finished saying these things, . . ." (Matt. 7:28; 11:1; 13:53; 19:1; 26:1). These discourses tie together the narrative sections by referring to themes found in the narratives that both precede and follow them. Thus, the discourses function to "interpret the previous narrative and prepare for the next."[2]

Sometimes the distinctions between narrative and discourse are not very pronounced. Matthew tends to focus on Jesus' teaching even in the narrative sections, and some contain substantial discourses. For example, the fifth narrative section has three lengthy parables (20:1–16; 21:33–46; 22:1–14). Furthermore, two discourse sections contain limited narrative elements (13:10, 36; 18:1, 21). Yet the alternating narrative-discourse arrangement of the Gospel is quite distinct and reveals a deliberate structuring of the material to conform to this pattern.

SECTION ONE: MATTHEW 1—4: BIRTH OF THE KING

Matthew 1—2: The Messiah Will Be Born in Bethlehem

Glancing through a Gospel parallels text reveals that all the passages in this section are M material. Matthew's account of

Jesus' birth contains none of the passages found in Luke's birth narrative. Each Evangelist carefully developed his description of the events surrounding Jesus' birth to set the stage for his story of Jesus. The narratives differ remarkably in tone and content.

1. Whereas Luke begins with a story about the parents of John the Baptist, Matthew begins with a genealogy. How does the format of Matthew's genealogy of Jesus differ from the format of the genealogy of Jesus in Luke 3:23–38? How does the content differ?
2. Whereas Luke focuses on Mary and rarely mentions Joseph, Matthew focuses on Joseph and says little about Mary. What qualities does Matthew emphasize in his comments about Joseph?
3. Matthew 1:18–19 states that Joseph had not yet married Mary. Why, then, does he need to divorce her? (See the material on betrothal under Luke 1:26–56, if necessary.)
4. What role do dreams play in the story?
5. According to Matthew, when was Jesus born? (Note: Herod was king of Judah from 37 B.C.E. until he died in 4 B.C.E. His son Archelaus reigned from 4 B.C.E. to 6 C.E.)
6. Matthew strongly emphasizes scripture fulfillment. Look up the following Old Testament passages he quotes and glance at the context surrounding each: Matt. 2:6⇒Micah 5:2; Matt. 2:15⇒Hosea 11:1; Matt. 2:17–18⇒Jeremiah 31:15. What seems to characterize the way in which Matthew uses the Old Testament?
7. What stories surrounding Jesus' birth are included in Matthew but not in Luke?
8. What differences are there between Matthew and Luke with respect to where Mary and Joseph lived at the time of Jesus' birth and how he came to be raised in Galilee? With respect to who comes to pay homage to the child Jesus and when they come?

THEOLOGICALLY MOTIVATED GENEALOGIES

Both Matthew and Luke trace their genealogies of Jesus back through Joseph, as authors would in patriarchal societies (Matt. 1:16; Luke 3:23). But Matthew begins Jesus' royal lineage with Abraham, the father of the Hebrew people (Matt. 1:1–2), whereas Luke traces Jesus' lineage by beginning with Joseph and working back to Adam, the son of God (Luke 3:38). These genealogies reflect the portrait of Jesus that each author developed. The lack of any indications of poverty in Matthew's story of Jesus' birth, for example, differs strikingly from Luke's description of the humble birth of Jesus, the Savior of the poor, the outcasts, and the Gentiles. Such details as the visit by foreign dignitaries (the Magi) and the escape to Egypt in Matthew contrast sharply with the description of the humble arrival of Jesus and the adoring visit by the shepherds soon after Jesus' birth in Luke.[3]

In addition to the differences from Luke, puzzling questions arise when studying the genealogy in Matthew 1:1–16. Matthew carefully divides the list into three sections that correspond to significant stages in Israelite history, each of which, he says in 1:17, contains fourteen generations. Yet the third division (1:12–16) contains only thirteen generations. Furthermore, to produce the desired number of fourteen involves leaving out some people; the three kings who actually reigned after Jotham (Ahaziah, Joash, and Amaziah) are omitted (1:9), and the king who reigned after Josiah (Jehoiakim) is also omitted (1:11). Matthew's major concern seems to have been theological in nature, formulating a list of kings in such a way as to show Jesus' royal lineage, which the Messiah should have.

Quite possibly the number 14 was chosen because in Hebrew the name David has a numeric value of fourteen. The letters in the Hebrew alphabet were assigned numeric values (first letter = 1, second letter = 2, etc.), so people could calculate the numbers of names (a practice called *gematria*). In the case of King David, the three Hebrew consonants that comprise his name are דוד (4 + 6 + 4 = 14). Ancient Hebrew was written solely with consonants, so David contains only three letters.

Enterprising Women

In light of the very Jewish nature of Matthew's genealogy of Jesus, the inclusion of five women runs completely contrary to custom. This is especially intriguing when we reflect on the background of these women. Each exercised initiative in a highly unusual situation, and the result was the continuation of the messianic line from Abraham to Joseph.

Tamar (1:3) was the daughter-in-law of Judah, whom Judah himself impregnated when she pretended to be a prostitute and he hired her services (Genesis 38). She took extraordinary measures to produce offspring for her dead husband, so that his name would not be blotted out of Israel. (See Deut. 25:5–10 for details on the levirate marriage law.)

Rahab (1:5) was a prostitute in Jericho who provided shelter for the Israelite spies and protected them from harm, in return for the lives of herself and her family when the Israelite army killed the inhabitants of the city (Josh. 2:1–21; 6:22–25).

Ruth (1:5), an honorable woman, was a hard-working, loyal

Moabite who married Boaz, a man close of kin to her dead husband, after she initiated a secret, nocturnal encounter (Ruth 1—4).

The *wife of Uriah* (1:6) was Bathsheba, whom David committed adultery with and got pregnant. David later arranged for her husband to be killed in battle as a way of covering up his sin, and he promptly married Bathsheba (2 Sam. 11:1–12:24). She later gave birth to Solomon, and her decisive intervention just before David's death saved the life of Solomon from his older brother Adonijah and ensured Solomon's position as king.

All four of these women were non-Israelites, and Matthew likely included them in the genealogy to pave the way for the amazing story of *Mary* (1:16) that follows. It is Matthew's way of showing that God sovereignly works out his purpose in history, not only through the use of alien women at times but also through the most miraculous of events, the virgin birth in which Mary delivers the Son of God.

JEWISH ESCHATOLOGICAL USE OF SCRIPTURE IN MATTHEW'S DAY

Although the genealogy presents sufficient problems for interpretation, most readers find comprehending the reason behind Matthew's use of scripture to be a greater challenge. Understanding something about the biblical interpretation employed during the first century helps tremendously in this endeavor.

During Matthew's time, eschatologically oriented Jews commonly employed a method of biblical interpretation called *pesher.* The term arises from the Aramaic *pᵉshar,* meaning "interpretation." (The Hebrew form, pronounced *pā'sher,* also means "interpretation.") This word is frequently used, for example, with Daniel's explanations of the meanings of dreams (e.g., Dan. 5:15–17, 26; 7:16), and eschatological Jews used it with reference to events pertaining to their own time. Because they believed they were living in the time immediately preceding the ushering in of the age to come, they concluded that all scripture was written for their time, and they interpreted it accordingly. In other words, all scripture referred in a veiled way to their situation, so they needed divine help to understand its secret meaning, which was formerly hidden but is now revealed to one of God's special servants.

Examples of this kind of biblical interpretation abound in the Dead Sea Scrolls. In the Habakkuk commentary, for example, the author first quotes an Old Testament passage, then gives the interpretation (*pesher*) of how the passage refers to some specific person or event of his own time. (Because the scrolls are often damaged, due to their extreme age, the translator has to decide by context which words are missing and supply them. These sections are set apart by brackets.)

> [*Oracle of Habakkuk the prophet. How long, O Lord, shall I cry] for help and Thou wilt not [hear]? (i, 1–2)*. [Interpreted, this concerns the beginning] of the [final] generation. . . .
>
> [*For the wicked encompasses] the righteous (i, 4a–b)*. [The wicked is the Wicked Priest, and the righteous] is the Teacher of Righteousness. . . .
>
> [*Behold the nations and see, marvel and be astonished; for I accomplish a deed in your days but you will not believe it when] told (1, 5)*. [Interpreted, this concerns] those who were unfaithful together with the Liar, in that they [did] not [listen to the word received by] the Teacher of Righteousness from the mouth of God. . . . And likewise, this saying is to be interpreted [as concerning those who] will be unfaithful at the end of days. They, the men of violence and the breakers of the Covenant, will not believe when they hear all that [is to happen to] the final generation. . . .
>
> *For behold, I rouse the Chaldeans, that [bitter and hasty] nation (i, 6a)*. Interpreted, this concerns the Kittim [who are] quick and valiant in war, causing many to perish. [All the world shall fall] under the dominion of the Kittim, and the [wicked . . .] they shall not believe in the laws of [God . . .].[4]

Cave 4 at Qumran, where some important Dead Sea Scrolls were discovered.

The Dead Sea Scroll commentary on Habakkuk illustrates how a *pesher* was seen to reveal the secret of the way in which a centuries-old saying mysteriously refers to the time of the author. Thus, in the Habakkuk commentary the Chaldeans, the Babylonians about whom Habakkuk wrote, are interpreted to mean the Kittim, a designation for the Romans. By taking this *pesher* approach, eschatological Jews found cryptic references to their own time throughout the scriptures.

Early Christians also implemented this approach to scripture. Acts 3:24, for example, records Peter as saying, "And all the prophets, as many as have spoken, from Samuel and those after him, also predicted these days." Also, Paul emphatically states in 1 Corinthians 10:11: "These things . . . were written down to instruct us, on whom the ends of the ages have come." So although Matthew's citations of biblical passages as messianic proof texts differ in form from the line-by-line interpretations seen above in the Habakkuk commentary, the approach to scripture does not differ substantially. We might say that Matthew and other early Christians read the Old Testament through Christ-colored glasses, seeing references throughout the scriptures to Jesus as the ultimate fulfillment of God's dealings with God's people.[5]

Summary Observations of Matthew 1—2

1. Summarize the overall differences between Matthew's and Luke's portraits of Jesus' birth.
2. How does Matthew's purpose in composing his account explain the differences between his version and Luke's?

Matthew 3—4: Preparation in the Wilderness

1. Compare Matthew 3:7 with Luke 3:7. How does Matthew's designation of the group of people singled out by John for special criticism differ from Luke's description?

This is but the beginning of Matthew's persistent attack on the Jewish religious leaders,[6] a theme that develops into an extremely important part of the Gospel. " 'Brood of vipers' (literally, 'offspring of snakes,' 'snake bastards') would be as insulting a label as one could imagine in a society in which social standing and the honor bound up with it are fundamentally a function of birth."[7] Notice also that Matthew leaves out Luke 3:10–14, John's exhortations on kindness and justice to people in the crowd who ask how they should live.

2. John's baptism for the forgiveness of sins posed a problem for early Christians in explaining why Jesus needed to be baptized. How does Matthew handle this problem?
3. Compare Matthew 3:17 with Mark 1:11 and Luke 3:22. What is different about the message of the voice from heaven in Matthew's account?
4. How are the temptations in Matthew 4:1–11 and Luke 4:1–13 both similar and different?
5. In 4:14–16, what do you notice once again about Matthew's use of scripture?
6. What do these early four chapters of Matthew emphasize about Jesus, and how does this differ from the focus of Luke's birth narrative?

SECTION TWO: MATTHEW 5—7: THE SERMON ON THE MOUNT
Matthew 5:1–12: "Blessed are you"

Matthew 1—2 presents the birth of the king, and Matthew 3—4 chronicles the beginning of his public ministry. After choosing his disciples in 4:18–22, Jesus preaches and heals in Galilee, attracting a great crowd of people, including Gentiles (4:23–25). After these opening chapters comes the *first discourse* section of Matthew, an extended example of Jesus' teaching. We could call this Jesus' inaugural address on the ethics of the kingdom of God (or the will of God) that he has come to proclaim. Note that Jesus goes up on a mountain to give this address, whereas Luke places it on a "plain" (Luke 6:17). Matthew apparently desires to make some sort of comparison between Jesus and Moses, who received the law from God on a mountain.

1. In Matthew 1—4, what other similarities are there between Matthew's portrait of Jesus and the life of Moses?
2. How do the Beatitudes in Matthew 5:3–12 differ from those in Luke 6:20–23?

Matthew 5:13–16: Salt and Light

1. How do these two sayings about the life of Jesus' disciples relate to the Beatitudes?

Matthew 5:17–20: I Did Not Come to Abolish the Law

The Hebrew Bible consists of three sections: the *Law* (Pentateuch), the *Prophets* (historical books such as Joshua, Judges, 1–2 Samuel, 1–2 Kings, as well as the actual books of the prophets, such as Isaiah and Jeremiah), and the *Writings* (Psalms, books of wisdom such as Proverbs and Job, and later works such as Daniel and 1–2 Chronicles). By Jesus' time, the Pharisees considered the Law and the Prophets to be inspired scripture (Sadducees accepted only the Law). The Writings, although nearly complete in terms of which books were considered inspired, were not yet canonized in final form; this took place after the destruction of Jerusalem in 70 C.E. Notice that in Matthew 5:17, Jesus designates only the Law and the Prophets.

1. What extremely important point does this passage assert about Jesus Messiah's attitude toward Mosaic law? About his disciples' relationship to Mosaic law?

The issue of Jesus' attitude toward the Mosaic law would be extremely important to Matthew's Jewish-Christian audience. The law occupied so central a place for Jews that they could not imagine past, present, or future without it. W. D. Davies points out that the rabbis believed the law was pre-existent "and instrumental in the creation of the world. . . . As the ground plan of the universe it could not but be perfect and unchangeable . . . no prophet could ever arise who would change it, and no new Moses should ever appear to introduce another Law to replace it."[8]

Basing their thoughts on the personification of wisdom in Proverbs 8:22–31, the rabbis connected the Mosaic law with this description of Wisdom's role in the creation of the world. Using architectural imagery, Rabbi Hosha'ya explains how he believes God used Torah:

> When a king builds a palace, he does not do it himself, but with the help of "the knowledge of a master builder." And the master builder in turn considers plans and drawings: in just the same way, "God looked into the Torah" when he created the world.[9]

So central was Torah in the thinking of the rabbis that they made no allowance for any alteration of it. The literature of the intertestamental period shows that many Jewish people expected the messiah to be taught by God and to rule with great wisdom (c.g., *Psalms of Solomon* 17:31, 35, 42). No indication exists that they expected the messiah to bring a new law.

There are indications, however, that first-century Jews realized the need for a *new interpretation* of the law to clarify unresolved questions. Like people today, they found the task of understanding many Old Testament passages extremely difficult; and they looked forward to the time when all would be clarified. For example, 1 Maccabees 4:41–46 reveals an expectation of a prophet who would come to resolve some issues of interpretation. And the Dead Sea Scroll community at Qumran believed that a new interpretation of the law would be a mark of the messianic age. In the age to come, people would study the law better, interpret it more correctly, observe it more fully, and even the Gentiles would reverence it.[10]

Since Matthew presents Jesus as the long-awaited Messiah, his Jewish readers naturally want to know Jesus' view of the law. Matthew describes him as the *one who brings a new and authoritative interpretation of the law,* not as one who brings a new law. Nowhere does Matthew use phrases such as "new teaching," as in Mark 1:27. He demonstrates in Jesus' life and teaching that Jesus fulfills the law's demands for righteousness (see, for example, 3:15). Thus, in 5:17–19, Jesus affirms the abiding validity of the law and pronounces authoritatively in 5:21–48 that his teaching represents the true will of God.

Of course, the non-Christian Jews in Matthew's community rejected his claim that Jesus is Messiah, and their teachers, the Pharisees, posed a threat to his credibility. The Gospel of

Matthew therefore consistently demonstrates that these rival teachers of the law do not understand the Bible and that their righteousness is substandard. Thus, in 5:20, Jesus asserts that the righteousness of his followers must exceed that of the Pharisees; and in the passages that follow, he shows how this is to be accomplished.

Matthew 5:21–48: The Greater Righteousness

In this section, each of the six areas that Jesus addresses begins with the same basic format: "You have heard that it was said . . . But I say to you . . . " Each of these six *antitheses* explains the greater righteousness of 5:20. Their aim is not to attack Torah but to demonstrate deficiencies in the ways in which others interpret it and to reveal the deeper righteousness that Jesus' followers are to observe.

1. In Matthew 5:21–26, how does Jesus press the prohibition of murder to a deeper level? (See Exod. 20:13; Deut. 5:17.)

"Fool" in 5:22 does not designate mental deficiency, like calling someone "idiot." In Matthew the term *fool* (Greek, *moros*) applies to those who are morally and spiritually deficient and thus are not part of the kingdom of God (7:26; 23:17; 25:2, 3, 8).

2. In Matthew 5:27–30, how does Jesus deepen the law against adultery? (See Exod. 20:14; Deut. 5:18.)
3. In Matthew 5:31–32, how does this saying limit the Jewish man's right to divorce, thereby deepening the Old Testament law? (See Deut. 24:1–4.)
4. In Matthew 5:33–37, how does Jesus deepen the Old Testament legislation? (See Exod. 20:7; Num. 30:2–15; Deut. 23:21–23.) What generally motivates people to swear oaths on valuable objects?
5. In Matthew 5:38–42, how does Jesus change this Old Testament law? (See Exod. 21:23–24; Lev. 24:19–20; Deut. 19:16–21.)

No Old Testament law commands hatred of enemies, corresponding to Matthew 5:43–48, although there are certainly passages in which people express hatred of enemies (for example, Pss. 137:7–9; 139:21–22). The Dead Sea Scroll community, however, had explicit instructions to hate the sons of darkness (1QS i 4,10). These sectarians anticipated destroying those who did not belong to their number, and they loathed their opponents, whom they believed were doomed for God's wrath.

6. How does God's example provide the standard for Christian treatment of enemies?

Application to Contemporary Issues

What would happen to the average church if its members took seriously the teachings of Jesus on being reconciled to other people (5:21–26)? How would worship services be different if Christians reconciled conflicts before they offered up their corporate praise to God?

How would family life change if husbands and wives radically removed tendencies to lust after other women and men (5:27–30)?

How would the business community be changed if Christians were always "as good as their word" (5:33–37)? How would relationships in general change if Christians gave up revenge as inappropriate in the kingdom of God (5:38–42)?

How would society change if Christians prayed for and sought the welfare of those with whom they come into conflict (5:43–48)? How would our nation change if Christians consistently loved and prayed for people in nations hostile to our own?

Matthew 6:1–18: Motivation for Pious Acts

The *three pillars of Jewish piety* were *almsgiving, prayer,* and *fasting.* Almsgiving, the giving of aid to the poor, was considered very meritorious. The apocryphal book of Tobit, for example, extols it highly:

> To all those who practice righteousness give alms from your possessions, and do not let your eye begrudge the gift when you make it. Do not turn your face away from anyone who is poor, and the face of God will not be turned away from you. . . . So you will be laying up a good treasure for yourself against the day of necessity. For almsgiving delivers from death and keeps you from going into the Darkness. Indeed, almsgiving, for all who practice it, is an excellent offering in the presence of the Most High.[11] (Tobit 4:7–11)
>
> Prayer with fasting is good, but better than both is almsgiving with righteousness. A little with righteousness is better than wealth with wrongdoing. It is better to give alms than to lay up gold. For almsgiving saves from death and purges away every sin. (Tobit 12:8–9)

Faithful Jews considered it their duty to give alms, and they were very careful to pray regularly. In addition, the Pharisees of Jesus' day fasted on Mondays and Thursdays (Luke 18:12; Didache 8:1).

1. What tendency does Jesus warn against in the performance of almsgiving, prayer, and fasting?
2. What relationship does Jesus' teaching in 6:1–18 have with his statement in 5:20?
3. Compare Matt. 6:9–13 with the Lord's Prayer in Luke 11:2–4. What are the differences between the two versions?

Matthew 6:19–34: "You cannot serve God and wealth"

1. What relationship does 6:19–24 have with 6:1–18?
2. How does 6:25–34 provide the motivation for obedience to 6:19–24?
3. What is Jesus' approach for living a life free from anxiety?

Matthew 7:1–12: "Take the log out"

1. What advice does Jesus give in this passage for overcoming a critical attitude toward others?

Although followers of Jesus are to avoid being judgmental, the proverbial saying in 7:6 counsels careful thought about how people are to relate with outsiders.

2. What foundation does 7:12 provide for how we should treat other people and thus fulfill the greater righteousness demanded of Jesus' followers (5:20)?

Reflection on Motivation
What is your motivation for performing acts of piety? How does this affect your attitude toward doing them? How does your typical focus in prayer compare with what Jesus emphasizes in 6:9–13?

Stress and Anxiety
What situations tend to cause anxiety in your life? Why do they produce stress for you? What changes would you like to make in light of Matthew 6:19–34?

Reflection on "Straightening Out" Others
When do you tend to be more judgmental toward others: when you feel good about yourself, or when you feel uptight about life? Why?

Matthew 7:13–29: The Solid Foundation

The contrasting of two ways—the way of life and the way of death or the way of righteousness and the way of wickedness—was quite common in antiquity. For example, the Didache (an early Christian set of teachings on various behaviors) begins by saying, "There are two ways, one of life and one of death, and there is a great difference between the two ways" (LCL). Note that each of the paragraphs in Matthew 7:13–29 makes such a contrast, and together they provide a powerful justification for obeying the teachings in the Sermon on the Mount: Enter through the narrow gate of his teaching (7:13–14); beware of those who do not follow his teaching (7:15–20); and recognize that not all who use Jesus' name obey him (7:21–23). To listen to Jesus and not obey is like building a house on the sand: It cannot stand against the storms of life (7:24–27). *The disciple of Jesus, therefore, is one who hears this authoritative teaching, understands it, and obeys (i.e., bears fruit).* Discipleship without obedience to Jesus is a contradiction in terms in Matthew's Gospel.

Dealing with Difficult Demands
Which of the teachings in the Sermon on the Mount do you find to be most challenging? Why?

1. False prophets were a problem in the early church. How does Jesus say one may detect such people?
2. What surprises does the last judgment bring for those people who do things in Jesus' name but do not follow his teaching?

SECTION THREE: MATTHEW 8—10: MESSIANIC MINISTRY IN GALILEE
Matthew 8:1–13: Heirs of the Kingdom

Matthew 7:28 concludes the first discourse section of the Gospel with people expressing amazement at the authoritative nature of Jesus' teaching. The *second narrative* section begins in 8:1, with Jesus coming down from the mountain.

1. Compare Matthew 8:1–4 with Mark 1:40–45. What does Matthew omit from the story, and on what note does he conclude it?
2. Matthew 8:5–13 is the same story as in Luke 7:1–10, but Luke positions the material in Matthew 8:11–12 in a later place (Luke 13:28–30). Why would Matthew 8:11–12 be offensive to many Jews in Jesus' audience?
3. What is "the outer darkness"? (Cf. 22:13; 24:51; 25:30.)

A standard Jewish expectation was that the righteous would sit down at a glorious banquet table with the messiah when he came and conquered the world. They called this the messianic banquet, and Jesus refers to it in Matthew 8:11. The sectarians at Qumran held a common meal daily in anticipation of this great banquet, and their scrolls describe how they believed it would be conducted: the messiah at the head of the table, the chiefs of the clans of Israel gathered close to him, and then all others, in the order of their dignity in the covenant community. Only the pure members of the covenant community would be allowed to attend.

Matthew 8:14–34: "Why are you afraid?"

Matthew 8:14–17 abbreviates the stories from Mark 1:29–34, removing some of the descriptive detail. In keeping with Matthew's style, the account adds a scripture citation in 8:17 to show once again that Jesus' actions conform to scripture. Matthew 8:18–22 is Q material, with certain differences from the parallel in Luke 9:57–61. (For example, Matt. 8:18–22 says a "scribe" wants to follow Jesus, whereas Luke 9:57 simply says "a man.")

The stories in Matthew 8:23–34 occur later on in Mark's account, but Matthew places them here in a different context and modifies the emphasis of the Markan arrangement.

1. Compare Matthew 8:23–27 with Mark 4:35–41. What does Matthew 8:26 do with the sequence of events in Mark 4:39–40 regarding when Jesus questions the faith of his disciples and when he stills the storm? (For "little faith" in Matthew, see also 6:30; 14:31; 16:8; and 17:20.)
2. How does the tone of the disciples' words in Matthew 8:25 differ from that found in Mark 4:38?
3. How does the number of demoniacs Jesus encounters in Matthew 8:28 compare with Mark 5:2?
4. Notice that Matthew 8:28–34 tremendously reduces the amount of material presented in Mark 5:1–20. What sorts of things does Matthew leave out?

Matthew 9:1–17: "And so both are preserved"

1. Matthew 9:1–8 leaves out many details from Mark 2:1–12, such as the four men digging through the roof. On what does Matthew focus?
2. In Matthew 9:9, the tax collector is called Matthew, instead of Levi as in Mark 2:14. Probably these were alternate names for the same person. How does the end of the story in Matthew 9:13 vindicate Jesus of the Pharisees' charges? (Note that this once again shows that Jesus does not break the law.)
3. How does the ending of the next story in Matthew 9:17 change the emphasis of the ending in Mark 2:22 and conform to a major Matthean theme?

Matthew 9:18–38: "The girl is not dead but sleeping"

1. Matthew 9:18–26 is substantially shorter than Mark 5:21–43. What kinds of details does Matthew omit? What is the effect of their omission?

2. What happens to the drama of Mark's account when Matthew begins the story with the father saying that his daughter has already died?

Note that the story of the blind man occurs much later in Mark's narration (Mark 10:46–50) than in Matthew's. Matthew's use of *two* blind men in 9:27 may well fit with his frequent use of Old Testament proof texts to show that Jesus' ministry was predicted by the prophets of old. Isaiah 35:5–6 predicts the day when "the eyes of the blind shall be opened, and the ears of the deaf unstopped; then the lame shall leap like a deer, and the tongue of the speechless sing for joy." Matthew may have specified two blind men to conform to the plural of Isaiah 35:5 and then added the story of the mute demoniac (Matt. 9:32–34), which is only found in Matthew, to reflect Isaiah 35:6.

3. From 9:35, Matthew's account diverges sharply from Mark's (cf. Mark 6:34). How does Matthew 9:37–38 both sum up chapters 8—9 and prepare for the disciples being sent out in chapter 10? (Cf., for example, 9:38 with 10:1–5.)
4. Although Matthew 8—9 basically follows Mark 1:40–2:22, it adds material from Mark 8:14–17, 23–27 and 9:18–31 to the series of stories. What characterizes all the miracle stories in this section of Matthew?

Matthew 10:1–23: "Go nowhere among the Gentiles"

1. After calling and commissioning his twelve apostles, what geographical and ethnic limits does Jesus place on their mission in 10:5–6?

The added material in 10:15–16 helps clarify both the nature of the judgment pronounced on the cities that reject the apostles and also the condition of the apostles among those who oppose their message (sheep among wolves). Interestingly, in 7:16 the image of wolves in sheep's clothing being among Christians was used for false prophets.

2. How would 10:16–23 help Matthew's readers, who live in a Jewish environment and have experienced division in their families because some follow Jesus and some do not?
3. Note the eschatological sound of 10:21–22 (cf. Mark 13:9–12). What understanding of the end of the age does 10:23 reveal?

Matthew 10:24–42: "A disciple is not above the teacher"

1. What comfort would 10:26–33 provide for Matthew's readers?
2. According to 10:34–42, what are the cost of and reward for following Jesus?
3. Summarize the central themes of Matthew 8—10 and explain how they build on the material presented in Matthew 1—7.

SECTION FOUR: MATTHEW 11:1–13:52: DIFFERENT RESPONSES TO JESUS' TEACHING ON THE KINGDOM

Matthew 11:1–19: Wisdom Is Vindicated by Her Deeds

After the discourse explaining the mission of his disciples in Matthew 10, Jesus seems to go alone on a preaching tour in 11:1, an event reported only by Matthew. One would expect some description of the success or failure of the apostles' mission for which Jesus prepared them and sent them out in Matthew 10, but the Gospel says not a word about this. Instead, one finds the story of John the Baptist questioning Jesus' identity. Evidently, for Matthew, recounting Jesus' instructions to the apostles in chapter 10 has greater importance than reporting the disciples' deeds. This again underlines Matthew's tendency to focus on the teachings of Jesus, sometimes at the expense of narrative coherence.

The discourse of Matthew 10 ties together the narrative of chapters 8—9, which consists predominantly of miracle stories, and the narrative of chapters 11—12, which consists primarily of conflict stories. Matthew 9:1–17 reveals that not everyone accepts Jesus' messianic authority, which he proclaimed in the Sermon on the Mount (chapters 5—7) and demonstrated by miracles in chapters 8—9. Matthew 10 shows the apostles' ministry to be continuous with that of Jesus and indicates that they, too, will suffer persecution for their ministry. This predicted persecution finds immediate illustration in the next narrative section with John the Baptist's imprisonment (11:2). And Jesus' words about reward for receiving him or his messengers (10:40–42) find immediate application in 11:6, when he pointedly tells John, "Blessed is anyone who takes no offense at me." In the narrative that follows, many take offense at Jesus.

John, the eschatological proclaimer of the powerful Messiah to come (3:1–12), who balked at baptizing Jesus because he recognized him as the Messiah (3:13–15), now sits in prison and wonders if he made a mistake. This provides occasion for Jesus to compare John's greatness with that of the kingdom of heaven.

1. Notice that the material in Matthew 11:12–15 is not in the parallel passage in Luke 7:24–35 (but cf. Luke 16:16). What does it reveal about John and the kingdom of heaven?

Matthew 11:12 deserves special comment due to its confusing nature. John baptized Jesus Messiah and thus initiated the messianic proclamation of the kingdom of heaven. Since that time, the kingdom has suffered violence from violent men: Herod arrested

John; the Pharisees oppose Jesus' ministry; and the apostles will suffer persecution (10:13–39). Jesus' messianic ministry differs substantially from the Zealots' attempt to establish the kingdom by force of arms. And although the Jews did not expect the messiah to be a healer, Jesus points to this aspect of his ministry as proof in answering John the Baptist's questions (11:4–5). The wisdom of Jesus' approach reveals itself in the success of his healing and teaching (11:19).

Matthew 11:20–24: More Tolerable for Sodom

1. The opposition that Jesus predicted in 10:13–39 has now happened (11:20–21). Why does he label their rejection inexcusable?
2. Locate the cursed cities of Chorazin, Bethsaida, and Capernaum on a map.

Matthew 11:25–30: "My burden is light"

In 9:3–6, 11–13 and 12:1–24, the Pharisees oppose Jesus on theological grounds. His actions do not conform to their standards of righteousness according to their interpretation of the Mosaic law.

1. According to this passage, how do people come to understand Jesus' identity and come to know the Father?
2. What dramatic difference does Jesus say there is between following his teachings and following the Pharisees' teachings?

When Jesus speaks of taking his *yoke,* he means submissively following his teachings. In rabbinic writing, *yoke* was used to designate the Mosaic law (cf. *Pirke Aboth* 3:6). Ben Sira, writing about 180 B.C.E., equates Wisdom with the law and says, "Put your neck under her yoke, and let your souls receive instruction; it is to be found close by. See with your own eyes that I have labored but little and found for myself much serenity" (Sirach 51:26–27). Jesus rejects the notion that people find rest in keeping the law as the Pharisees teach it (see Matt. 23:3). He asserts that following the Pharisees' teaching is a burden too heavy to bear, whereas following his instruction will truly bring rest for their souls.

Jesus' point may be illustrated by reading through the tractate called *Shabbath* (Sabbath) in the Mishnah. It specifies numerous activities that one should shun on the Sabbath to avoid working on the day of rest. A tailor must not carry a needle out of his shop if the time is near sundown on Friday, lest he forget that it is in his pocket and thus be guilty of carrying it on the Sabbath (*Shab-*

130

bath 1.2). One must not let clothes soak in dye over the Sabbath (1.5). "Camels may not be led along tied together, but a man may hold their ropes in his hand provided that he does not twist them together" (5.3).[12] One must not wear sandals "shod with nails" on the Sabbath, for that would be bearing a burden (6.2). An amputee may go out with a wooden stump on the Sabbath, but only if it does not have knee pads, which are susceptible to uncleanness (6.8). One is guilty of breaking the Sabbath if one takes "milk enough for a gulp, or honey enough to put on a sore, or oil enough to anoint the smallest member [little toe of a one-day-old child], or water enough to rub off eye plaster" (8.1). "[He is culpable] that takes out [on the Sabbath] wood enough to cook the smallest egg, or spices enough to flavour a light egg" (9.5). These regulations extend through twenty-four sections, vividly illustrating the minutiae that the rabbis sought to legislate. How many such laws were operative during the time of Jesus is impossible to know, but the tendency toward amassing such regulations was evidently well under way in the first century.

Matthew 12:1–14: "If you had known what this means"

With this story, Jesus begins to enter into theological debate with the Pharisees. Such passages are extremely important for Matthew, for in them he demonstrates Jesus' superior understanding of the scriptures. If his readers want to follow God's will, they must follow Jesus, the authoritative interpreter of scripture. (For other background information on Sabbath observance, see under Mark 2.23–28 and Luke 13:10–21; 14:1–6.)

1. How does Matthew's addition of 12:5–7 (cf. Mark 2:23–28) emphasize the Pharisees' ignorance? (See also 12:3: "Have you not read . . . ?") Through what means does it show Jesus' innocence of wrong? Jesus' greatness?
2. Why does Matthew delete Mark 2:27?

Matthew 12:10 changes the silent watching by the Pharisees of Mark 3:2 to a direct question: "Is it lawful to cure on the sabbath?" In this way Matthew allows Jesus to teach more forcefully on this issue, as is evidenced by the addition of the saying in 12:11–12. (Note that Luke 14:5 places this Q saying in an entirely different context.) Jesus then makes the direct pronouncement: "So it is lawful to do good on the sabbath" (12:12). Thus, Matthew again demonstrates that Jesus is without blame with respect to the law by changing the question of Mark 3:4, "Is it lawful . . . ?" to a statement, "It is lawful . . . " (Matt. 12:12). (Note also that

Matthew omits the comment on Jesus' emotions from Mark 3:5 and the involvement of the Herodians in Mark 3:6. In so doing, he emphasizes Jesus' teaching over other elements of the story.)

Matthew 12:15–21:
"To fulfill what had been spoken through the prophet Isaiah"

1. Most of this passage is found only in Matthew. What typical Matthean approach to describing Jesus' actions does it represent?
2. Review the places Jesus ordered his disciples to go (and not to go) in 10:5. What new dimension does 12:17–21 bring to Jesus' ministry?

Matthew 12:22–37: "Make the tree good, and its fruit good"

1. What does Jesus' response to the Pharisees' charge against him reveal about himself and the kingdom of God?
2. Compare 12:33–37 with 7:15–23. What similarities are there? (Note the emphasis on evil words in 12:33–37. Jesus' opponents teach evil words, which reflects their inner condition.)

Matthew 12:38–50:
"An evil and adulterous generation asks for a sign"

1. Compare Matthew 12:38 with Luke 11:29. How does Matthew's designation of the identity of the "evil generation" differ from Luke's? (Cf. also Matt. 3:7 with Luke 3:7 in this regard.)
2. Compare Matthew's statement about the sign of Jonah with that found in Luke 11:30. How does Matthew's additional material alter the meaning of the passage as it appears in Luke?
3. Of what significance for this Gospel is the fact that Gentiles (people of Nineveh and the queen of the South) will judge the scribes and Pharisees?
4. Matthew applies the story of the demon in 12:43–45 to "this evil generation" (12:45). What judgment does it therefore make on the Jewish religious leaders?

Matthew repositions the story of Jesus' family (12:46–50; cf. Mark 3:31–35) so that it occurs in the context of judgment on the Pharisees. Note also that in Matthew 12:49, Jesus designates his "disciples" as his family.

5. How does the story effectively eliminate Jesus' opponents from the kingdom of heaven?

Matthew 13:1–23: "Blessed are your eyes, for they see"

This passage begins the *third discourse* in Matthew, which connects the Pharisees' hostility toward Jesus in the third narrative section (Matthew 11—12) with similar hostility in the fourth narrative section (Matt. 13:53–17:27) by explaining how the same messianic message can produce diverse results in various people. Notice how Matthew makes this connection initially by specifying a more precise time framework in 13:1: "That same day . . ." (cf. Mark 4:1).

Of the seven parables that form the third discourse in Matthew 13:1–52, only three are found in Mark or Luke. The others are uniquely Matthean. And in contrast to Mark's portrait of the disciples as lacking in understanding, Matthew stresses that Jesus' disciples are those who hear their master's words and *understand.* This comes as no surprise, given Matthew's portrait of Jesus as the authoritative interpreter of the law; a description of the disciples as not understanding might cause the reader to question Jesus' effectiveness as a teacher.

1. What distinction does 13:10–11 make between Jesus' disciples and the rest of the crowd?
2. What do 13:11, 16–17, 19, 23, 51 reveal about the disciples' understanding of Jesus' teaching? (Cf. Mark 4:10–13.)
3. How does Matthew 13:13 soften the harshness of Mark 4:11–12?
4. How does the addition of the Isaiah 6:9–10 quotation in Matthew 13:14–15 explain both Jesus' use of parables and his opponents' failure to believe him?

Matthew 13:1–23 reinforces this Gospel's theme that a disciple is one who *hears, understands,* and *responds* in obedience to the teaching of Jesus Messiah.

5. How might Matthew's reversal of the order of magnitude of the yield in 13:23 (cf. Mark 4:20) reflect his emphasis on the disciple being one who bears fruit?

Matthew 13:24–43: Parables of the Kingdom

The six parables in 13:24–50 are *similitudes,* comparing the kingdom of heaven to various things. Some are found only in Matthew (13:24–30, 36–43, 44–46, 47–50).

1. What do 13:24–30 and the allegorical interpretation in 13:36–43 reveal about the composition of the church, the gathering of those who claim to be Jesus' disciples? (Cf. 7:15–23.)
2. When will those who bear fruit be separated from those who do not?
3. How does the symbolism of 13:31–32 tie it to the preceding parables?
4. How is the message of 13:33 similar to that of 13:31–32?
5. What is Matthew's purpose in placing 13:34–35 in this context?

Matthew 13:44–52: At the End of the Age

The parables in 13:44–46 continue the theme of the secret nature of the kingdom of heaven from 13:31–33, but 13:44–46 adds the dimension that the kingdom has such surpassing value that one should sell everything to gain it.

1. How does the parable in 13:47–50 repeat the message of 13:24–30, 36–43?
2. Matthew 13:51–52 shows that the disciples understand Jesus' parabolic speech. What equips them to be scribes (13:51–52), accurate exponents of the kingdom of heaven, whereas the Pharisaic scribes are not even members of the kingdom?
3. In 13:51–52, the Christian scribe draws on what is old (the scriptures) and what is new (Jesus' teachings) to present the treasures of the kingdom. Why does the new build on the old instead of replacing it? (Cf. 9:17.)

SECTION FIVE: MATTHEW 13:53–18:35: LIFE IN THE KINGDOM OF HEAVEN

In the *fourth narrative* section of Matthew (13:53–17:27), the disciples steadily grow in understanding while the Pharisees and scribes grow in hostility toward Jesus. These developments are important for Matthew's demonstration of who belongs in the kingdom of heaven.

Matthew 13:53–14:12: "Is not this the carpenter's son?"

After the parables in 13:1–50, Jesus returns to his hometown of Nazareth, only to be rejected there by his former neighbors (13:53–58). This story follows Mark's account fairly closely.

1. Compare Matthew 13:58 with Mark 6:5. What slight modification does Matthew make to eliminate any notion that people's responses may limit Jesus' power?
2. Matthew 14:1–12 abbreviates the account of John's death in Mark 6:17–29. What does his modification of the details in 14:5 (cf. Mark 6:19–20) do to change Mark's picture of Herod's attitude toward John?
3. How does Matthew's reason for Herod's not executing John at first (14:3–5) compare with the reason given in Mark 6:17–20? What tension does this create in Matthew's telling of the story when in 14:9 he maintains the picture of Herod presented in Mark 6:26?

Matthew 14:13–36: "Truly you are the Son of God"

Whereas in Mark 6:30–33, Jesus goes with his disciples to a lonely place so that they might rest after returning from a hectic time of ministry, in Matthew 14:13–14, Jesus goes to a lonely place in response to hearing about John the Baptist's death. (The sending out of the Twelve in Matthew occurs in chapter 10.) Matthew then proceeds to modify substantially Mark's emphasis on the disciples' failure to learn their lesson about being good shepherds in the story of the feeding of the five thousand. In Matthew's account, the disciples are much more in tune with Jesus.

1. Compare Matthew 14:16–17 with Mark 6:37–38. How does Matthew alter the portrait of the disciples?
2. How does Matthew change the focus of the stilling-of-the-storm story in Mark 6:45–52 by adding the material about Peter in 14:28–31?
3. In Mark 6:51–52, the story of the stilling of the storm concludes with the disciples in fearful ignorance. How does Matthew 14:33 change this picture?

Note that Matthew 14:22 omits the statement in Mark 6:45 that Jesus told the disciples to go to Bethsaida; so when they arrive in Gennesaret in Matthew 14:34, one might assume this was their intended destination. Perhaps the "lonely place" of 14:13 is supposed to be understood as being on the east side of the lake.

Matthew 15:1–20: "They are blind guides"

This passage provides an excellent example of Matthew's redaction of Mark in order to communicate more effectively to his Jewish audience. Matthew omits the editorial explanation of the customs of the Pharisees in Mark 7:3–4 and the explanation of the meaning of corban in Mark 7:11 (cf. Matt. 15:5), because his readers already understand these things.

1. How does the Pharisees' response to Jesus differ from that of the people in Gennesaret in Matthew 14:34–36?
2. For what do the Pharisees criticize Jesus?
3. For what does Jesus criticize them?
4. How does the addition of Matthew 15:12–14 intensify Matthew's portrait of the Pharisees? What warning do these verses provide for Matthew's readers in their own situation of living in a Jewish community? (Also compare the imagery in the parable of the weeds [13:24–30] with 15:13.)
5. Why does Matthew's omission of the editorial comment in Mark 7:19 fit with his attitude toward the law of Moses?
6. How does 15:20 vindicate Jesus' disciples of the accusations by the Pharisees?

Matthew 15:21–28: A Canaanite Woman

Matthew 15:22 calls the woman in this story a *Canaanite* (15:22), a term more likely to be used by his Jewish audience than

Syrophoenician, used in Mark 7:26 for Mark's Gentile readers. The words are synonymous.

1. Matthew 15:23–24 adds to the drama of the story. How does it further explain Jesus' harsh response to the woman's request?
2. For what is the woman commended? (Cf. Peter in 14:31.)
3. How does this story alter the scope of Jesus' ministry presented in 10:5, even though, in 15:24, Jesus states that he was sent only to Jews?

Matthew 15:29–39: On a Mountain by the Sea

Mark 7:31 locates the feeding of the four thousand in the Decapolis, a Gentile area. Although Matthew adopts Mark's sequence of events in this section, he does not specify the region but merely says Jesus "passed along the Sea of Galilee" (15:29). If Matthew means for us to understand a Gentile setting, as the statement "they praised the God of Israel" (15:31) may indicate, then Jesus' messianic ministry broadens to include non-Jews after his encounter with the Canaanite woman in 15:21–28.

1. How does Matthew 15:29–31 modify the healing story in Mark 7:31–37?
2. Locate the region of Magadan (Matt. 15:39) on a map, noting that this name is synonymous with Dalmanutha (Mark 8:10).

Matthew 16:1–4: The Sign of Jonah

Determining whether Matthew substantially reworked this story by adding the material in 16:2b–3 is quite difficult. Some of the more reliable Greek manuscripts that are used to determine the best reading of the text omit these verses, which might be an early addition by some scribe who copied the Gospel. Early scribes in Alexandria, however, an area from which we obtain some of the best Greek manuscripts, might well have omitted this material about weather. In contrast to Palestine, where a red sky in the morning indicates rain, in Egypt such conditions do not portend rain. It is entirely consistent with Matthew's agenda to show that the Pharisees and Sadducees are incapable of understanding what God is doing in the world. So the addition of 16:2b–3, asserting that they can interpret physical facts about weather but "cannot interpret the signs of the times," fits quite well with Matthew's emphasis that the Pharisees are blind guides (15:14). The only sign they will receive is the sign of Jonah (16:4, cf. 12:39–40; note that Mark 8:12 says "no sign").

Matthew's Jesus

Matthew 16:5–12: "Then they understood"

1. How does this story supplement the negative picture of the Pharisees and Sadducees in 16:1–4?
2. How does Matthew soften the negative portrait of the disciples presented by Mark 8:17–21?
3. Although Mark 8:21 leaves the reader to interpret the meaning of the story, how does Matthew 16:11–12 interpret it?

Matthew 16:13–23: The Keys of the Kingdom

Probably not wanting to imply that Peter has been blind to Jesus' teaching, Matthew omits the story of the blind man at Bethsaida (Mark 8:22–26) and goes directly to Peter's extremely important confession (to which Matt. 16:16 adds "the Son of the living God").

1. How does Matthew's addition of 16:17–19 reinforce his positive portrait of the disciples and further stress the significance of Peter's confession?

The word *church* (*ekklesia*) is used in the four Gospels only in Matthew 16:18; 18:17, and scholars debate the origin of these sayings. Although Christians commonly used *church* as a title for the Christian movement by the time Matthew wrote his Gospel, there is little evidence that Jesus himself used the term in reference to a future institution. But deciding whether Matthew 16:17–20 originated in the life setting of Jesus or in that of the author of the Gospel poses less difficulty than interpreting the meaning of 16:18. The name Peter (*Petros* in Greek) is a masculine form of the feminine noun *petra*, which means "rock." Jesus' proclamation reads: "You are *Petros*, and on this *petra* I will build my church" (16:18).

Christians debate whether *Peter himself* is the rock on which Jesus will build the church or whether *Peter's confession*, "You are the Messiah, the Son of the living God" (16:16), is its foundation. Understanding Peter as the rock enables some Roman Catholic scholars to substantiate papal authority over the church by tracing the institution back to Peter. Protestants, by contrast, pointing out that Jesus calls Peter "Satan" in 16:23 in reaction to his rebuke (cf. 26:69–75), usually argue that the rock is Peter's confession of truth, which is quite distinct from Peter the man. Thus, those who belong to the church are those who, like Peter, confess that Jesus is the Christ.

Whichever way one interprets the passage, the wordplay between *Petros* and *petra* is obvious. Peter's name in Aramaic, Cephas, also means rock, so the wordplay works in both languages.

That Jesus earlier compared his teachings in the Sermon on the Mount to a firm foundation on which all disciples must build their faith (7:24–27) lends credibility to viewing Jesus' teachings as the rock. But if Peter is not the rock, what are the keys of the kingdom, and why are they given to him along with the authority to bind and loose on earth (16:19)? Robert H. Gundry provides an interesting possibility for interpretation:

> The identification of "this rock" with "these my words" provides a beautifully natural lead into the portrayal of Peter as a Christian scribe who uses keys—i.e., Jesus' words—and binds and looses things—i.e., prohibits and allows various kinds of conduct and disciplines church members according to the law of Christ. . . . It is not as a hierarch that Peter will use Jesus' words. For Peter is not the foundation, and Matthew portrays every Christian as a scribe (. . . 13:52).[13]

Exegetical problems remain, and the debate continues.

2. How do you interpret 16:18–19? Why?

Matthew 17:1–13: "There appeared to them Moses and Elijah"

After Peter's confession, Jesus' glory is further revealed on the mount of transfiguration.

1. Compare Matthew 17:4 with Mark 9:5–6. What does Matthew leave out of the description of Peter?
2. What from Mark 9:10 does Matthew 17:9 omit?
3. How does the added statement of clarification in 17:13 make sure this story fits Matthew's ongoing portrait of Jesus' disciples?

Matthew 17:14–27: "Does your teacher not pay the temple tax?"

Matthew substantially shortens the account in 17:14–19 (cf. Mark 9:14–29) and once again adds a concluding explanation to clarify the meaning of the story (cf. Matt. 17:20–21 with Mark 9:29).

1. How does what 17:14–21 both leaves out of the story and adds at the end fit Matthew's normal pattern of redacting Mark?

Jesus' third mention of his coming passion (17:22–23) is followed by a story found only in Matthew, in which people question whether Jesus pays the required temple tax (Exod. 30:11–16). The setting of the story, Capernaum (17:24), seems to arise from Mark 9:33.

2. What does 17:24–27 reveal about Matthew's viewpoint on whether or not Christians should belong to and support the Jewish institutions of his day?

Matthew 18:1–14: "Do not despise one of these little ones"

Matthew's *fourth discourse,* chapter 18, focuses on church discipline, and in addition to the time reference ("at that time," 18:1), the power to bind and loose in 18:18 connects this material with the previous narrative section (16:19). Notice again how Matthew eliminates narrative elements of stories from Mark in order to focus on Jesus' words. (For example, cf. Matt. 18:1–2 with Mark 9:33–37.)

1. Compare Matthew 18:1–5 with Mark 9:33–41. How does Matthew improve the image of Jesus' disciples while still emphasizing the point about greatness in the kingdom?

"Children" and "little ones" in 18:5–6, 10 seem to refer to average church members, and the material that follows deals with relationships within the church (cf. 10:42).

2. What does 18:10–14 reveal about God's attitude toward the little ones? (Note that this Q material is located in a very different context in Luke 15:3–7.)

The "little ones" in 18:10 seem to be distinct from the plural "you" in this command, which may indicate that the text addresses church leaders and their treatment of Jesus' disciples.

3. How do God's actions here provide a model for Christian leaders to restore those who have gone astray? (Remember that false teachers lead people astray; 7:15–20.)

Matthew 18:15–35: "How often should I forgive?"

This passage consists of M material and pursues further the theme of relationships within the church that characterizes this discourse.

1. According to 18:15–17, what steps should a Christian follow when another Christian sins against him or her (goes astray)?
2. How does the binding and loosing in 18:18 connect with God's helping to reconcile Christians through their agreeing in prayer in 18:18–20?
3. For reconciliation to occur, what needs to happen on the part of the one offended and on the part of the one who did the offending?
4. The parable in 18:23–35 reinforces the teaching of 18:21–22 concerning the extent to which forgiveness should go. What does it reveal about the consequences of failure to forgive?

The immensity of the monetary figures in this parable reveals the connection with Jesus' teaching on unlimited forgiveness in the preceding story ("seventy times seven"). The magnitude of the servant's debt vastly exceeds the yearly income of a prosperous province. Josephus (*Antiquities* 17.11.4 [§§317–20]) gives a figure of six hundred talents for the total amount of taxes collected by the Romans from Judea, Idumea, and Samaria. A single talent would be worth more than fifteen years' wages for a common worker, so the total value of ten thousand talents is astronomical. Thus, the exaggerated amount of the debt stresses Jesus' point: The servant could never repay such a debt.

By contrast, a denarius is a day's wage for a common laborer. The contrast between the debt forgiven the servant, ten thousand talents, and the amount the fellow servant owed him, one hundred denarii, symbolically stresses the absolute necessity of forgiving others in light of what God has forgiven us. To be ruthless over small debts in light of the magnitude of what we have been forgiven is unforgivable.

Dealing with Conflicts in the Church
If Matthew wrote for a church experiencing difficulties with forgiveness among its members, how would chapter 18 minister to the needs of its members? What are the effects on a church when members refuse to forgive each other?

SECTION SIX: MATTHEW 19—22: OPPOSITION TO THE KINGDOM OF HEAVEN

The *fifth narrative* (chapters 19—22) is connected to the preceding material in several ways. It culminates the opposition begun in the second narrative. The Pharisees function as representatives of Israel, rejecting the kingdom of heaven, and Jesus pronounces that the kingdom will be "given to a people that produces the fruits of the kingdom" (21:43). This transferal of the kingdom to Gentiles and others not previously part of it enhances Jesus' emphasis on forgiveness and acceptance in the fourth discourse (chapter 18) and connects his teaching material to chapters 19—22, where such people as the unmarried, Gentiles, the blind, the lame, tax collectors, and prostitutes are part of the kingdom of heaven.

Matthew 19:1–15: "Have you not read?"

One area of life that often provides an arena for forgiveness is the home, where constant interactions among family members produce tensions. A successful marriage involves forgiveness. Right after preaching about forgiveness without limit in Matthew 18:15–35, Jesus confronts the question of divorce.

1. How has Matthew rearranged the dialogue in 19:1–9 by changing the sequence of events in Mark 10:1–10?
2. Of what significance is the reversal in Matthew 19:7–8 of who uses the terms *command* and *allow* from those using these words in Mark 10:3–5?

Because the Pharisees are the main teachers in the Jewish community in which Matthew lives, they are a threat to the existence of his church. Matthew stresses repeatedly that these men are blind guides who are not in tune with God's will, and in this story they approach Jesus insincerely, to test him. This Gospel also phrases their question in a way that fits the Jewish setting in which Matthew's community lives: Matthew 19:3 alters the scope of their initial question from "Is divorce legal?" (Mark 10:2) to "Is divorce legal for just any old reason?" (an issue of debate among Pharisaic leaders). The net effect of the dialogue is to show that Jesus understands scripture and the Pharisees do not.

Jesus begins by pointing out their ignorance of scripture ("Have you not read . . . ?"; Matt. 19:4) and explaining from Genesis 1:27 that divorce is not God's will. The Pharisees are confused over this, and they question if the scriptures contradict each other, since Moses *commanded* divorce. Jesus then explains the reason for Moses' *allowing* divorce, and in 19:9 he adds the exception clause "except for unchastity," which does not occur in Mark 10:11. The teaching delivered only to the disciples in Mark 10:10–11 becomes part of the public debate with the Pharisees in Matthew 19:9, and the private teaching in Matthew concerns celibacy (19:10–12).

Some eschatological Jews remained celibate, such as the members of the Dead Sea Scroll community at Qumran, but most Jews believed marriage to be a commandment of God. Jewish men considered Genesis 1:28, "Be fruitful and multiply, and fill the earth and subdue it," to be a mandate for them to have children. In the second century C.E., the Mishnah said that one of the few valid reasons for a man not to marry by age twenty was that he desired time for intense study of the scriptures first (Mishnah *Aboth* 5:21). And if a man's wife bore him no children after ten years, some taught that he was to divorce her and marry someone fertile:

> No man may abstain from keeping the law *Be fruitful and multiply*, unless he already has children; according to the School of Shammai, two sons; according to the School of Hillel, a son and a daughter, for it is written, *Male and female created he them.* If he married a woman and lived with her ten years and she bare no child, it is not permitted him to abstain. If he divorced her she may be married to another and the second husband may live with her for ten years. If she had a miscarriage the space [of ten years] is reckoned from the time of the miscarriage. The duty to be fruitful and multiply falls on the man but not on the woman. R. Johanan b. Baroka says: Of them both it is written, *And God blessed*

them and God said unto them, Be fruitful and multiply.
(Mishnah *Yebamoth* 6:6)[14]

3. What does Matthew 19:10–12 explain about the place of celibacy in the kingdom of heaven?

Matthew 19:16–30: "If you wish to be perfect"

1. How do Matthew's modifications in 19:21 (cf. Mark 10:21), 19:23–24 (cf. Mark 10:24), and 19:28 (cf. Mark 10:28) fit his theme of discipleship?

Matthew 20:1–16: "Are you envious because I am generous?"

Jewish law required employers to pay their workers at the end of each day (Deut. 24:14–15). Work began at sunup and continued until sundown.

1. This parable, found only in Matthew, begins with "For," indicating its connection with the previous material. How does it help to explain the meaning of 19:23–30? (Hint: Compare 19:30 with 20:12, 14, 16.)

Comparing Israel to a vineyard is a motif taken from the scriptures. See, for example, the song of the vineyard in Isaiah 5:1–7 and the judgment proclamation in Jeremiah 12:10.

2. What does the parable reveal about Jews and Gentiles in the kingdom of heaven?

Matthew 20:17–28: The Mother of the Sons of Zebedee

1. Compare the passion prediction in 20:17–19 with the previous ones in 16:21 and 17:22–23. What new details are added here?
2. From whom does the request for positions of power come in Matthew 20:20–21, and how does this differ from Mark 10:35? Why might Matthew's portrait of Jesus' disciples have motivated this change?
3. To whom does Jesus direct his response? ("You" in Matt. 20:22 is plural and matches "they" in this verse, following Mark 10:38, not Matthew's change in 20:20.)

Matthew 20:29–34: Two Blind Men

As with the two demoniacs in 8:28 and the two blind men in 9:27–31, Matthew once again doubles the number in this story. Here, two blind men proclaim Jesus the Son of David (20:29) instead of one, Bartimaeus, as in Mark 10:46. The story illustrates discipleship, as the lowly blind men follow Jesus.

Matthew's Jesus

Matthew 21:1–11: The King on a Donkey

1. How does the number of animals that the disciples bring to Jesus in 21:2, 7 compare with Mark 11:2, 7?

Note that Matthew adds a scripture citation in 21:5 (not found in Mark 11:3).

2. How does this quotation from Zechariah 9:9 and Isaiah 62:11 provide a possible explanation for Matthew's modification of the donkey and her colt being brought to Jesus?

Matthew 21:12–22: "Have you never read?"

In this story, Matthew eliminates Mark's connection of the temple with the fig tree by having Jesus go directly to the temple after the triumphal entry into Jerusalem and drive out the merchants (21:12–13). The encounter with the fig tree does not occur until the next day, and when Jesus curses the tree, it withers "at once" (21:18–19).

1. How does the description of the chief priests and scribes in the M material in 21:14–16 compare with Matthew's depiction of the Pharisees?
2. What is the purpose of the story of the fig tree in 21:18–22?

Matthew 21:23–46: "He will put those wretches to a miserable death!"

These passages illustrate in part why Joachim Jeremias argued that parables were Jesus' weapons of war against his opponents. (See chapter 3, section 8, "Interpreting the Parables of Jesus," above.) The religious leaders' refusal to give an honest reply to Jesus' question about John the Baptist in 21:23–27 reinforces Matthew's portrait of them.

1. What does 21:28–32 (M) add to this negative portrait? What does it reveal about the kingdom of God?
2. What does 21:33–46 assert about the religious leaders? (Remember the imagery of the vineyard in 20:1–15.)
3. To whom does Matthew's addition in 21:43 say the kingdom will be given? What Matthean theme does this reinforce?

Matthew 22:1–14: "He . . . destroyed those murderers, and burned their city"

This parable continues the polemic against the religious leaders seen in the preceding material, this time using the imagery of the messianic banquet to describe Jesus' ministry. The vivid description in 22:7 of the destruction of those who refused the invitation probably points to a time of composition for this Gospel after the destruction of Jerusalem in 70 C.E.

1. In this allegory, which people are invited but refuse to come? How do they treat the king's messengers who bring the invitation to attend the marriage feast? (Remember that Jesus referred to his work as a wedding feast in 9:14–17.)
2. How does the king's response compare with 21:40–41?
3. How does the presence of good and bad among the invited guests (22:10) compare with the parables of the weeds (13:24–30, 36–43) and the fish (13:47–50)? What does this say about the church?
4. How might 7:21–23 help in understanding the meaning of 22:11–14?
5. What are the main differences in detail between Matthew 22:1–14 and Luke 14:16–24? Are these different versions of the same parable or different parables entirely?

Matthew 22:15–46: "You know neither the scriptures nor the power of God"

Matthew 22:15 directly connects these passages to Jesus' preceding attacks against the Pharisees. Now his opponents take the offensive.

1. How do Jesus' opponents' actions show that they, like those in the parable of 22:1–10, will not participate in the messianic banquet?
2. How do these stories once again prove that Jesus is the authoritative interpreter of the Mosaic law? (Note how 22:29, 31 asserts his opponents' ignorance of the Bible.)
3. Compare Matthew 22:34–40 with Mark 12:28–34. What block of material does Matthew omit? Why?
4. How does Matthew 22:41–46 modify Mark 12:35–37a to reinforce Matthew's depiction of the Pharisees' ignorance of scripture?

The positive encounter between Jesus and the scribe in Mark 12:28–34 becomes merely another hostile encounter in Matthew 22:34–40. Matthew carefully excises the commendation of the scribe in 22:34, seemingly because it does not fit his agenda of showing the ignorance of the Pharisees. Matthew also moves this section of Mark 12:34 to the end of his debate section with the Pharisees in Matthew 22:46. All questioning is now over. Jesus has demonstrated himself superior to his opponents in his ability to understand and interpret the law. They have no further ability to confute. Now they can merely plot his death.

SECTION SEVEN: MATTHEW 23—25: OPPOSITION AND THE TIME OF THE END

The *fifth,* and last, *discourse* (chapters 23—25) continues Jesus' condemnation of the Pharisees from the fifth narrative with a lengthy and scathing denunciation in Matthew 23. Then it outlines the future of those who follow Jesus and those who reject him, providing an eschatological look at the persecution of his disciples and parables that describe how people will be evaluated at the last judgment.

Matthew 23:1–12: Do What They Say, but Not as They Do

This condemnation of Pharisaic leaders mentions that they "sit on Moses' seat" (23:2). As we saw in Luke 4:16–21, teachers of that time stood to read the scriptures and sat to teach them. Jesus follows this pattern in Matthew, sitting to teach in 5:1; 13:1–2; 15:29; 24:3; and 26:55. Synagogue teachers sat in front of the congregation, but we do not know for sure if the seat on which they sat was called "Moses' seat." No further mention is made of such a seat until the fourth century, when a reference emerges in rabbinic literature to the seat reserved for the president of the Sanhedrin (*Pesikta* 7a).

Consequently, we do not know whether Moses' seat in Matthew 23:2 is a technical term for the chair from which men taught the law or merely a symbolic expression for teaching the law. Either way, the statement refers to the exposition of Mosaic law, an area in which Jesus previously has demonstrated the Pharisees' incompetence. Interestingly, Jesus does not say that people should obey what the scribes and Pharisees "teach" (*didáskō*) but rather what they "say" (*légō*). If the avoidance of *didáskō* is deliberate, this probably forms a striking contrast with Jesus' teaching. Matthew might mean that, unlike the authoritative teaching of Jesus, the words of the scribes are not suitable to be called teaching. Through their pseudoteaching, they simply burden people with the weight of their commands (23:4). If this is the case, Matthew might mean Jesus' remark in 23:2 ironically. However, 23:2 might follow Jesus' assertion in 5:17–20, that disciples are to keep the law even better than the Pharisees. Therefore, "practice and observe whatever they tell you, but not what they do; for they preach, but do not practice" (23:3, RSV.).

1. What are Jesus' basic criticisms of the Pharisees in this passage?
2. The Pharisees are used as a foil for showing what Christian leaders should be like. What is to characterize Christian

leadership? (Cf. the scribes trained for the kingdom of heaven in 13:52.)

Phylacteries are the small, leather cases containing texts of the Law that Jews sometimes wear strapped to their forehead, following a literalistic application of Deuteronomy 6:4–9; 11:18–21. Some also wear *fringes* on the corners of their outer garments in obedience to Numbers 15:37–39 and Deuteronomy 22:12, a practice Jesus himself kept (Matt. 9:20; 14:36). *Rabbi* is the term of respect used by disciples for their teachers, and it is also the official title for scribes.

Matthew 23:13–39: Blind Guides! Snakes!

Note the repeated charge of hypocrisy that begins each section, in spite of the numerous signs of religious zeal among the Pharisees.

1. In 23:13–15, how would the actions of the scribes and Pharisees keep people from entering the kingdom of heaven?
2. Compare 23:16–22 with 5:33–37. What is the combined message of the two passages?

Jesus uses a common principle of interpretation called *Qal Wahomer* (from the lesser to the greater): "What applies to the lesser applies also to the greater." He charges that his Pharisaic opponents ignorantly think that lesser objects in the temple, such as gold or a gift on the altar, are of more value in oath taking than greater objects, such as the temple in which the gold is located or the altar that makes the gift sacred. Jesus, the authoritative teacher, judges their rulings to be invalid.

3. How do you explain Jesus' evaluation of the Pharisees' meticulous concern with keeping the law (e.g., 23:23–24) in light of 5:17–20?

The Pharisees may have strained their drinking water to avoid the possibility of swallowing insects, such as gnats, that were unclean according to Mosaic law. More probably, however, Jesus' sarcastic statement in 23:24 merely reflects a humorous wordplay between the Aramaic words for gnat (*qalma*) and camel (*gamla*).

4. In 23:25–26, Jesus criticizes the religious leaders for cleansing their eating utensils but then filling their plates with food obtained by self-indulgent motivation. How is the same blindness to true religious significance seen in 23:27–28?
5. How is the seventh woe in 23:29–36 much like the sixth woe? (Note 23:29.)

6. What does 23:34 say about the work of Christian missionaries among the Jewish people?

Ironically, although Jerusalem is the center of Jewish religious life, it is the place where God's prophets are killed (23:37; cf. 21:33–22:10). Matthew sees the results of its people's refusal to respond to Jesus Messiah as devastating.

Matthew 24:1–14: "What will be the sign of your coming and of the end of the age?"

Jesus gives the *apocalyptic discourse* in Matthew 24 in response to the disciples' question about when the temple will be destroyed and what the sign will be of Jesus' coming and the close of the age (24:3). The disciples seem to associate the three events with the same time period. (Note that Matthew moves the apocalyptic material in Mark 13:9–12 back to the account of the sending out of the apostles in Matt. 10:17–21.)

1. In 24:4–5, Jesus stresses the necessity of not being deluded by false teachers with respect to his second coming. How might his instructions that follow provide guidance for the missionaries in Matthew's church? (Cf. 24:14 with 10:5–6.)

Matthew 24:15–31: "They will see 'the Son of Man coming on the clouds of heaven' "

Matthew 24:20, unlike the parallels in Mark and Luke, reveals concern for the faithful Jewish Christians who continue to observe the Sabbath. Matthew also sees the *desolating sacrilege* of Daniel 9:27; 11:31; 12:11 (the abominable action that occurred in 168 B.C.E. when Antiochus IV Epiphanes erected an altar to Zeus over the altar of the Lord and sacrificed pig flesh on it) as a foreshadowing of a coming event so terrible that God's people will abandon the temple.

1. Although false Christs and false prophets seek to lead astray the followers of Jesus, what will keep his disciples secure? (Notice again how dramatic and visible to the entire world the second coming will be; cf. 24:31 with 13:41–42, 49–50.)

Matthew 24:32–51: The Son of Man Comes at an Hour You Don't Expect

In 24:32–33, Jesus says that reading the signs of the times is somewhat like observing a fig tree. Those who are familiar with fig trees know that once their leaves begin to appear, summer is near. In like manner, when Jesus' disciples see the things he predicts, they will know his coming will soon follow. Knowing something is

147

near does not mean knowing the exact time of arrival, however, and Jesus admits that even he is not aware of when he will return (24:36). For Christians to predict such things is a hazardous endeavor, and history (especially recent history) provides ample examples of why people should avoid such activities. So far, such guesses have always proven an embarrassment.[15]

1. How do these passages seek to inspire faithfulness to Jesus and his teachings?

Matthew 25:1–13: "The bridegroom was delayed"

1. The "Then" of 25:1 (NIV, "At that time") seems to refer to the day of judgment (24:51). How does this parable continue the theme from 24:45–51?

Many have speculated what the oil for the lamps in 25:3 symbolizes and why it is not transferable to other disciples. Quite likely, however, this is one of those parables that simply seeks to make one point, in this case about diligence in preparing for Christ's parousia (return). The wise person prepares for unexpected delays; the foolish person fails to consider unforeseen circumstances.

Matthew 25:14–30: Trustworthy and Wicked Servants

The parallel story in Luke 19:12–27 utilizes a much smaller monetary unit, the pound, than the talent employed here. The pound was equivalent to about three months' wages for a common laborer, whereas the talent was equivalent to nearly sixteen years' wages for the laborer (one talent = sixty pounds = six thousand denarii). This interesting difference represents a trend in Matthew to use larger monetary values than in Luke or Mark, perhaps because his readers were used to larger incomes. (See also the use of the talent in Matt. 18:24.)

1. How does this parable fit the theme of fruit bearing (hearing and doing) presented elsewhere in the Gospel (e.g., 7:15–20)?

Matthew 25:31–46: "Lord, when was it that we saw you hungry . . . or thirsty?"

This passage concludes Matthew's eschatological discourse and deals with the theme of the last judgment. In the story, both the righteous and the wicked are surprised at what they learn about themselves. Judgment in Matthew brings surprises: In 7:21–23, the false prophets are astonished that Jesus does not know them, and in 22:12–13, the man without the wedding garment is flabbergasted.

1. What separates the sheep from the goats? (Cf. 21:28–32.)
2. What does this story reveal about the relationship between proper belief and proper behavior? (Note that it is not enough merely to abstain from sinning.)
3. What does this passage have in common with the parable of the weeds in the field (13:24–30, 36–43) and the parable of the catch of good and bad fish (13:47–50)?

SECTION EIGHT: MATTHEW 26—28: THE PASSION NARRATIVE

Jesus' prediction of intense opposition for his followers, which he explains in the fifth discourse (chapters 23—25), prepares for the persecution Jesus suffers in the passion narrative. Although Matthew gives the story of Jesus' time in Jerusalem his own characteristic touches, he follows Mark's narrative quite closely, maintaining exactly the same order of events. In his efforts to integrate the material into a unified presentation of Jesus Messiah, he modifies the stories in the passion narrative very little.

Matthew 26:1–16: Loving Service and Bitter Betrayal

Matthew 23—25 concludes with the same formula used in 7:27; 11:1; 13:53 and 19:1, with one small yet important difference. Matthew here adds the word *all*: "When Jesus had finished saying *all* these things . . . " This effectively signals the end of Jesus' discourses, and perhaps it is designed to echo Moses' words at the end of his final speech to the Israelites in Deuteronomy 32:45: "When Moses had finished reciting all these words to all Israel. . . . " The one greater than Moses now concludes his public address and prepares for his death.

Note that 26:2 modifies the editorial transition of Mark 14:1, which merely states when the events occur, to another instance of Jesus *teaching* his disciples about his coming death.

1. How does the identity of the high priest in 26:3 compare with Luke 3:2 and Acts 4:6? With John 11:49?

Josephus (*Antiquities* 18.2.2 [§35]) states that Caiaphas was high priest from 18 to 36 C.E. Annas was formerly a high priest but was deposed in 15 C.E. Evidently, however, he continued to exercise considerable influence in priestly matters.

2. After the story of the woman's beautiful act of love in 26:6–13, how does Matthew 26:15 modify Mark 14:10 to make Judas look even worse?

Personal Reflection
How do you respond to the insistence in Matthew 23—25 that the kind of faith God finds acceptable is that reflected in a life wholly transparent and consistent with one's profession? In what ways are you tempted to live day by day in ways that betray what you claim to be your highest ideals for human life? What do you need to do to live consistently?

Matthew 26:15 alludes to Zechariah 11:12, a passage in which the prophet describes his sharp confrontation with Jewish rulers:

> I then said to them, "If it seems right to you, give me my wages; but if not, keep them." So they weighed out as my wages thirty shekels of silver. Then the LORD said to me, "Throw it into the treasury"—this lordly price at which I was valued by them. So I took the thirty shekels of silver and threw them into the treasury in the house of the LORD. (Zech. 11:12–13)

3. Compare Matthew 26:15 with Mark 14:11. How has Matthew modified the story to conform to Zechariah 11:12? (See also Matt. 27:3–5.)

Matthew 26:17–29: The Passover

Review the material under Mark 14:12–31 in chapter 2 on how Jewish people celebrated the Passover.

1. What details does Matthew 26:17–19 omit from Mark 14:12–16? How does this slightly change the picture of how the two disciples located the place where Jesus wanted them to prepare for the Passover?
2. Jesus' movements in Matthew 26:20 are perhaps less secretive than in the parallel of Mark 14:17. In the betrayal prediction that follows, how do divine sovereignty and human responsibility merge together?
3. According to Matthew 26:26–29, what is the significance of Jesus' death?

Example of an olive press. The name Gethsemane means "oil press," and the garden there grew olive trees.

Matthew 26:30–56: "The spirit indeed is willing, but the flesh is weak"

In first-century Palestine, Jews divided the night into four watches. The third watch lasted from midnight to 3 A.M., and toward the end of this time roosters might begin to crow in anticipation of the dawn. Matthew's account of the events in this section closely follows Mark's version. Matthew 26:39–45, for example, maintains the struggle in prayer recorded by Mark 14:36–41 but omitted by Luke 22:42–45.

1. In the story of the betrayal, Matthew adds a saying of Jesus in 26:52–54. What does this addition contribute to Matthew's portrait of Jesus?

2. How does the Matthean modification in 26:56 accomplish the same effect? (Cf. Mark 14:49.)

Matthew 26:57–75: "You will see the Son of Man seated at the right hand of Power"

1. What effect does Jesus' silence in 26:62–63 have on the high priest?

While Jesus is on trial, Peter sits outside by a fire, periodically questioned by others about his relationship to Jesus. Aside from the minor difference of the number of times the cock crows before the denial (cf. Matt. 26:34, 75 with Mark 14:30, 72), Matthew's portrayal of Peter here is the same as Mark's.

2. How does this story of Peter contrast with earlier portraits of the disciples in Matthew?

Matthew 27:1–10: "I have sinned by betraying innocent blood"

1. The material in 27:3–10 is found only in Matthew. What new information does it provide about the result of Judas' treachery?
2. What does 27:3–10 contribute to Matthew's negative portrait of the Jewish leaders?

For the scripture quotation in 27:9–10, see Jeremiah 32:6–15 and Zechariah 11:12–13. Although Matthew calls the event a fulfillment of Jeremiah, his quotation comes primarily from Zechariah.

3. Which details in Matthew 27:3–10 differ from the account of Judas's death in Acts 1:15–20?

Matthew 27:11–26: "His blood be on us and on our children!"

Pilate recognizes Jesus' innocence, so he offers the people a choice of which prisoner they would have released. Some Greek manuscripts of Matthew 27:16, 17 specify that the notorious criminal's name was Jesus Barabbas, and if this is the original reading of the text, then Pilate is asking in 27:17 which Jesus they want him to release. He probably thought they would choose Jesus the Christ, rather than have Jesus Barabbas released back into society. He was wrong. The Jewish leaders successfully incite the people to reject Jesus Christ (27:20), fulfilling his earlier warning about the blind leading the blind. Following these men leads the people into disaster.

151

1. What does the Matthean addition of 27:19 contribute to the story?
2. Why is Matthew's addition of 27:24–25 an extremely ominous charge against the Jewish leaders and their descendants?

Matthew 27:27–54: King of the Jews

For details on crucifixion, see the material on Mark 15:21–41 in chapter 2. Matthew's version of this event closely follows  Mark's account, including the painful cry in 27:46. Matthew uses none of the brave words that Jesus delivers in Luke's account.

Matthew adds further words of derision from Jesus' opponents in 27:43, ridiculing the claim that Jesus is the Son of God. But their contemptuous insults melt into insignificance when the tombs break open in 27:51b–53, and the righteous dead walk the streets of Jerusalem, and the Roman centurion declares in 27:54: "Truly this man was God's Son!" Only Matthew records the bizarre account of the tombs yielding their dead for a time. Historically speaking, one can hardly imagine such an event would not have made quite a stir in Jerusalem. Quite probably Matthew's concern here is more theological than historical, showing that Jesus' death begins to usher in the promised resurrection of the dead that will occur in the last times. Once again, Matthew's tendency to show that Jesus fulfills the Old Testament manifests itself.

Reconstruction of a tomb at the Biblical Resources Study Center in Jerusalem.

Matthew 27:55–66: "Make it as secure as you can"

It appears that some of the Jewish leaders in Matthew's community were claiming the reason Jesus' body was missing from the tomb was that his own disciples stole it and then perpetrated the hoax. Note the similar accusation specified in 28:15.

1. How does the M material in 27:62–66 answer these charges?
2. How does this Matthean claim that Jesus' enemies knew he predicted that he would rise from the dead compare with Jesus' own disciples' knowledge of this event in Mark's account?

Matthew 28:1–10: With Fear and Great Joy

1. What details does this story add to and delete from Mark 16:1–8?

2. Why would the addition of 27:62–66 also cause Matthew to add the description of the angels and the guards in 28:2–4?
3. How does the picture of triumph and joy in Matthew 28:8–10 compare with Mark 16:8?

Matthew 28:11–15: Bribing the Soldiers

1. This passage is found only in Matthew. What relationship does it have to the Matthean addition in 27:62–66?
2. What important answers does it provide for Christians in Matthew's community as they face charges from their non-Christian neighbors?

Matthew 28:16–20: "Teaching them to obey everything that I have commanded you"

1. Matthew describes the meeting predicted in Mark 16:7. In what different ways do the disciples respond to Jesus' appearance?
2. How does Jesus' command in 28:18–20 forcefully summarize Matthew's overall portrait of Jesus Messiah?
3. How does the command fit the understanding of discipleship presented throughout Matthew?
4. Of what significance would this charge be to the members of Matthew's church community?
5. How has Matthew's Gospel prepared us for this final charge, in which Jesus clearly indicates the presence of Gentiles in the church?

REVIEW OF MATTHEAN THEMES AND CHRONOLOGY

1. What characteristics dominate Matthew's portrait of Jesus?
2. What characteristics dominate his portrait of Jesus' disciples?
3. Why is his portrait of the disciples vitally connected to his portrait of Jesus, in a cause-and-effect relationship?
4. How does the overall structure of Matthew's Gospel reveal his emphasis on the significance of Jesus Messiah?

FURTHER READING ON THE GOSPEL OF MATTHEW

Albright, William, and C. S. Mann. *Matthew*. Anchor Bible. Garden City, N.Y.: Doubleday & Co., 1971.

Barr, David L. "The Drama of Matthew's Gospel: A Reconsideration of Its Structure and Purpose." *Theology Digest* 24 (1976): 349–59.

Beare, F. W. *The Gospel according to Matthew*. New York: Harper & Row, 1982.

Brown, Raymond E. *The Birth of the Messiah: A Commentary on the Infancy Narratives in Matthew and Luke*. Garden City, N.Y.: Doubleday & Co., 1977.

Davies, W. D. *The Setting of the Sermon on the Mount*. Cambridge: Cambridge University Press, 1964.

Edwards, Richard A. *Matthew's Story of Jesus.* Philadelphia: Fortress Press, 1985.

Ellis, Peter F. *Matthew: His Mind and His Message.* Collegeville, Minn: Liturgical Press, 1974.

Gundry, Robert H. *Matthew: A Commentary on His Literary and Theological Art.* Grand Rapids: Wm. B. Eerdmans Publishing Co., 1982.

Hagner, Donald. *Matthew.* 2 vols. Word Biblical Commentary, 33A–33B. Dallas: Word Books, 1993, 1995.

Harrington, Daniel J. *The Gospel of Matthew.* Sacra Pagina. Collegeville, Minn.: Michael Glazier, 1991.

Hill, David. *The Gospel of Matthew.* The New Century Bible. London: Oliphants, 1972.

Kingsbury, Jack D. *Matthew as Story.* Philadelphia: Fortress Press, 1986.

————. *Matthew: Structure, Christology, Kingdom.* Philadelphia: Fortress Press, 1975.

Mays, James L. *The Gospel of Matthew.* Harper's Bible Commentary. San Francisco: Harper & Row, 1988.

Minear, Paul. *Matthew: The Teacher's Gospel.* New York: Pilgrim Press, 1982.

Mounce, Robert H. *Matthew.* New York: Harper & Row, 1985.

Schweizer, Eduard. *The Good News according to Matthew.* Atlanta: John Knox Press, 1975.

5

John's Jesus

The Descent and Ascent of the Eternal Logos

Leaving the Synoptic Gospels and entering the Fourth Gospel in some ways is like entering a different world. Whereas the Synoptics share much of the same material and produce similar portraits of Jesus, John follows a completely different agenda. Only a few of the stories in John are also found in the Synoptics, such as the cleansing of the temple (John 2:13–22) and the feeding of the five thousand (6:1–21). And John uses these stories in very different ways from the other Gospels: The cleansing of the temple is located at the beginning of Jesus' ministry instead of during the final week, as in the Synoptics; and the multiplication of the loaves is a prelude to a discourse on Jesus as the true bread from heaven (6:25–71). John makes no mention of Jesus' birth, temptation by Satan in the wilderness, or the Last Supper where he says "This is my body." John does not even specifically mention Jesus' baptism or agonized prayer in Gethsemane.

In the Synoptics, Jesus spends most of his ministry time in Galilee and makes only one fateful trip to Jerusalem, which culminates in his crucifixion and resurrection. In John he makes numerous trips with his disciples back and forth from Galilee to Jerusalem. Encounters with demoniacs are frequent in the Synoptics, but not a single account of Jesus encountering or casting out a demon appears in John. And whereas parables are a major source of Jesus' teachings in the Synoptics, John records not a single parable, although Jesus does employ highly symbolic speech in the Fourth Gospel.

John's Jesus delivers lengthy discourses in which the style of speaking is quite distinct from that in the other Gospels. And instead of focusing on the kingdom of God as he does in the Synoptics, Jesus' discourses in John focus on his own identity and his relationship to God, his Father. Indeed, the description of Jesus' public ministry in John 1—12 contains no explicit ethical teaching; every story in these chapters focuses on his identity as the Son of God, who descended from heaven. (Compare this, for example, with the Sermon on the Mount in Matthew 5—7 for a striking contrast.) The theme of Jesus' descent to earth and ascent back to heaven plays a dominant role in the Johannine narrative.

John's unique portrait of Jesus represents a later perspective on the significance of Jesus Messiah. From Acts 1—15 it is clear that the early Christians required substantial time to understand the person and ministry of Jesus. And extended reflection on the significance of Jesus affects the way in which one tells the story of his earthly life. Consider, for example, some important event that happened in your life during your early teenage years, such as a broken romance. Your perspective on that event today probably differs substantially from your response to the situation at the time it occurred. If you were to tell someone that story today, you would most likely focus on what you learned from the circumstance. But right after it happened, you probably focused on the pain of the experience and the despair you felt. Distance from a situation changes our perspective on what we consider important and changes the details we choose to recount.

For example, in June 1972, when I was twenty-two, I spent a month in Guatemala on an overseas missionary-training program sponsored by InterVarsity Christian Fellowship. During that time I suffered an accident while playing soccer, tearing a ligament in my left knee. Consequently, on the same day the other participants in the camp left to work with various missionaries for a week, the part of our program called "Operation Involvement," I went to a Guatemalan hospital for "involvement operation."

I had no idea how painful the knee surgery would be, so coping with that factor was difficult in itself. What complicated this was my isolation. Virtually no one in the hospital spoke English, and I spoke no Spanish. My fellow campers and our supervisors were off on their missionary learning experiences, and I lay alone in a foreign hospital bed, trying to communicate to my Spanish-speaking nurse that I had contracted Montezuma's revenge. The combination of muscle spasms in my knee, frequent trips to the bathroom with diarrhea, loneliness, and inability to communicate made the whole experience extremely difficult.

John's Jesus

In the months after that memorable event, when I told it I would recount the gory details that were so fresh in my memory. I could see no particular meaning in the episode. It was simply something I endured. But from a later perspective, the event proved significant in the future direction of my life. Normally, during the summers I worked on electric power-line construction as a means of earning money to pay my way through another year at the University of Montana, where I was working on a degree in wildlife biology. But recovering from knee surgery eliminated that as a possibility, and I spent a lot of time reading that summer. This started a chain of events that finally culminated in my becoming a campus staff member for InterVarsity instead of pursuing work in wildlife management.

So, from a later perspective, seeing what happened as a result of an accident on a soccer field, I tell the story much differently now than I did then; for now I see implications of that event that I then had no way of knowing. Consequently, when I tell about the injury now, I weave into my account of the story the action of God, guiding me through the situation into a very different line of work from that I embarked on when I entered college. I see the past through subsequent events and a more developed understanding, and this substantially affects my telling of the story. No longer do I tell in vivid detail the suffering I endured. Now I focus on the new direction in life which resulted from that difficult experience in June 1972. I speak about God's work even in a painful situation, setting the stage for my one day becoming a professor of New Testament.

Similarly, when the apostles went through the dark days immediately after Jesus' crucifixion, they did not see the significance of that terrible event. They saw only the pain and disappointment, and when they told the story then, these factors naturally dominated. But later, in the light of Easter, they understood the sacrificial nature of Jesus' death to be a mighty victory won by his hideous suffering, and their telling of the story changed substantially. When they came to the conclusion that Jesus was the pre-existing Son of God, who descended into history in human form, this belief entered into their telling the story of Jesus. Now they focused on the plan of God working through the death and resurrection of Jesus, not just the details of the suffering.

John's Gospel represents such a telling of the story of Jesus from a later perspective, even more obvious than in the Synoptics. By the time it was written (the majority of scholars date it around 90–95 C.E.), many years had elapsed since Jesus' earthly

157

existence, and his disciples had reached many conclusions about the Son of God. These conclusions are apparent as one reads John, for the story reflects an understanding about Jesus that his disciples did not yet have during Jesus' actual time on earth. Thus, later understandings of the significance of Jesus' existence are woven into the story itself, allowing the reader to see deeper meanings. Note, for example, the more obvious indications of this in the narrator's explanations:

> After he was raised from the dead, his disciples remembered that he had said this; and they believed the scripture and the word that Jesus had spoken. (2:22)

> His disciples did not understand these things at first; but when Jesus was glorified, then they remembered that these things had been written of him and had been done to him. (12:16)

It is also obvious in the characters' dialogues:

> He came to Simon Peter, who said to him, "Lord, are you going to wash my feet?" Jesus answered him, "You do not know now what I am doing, but later you will understand." (13:6–7)

> "I still have many things to say to you, but you cannot bear them now. When the Spirit of truth comes, he will guide you into all the truth; for he will not speak on his own, but will speak whatever he hears, and he will declare to you the things that are to come. He will glorify me." (16:12–14)

Simply stated, the Gospel of John represents the end product of what the Spirit had been revealing to the Johannine community during the past decades, stressing the glory of Jesus Christ. The teaching on the Holy Spirit, which is unique to this Gospel, provides the basis for how John tells the story of Jesus.

As in the other Gospels, the author of John does not identify himself. He does, however, provide a statement of purpose for his work:

> Now Jesus did many other signs in the presence of his disciples, which are not written in this book. But these are written that you may come to believe that Jesus is the Messiah, the Son of God, and that through believing you may have life in his name. (20:30–31)

The last words of the Gospel echo the same theme:

But there are also many other things that Jesus did; if every one of them were written down, I suppose that the world itself could not contain the books that would be written. (21:25)

Indicating that he has been highly selective in what he has chosen to tell about Jesus, the author reveals that his mission is to bring about belief. He has no desire to tell stories about Jesus just to entertain. His agenda is to tell the story of Jesus in such a manner as to convince the reader to respond in belief to the message. We will see as we work through the Gospel, however, that John wrote his witness not to inspire non-Christians to place their faith in Jesus but to promote a certain kind of Christology among people who already believe.

SECTION ONE: JOHN 1—3: THE ETERNAL LOGOS COMES IN THE FLESH
John 1:1–18: "In the beginning"

1. Compare the Prologue to John's Gospel (1:1–18) with the approaches used in the Synoptic Gospels to begin their stories of Jesus. How does John's approach differ from theirs?

This highly theological prologue stresses the eternal existence and identity of Jesus. Quite possibly it is based on a hymn about Christ sung in the Johannine community, for some of the lines are poetic in structure and present very carefully worded, creedal formulations. Note the strophic composition of 1:1–5 in the following, very literal translation, which shows the approximately equal length of the phrases, the repetition of words and phrases, and the structure of the statements:

> *In the beginning was the Word,*
> *and the Word was with God,*
> *and the Word was God.*
> *He was in the beginning with God;*
> *all things through him came to be,*
> *and without him came to be not one thing.*
> *What came to be in him was life,*
> *and the life was the light of men;*
> *and the light in the darkness shines,*
> *and the darkness did not overcome it.*

Although the prologue foreshadows the Gospel's main themes, some of the vocabulary is not found elsewhere in John, which further indicates an independent existence before being incorporated into the Gospel. The central concept of the prologue is that

159

Jesus is the eternal "Word" (*logos*), yet this term does not occur elsewhere in the Gospel as a title for Christ. Similarly, "grace" (*charis*) in 1:14, 16, 17 and "fullness" (*pleroma*) in 1:16 occur nowhere else in John.

The practice of using parts of hymns to aid in expressing theological points is not uncommon in the New Testament. As pastors today use the words of hymns in their sermons, so the New Testament authors sometimes used hymns to help establish their points. Paul, for example, quotes a hymn in Philippians 2:6–11 that presents the same sort of theology as does John 1:1–18, explaining succinctly how Christ humbled himself from a heavenly existence to become a man and then was exalted back to his glorious heavenly existence. (Other instances of hymnic material may be seen in such passages as Col. 1:15–20, 1 Tim. 3:16, and Heb. 1:2–5.) Thus, instead of beginning with a birth narrative to reveal something about Jesus' parents and the events surrounding his birth, John begins with a hymn of praise, showing the eternal existence and glory of the Word become flesh.

2. What echoes of Genesis 1 do you hear in John 1:1–5? What does this passage reveal about the nature of the Word and his relationship to all created things?
3. How does 1:6–8 contrast John the Baptist with the Word?
4. What does 1:9–14 reveal about the reception of the Word by the Jewish people? What is the result of believing in the Word?
5. What contrast does 1:15–18 draw between the significance of the Word and the significance of the law of Moses?

A great deal of research has been devoted to understanding what John intended to communicate by using Word (*logos*) as a title. Commentaries on the Fourth Gospel usually contain a section attempting to explain this concept. Some explain *logos* in light of Greek philosophy, because ancient Greek philosophers used *logos* to express important concepts pertaining to the relationship of divine order and thought with the physical world. Increasingly, however, scholars have seen affinities between John's use of *logos* and the thought world found in Jewish writings such as the Dead Sea Scrolls.[1]

John 1:19–51: "Come and see"

John's prophetic ministry in the wilderness raises questions about his identity, and officials come to question him.

1. What do 1:6–8, 15, 19–36 emphasize about the role of John the Baptist?

John's Jesus

2. In 1:29–36, what does John assert about the person and work of Jesus?
3. How does John's knowledge of Jesus' ministry here compare with that which he exhibited in the Synoptics (e.g., Luke 3:15–17; 7:18–19)?
4. In 1:35–51, what do the men who begin to follow Jesus affirm about him? (List the various titles used for Jesus.)
5. How does this initial knowledge of Jesus' identity, and Jesus' lack of secrecy about himself, contrast with Mark's presentation?

THE INTENDED READERS

John's audience already knows the story of Jesus. For example, John the Baptist appears without introduction in 1:19, answering a question about his identity. (Also, he is called only John, without adding "the Baptist.") John 3:24 comments, "John, of course had not yet been thrown into prison," although this Gospel does not describe John's arrest or execution. The Evangelist therefore presupposes that the reader knows the story of John the Baptist's life. Similarly, Andrew is identified as Simon Peter's brother in 1:40, with the assumption that the reader already knows who Peter is. Conversely, the author does not assume the reader knows the meaning of such names as Rabbi (1:38) and Messiah (1:41) and Cephas (1:42). This contrasts sharply with what we saw in the Gospel of Matthew, whose author presupposes that his Jewish-Christian audience knows the meaning of Aramaic expressions and so typically does not provide translations for these.

Another window into the historical setting of the Fourth Gospel may be the way in which the author so strongly stresses that John the Baptist was only a man who bore witness to Jesus (1:6–8, 15, 19–23, 30–34; see also 3:22–36 in this regard). Among the intended readers may well have been those who placed too much emphasis on John. The Baptist was a powerful figure and commanded a substantial following. For example, Paul encountered disciples of John in Ephesus during his third missionary journey around 52 C.E. (Acts 19:1–7). The Fourth Gospel may therefore downplay the significance of John in order to correct mistaken beliefs about him, emphasizing that he was only a witness, just a man, whereas Jesus is the eternal Word (1:1–8). This historical reconstruction is speculative; but through such reconstructive efforts, scholars seek to determine the life setting of the author and to determine his goals in writing.

John 2:1–11: When the Wine Gave Out

1. How does this story fulfill the prediction of 1:50?
2. What does the interchange between Jesus and his mother reveal about him?

Personal Reflection

When faced with Nathanael's difficult question in 1:46, Philip responds, "Come and see." How might this approach be helpful to you if someone asks a question about your faith that you presently are not capable of answering?

3. Approximately how many gallons of wine does Jesus make? Of what quality is it?
4. What effect does the miracle have on the disciples? (Notice that it is called a sign, not a miracle.)

Jesus' first miracle in John occurs at a wedding, and 2:1 specifies that it happened on the "third day." This does not appear to follow the "next day" designations in 1:29, 35, 43, because the sum of these days yields a number higher than three for 2:1. Perhaps this is the third day after Jesus and the disciples left the region of the Jordan River, indicating a three-day trip. Raymond Brown speculates that, since Mishnah *Kethuboth* 1 stipulates a virgin's wedding should occur on Wednesday, Jesus arrived with his disciples in Cana on Tuesday evening or Wednesday morning.[2] In any event, the replacement of purification water with the wine of celebration for a wedding seems to signal the advent of Jesus' messianic ministry.

In the other Gospels, Jesus compares his ministry to a wedding banquet (for example, Mark 2:18–22), and a common expectation among the Jews was that the faithful would attend a great banquet given by the messiah (a belief reflected, for example, in Matt. 8:11; 22:1–14). This banquet was to have all good things in abundance, including wine. Thus the abundance of wine produced by Jesus is a messianic sign. A good example of this belief may be seen in *2 Baruch,* an apocalyptic document from the same time period, which explains, "The earth will also yield fruits ten thousandfold. And on one vine will be a thousand branches, and one branch will produce a thousand clusters, and one cluster will produce a thousand grapes, and one grape will produce a cor of wine"[3] (one cor = 60.74 gallons).

That You May Believe

John's Gospel records few miracles when compared with the Synoptic accounts, and the miracles function as *signs*, indicating Jesus' identity (see 2:11; 5:36; 6:14; 7:31; 10:25; 11:45; 20:30–31). In so doing, they combine their witness with the narrator's witness (19:35), the Spirit's witness (15:26), the Father's witness (8:18), and Jesus' witness to himself (3:32; 8:14; 18:37). The author seeks to inspire belief in Jesus (20:31), and he is highly selective in what he reports. Over the approximately two and a half years that elapse in the story told in John 1—21, events occupying only about two months of that time are recorded. John recounts only a small part of the total story, events that function to demonstrate what he wants the reader to know about Jesus.[4]

John's Jesus

John 2:12–25: "Destroy this temple, and in three days I will raise it up"

1. This is one of the few stories in John that also occurs in the Synoptics. How does the time during which it happens in Jesus' ministry differ here from that in the other Gospels?
2. How has the postresurrection realization mentioned in 2:22 shaped the telling of the story?
3. Why does Jesus not entrust himself to those who believe in him because of his signs (2:23–25)?

Although a few scholars argue that Jesus cleansed the temple twice, once at the beginning of his ministry and again during the final week in Jerusalem, most believe that John placed the story here for theological rather than historical reasons. The passage introduces a major Johannine motif, *the replacement of Jewish religious institutions by Jesus.* The Son of God, not the temple, is now the focus of God's dealings with his people. Messiah has come.

John 3:1–21: "You must be born from above"

There is a strong connection between 3:1 and 2:25 through repetition of the term *man:* "He knew all *men* and needed no one to bear witness of *man;* for he himself knew what was in *man.* Now there was a *man* of the Pharisees, named Nicodemus. . . . " The NRSV loses this connection because it eliminates the word *man* in the interests of inclusive language.

1. What does this connection communicate about Nicodemus?
2. What role does Nicodemus play in this story? Is he an active dialogue partner or merely someone who asks Jesus the right questions so that Jesus can speak about important matters? When is Nicodemus last mentioned in the passage?
3. What do Jesus' short sermons to Nicodemus reveal about the requirements for entry into the kingdom of God?

Irony and the Two Levels of Communication in John's Gospel

Irony permeates the Gospel of John. Often this takes the form of Jesus speaking on a spiritual level but his audience misunderstanding his words because they interpret them on a physical level. In 3:1–21 this emerges in the double meaning of *anothen,* which can mean either "from above" or "again," and *pneuma,* which can mean "spirit" or "wind" or "breath." In this context, when Jesus speaks of spiritual birth, he means being born "from above." (John the Baptist employs the same meaning for *anothen* in 3:31 when he calls Jesus the one who comes "from above"; and Jesus tells Pilate in 19:11, "You would have no power over me unless it had been given you *from above* [*anothen*].") Nicodemus, however, understands Jesus to be saying "born again," which shows his dullness toward spiritual realities. So, in a very confused state of mind, he asks about entering again into his mother's womb.

This is all part of Johannine irony. Perhaps an even greater irony is the number of English translations that duplicate Nicodemus's ignorance and translate Jesus' statement with "born again" instead of "born from above" in an attempt not to confuse the reader who does not know Greek and therefore cannot see the wordplay. It is also interesting that this wordplay works only in Greek. No equivalent Hebrew or Aramaic term exists that means both "from above" and "again."

4. What does the ambiguity of Jesus' words, which fosters misunderstanding by Nicodemus, as well as the ascent/descent language in 3:13, contribute to John's portrait of Jesus?
5. In the context of John 3, what does being "born from above" seem to mean?
6. What does this story reveal about Jesus' role in the salvation or condemnation of people?

Translations vary as to where in this passage they place quotation marks to conclude the words of Jesus. The RSV ends Jesus' discourse at 3:15, whereas other translations, such as the NRSV and NIV, extend Jesus' words through 3:21, placing the quotation marks at the end of that verse. Deciding where Jesus quits preaching to Nicodemus and where (or if) the author begins preaching to his readers about Jesus is quite difficult, since the style of speaking and vocabulary are the same throughout the passage. This is also true throughout the rest of the Gospel. In other words, one cannot distinguish between the speaking style of Jesus and that of the narrator. The two are one. Alan Culpepper provides a very valuable analysis of the style of narration in John's Gospel.[5] He explains that "when Jesus . . . speaks, he speaks the language of the author and his narrator," and Culpepper observes that "it is impossible to tell when Jesus or John the Baptist stops speaking in chapter 3 and when or if the narrator speaks."[6]

John 3:22–36: "He must increase, but I must decrease"

1. What concerns the disciples of John about the baptizing activity of Jesus' disciples?
2. This concern gives John an occasion to preach about Jesus. What does 3:31–36 reveal about Jesus and about salvation? (The content and style of speaking in this sermon are very similar to 3:11–21; and for reasons similar to those encountered in 3:11–21, translations vary as to whether the words of John extend through 3:30 or 3:36.)

John's Jesus

A confusing element exists here in the account of Jesus' movements. In 2:1 he arrives in Galilee, and in 2:13 he returns to Judea for the Passover celebration in Jerusalem, where he encounters Nicodemus (3:1–21). The transition at 3:22, which states that Jesus went into the land of Judea, is curious, for the events of 3:1–21 take place in Judea. Commentators explain this conundrum in various ways. For example, some say the author used different sources of information about Jesus, and here he draws from a source different from that used in the previous passage, which explains the problem. Others simply say the author is indicating that Jesus left the city (Jerusalem) and went into a rural area of Judea. This approach may be seen in the NRSV, which translates it "Judean countryside." Because we can only speculate on the answer in light of careful observation of the text, the "correct" solution to the problem depends on individual discretion.

SECTION TWO: JOHN 4—7:
BELIEVE IN THE SON OF GOD!

John 4:1–30: "Sir, you have no bucket"

There seems to be an element of divine mission as Jesus leaves a successful baptizing ministry. John 4:4 says, "He *had* to go through Samaria" (emphasis mine), although geographically speaking, he could have gone around this region. Indeed, many Jews deliberately went around Samaria to avoid contact with Samaritans. Jesus does not. Tired and thirsty, he stops beside the well at the "sixth hour." In the Jewish reckoning of time employed in Judea this would be noon, for there they calculated the hours beginning at approximately 6 A.M. This scenario would nicely fit the story of Jesus needing to stop after walking quite a distance.

Since the Fourth Gospel was probably written outside of Judea, some scholars argue that the author used the Roman reckoning of time, where the hours were calculated beginning at midnight instead of at 6 A.M. (cf. 19:14, which states that Pilate delivered Jesus to be crucified at the sixth hour). But this places a travel-weary Jesus by the well at 6 A.M., a time when women normally went to gather water, and this simply does not fit the Johannine description.

The diversity of ways in which ancient people calculated time may be seen clearly in the following quotation from Pliny the Elder:

> The Babylonians count the period between two sunrises, the Athenians that between two sunsets, the Umbrians from midday to midday, the common people everywhere from dawn to dark, the Roman priests and the authorities

Coming to the Light
In what matters have you observed people choosing to hide their actions instead of coming into the light and allowing their deeds to be visible? What effect does doing things that need to be hidden have on your relationship with God? On your relationships with other people? What would help you to live a more transparent life in the light?

who fixed the official day, and also the Egyptians and Hipparchus, the period from midnight to midnight. (Pliny, *Natural History* 2.79.181; LCL)

Days in Judea were calculated from sundown to sundown, as among the Athenians. Thus, instead of the way in which we connect a night with the preceding day (Friday night comes at the end of Friday), Jews connected the night with the following day (Saturday night begins at sundown on Friday and leads into Saturday; this form of calculating time remains true today for the Sabbath). But the actual hours of the day were counted beginning with sunrise.

Whether time in John's Gospel reflects Judean hour designations or the "official day" according to the Romans remains a matter of debate. Scholars argue in favor of both interpretations, and

at this point no consensus exists as to the best understanding. I favor interpreting the sixth hour as noon, because it fits the story line of John 4 better. A thirsty Jesus, wearied from hours of walking that day, stops by a well to tell an outcast woman about living water.

The woman is surprised that Jesus speaks to her and suspicious of his intentions. (Note also that his own disciples are shocked at his speaking with her, when they return from town in 4:27, but they are too embarrassed to ask about his motive.) Speaking to a strange man would be socially unacceptable, but that provides only the first astonishing part of the encounter. The woman expresses surprise that a Jew would condescend to speak with a Samaritan, and the narrator explains, "Jews do not share things in common with Samaritans" (4:9). For centuries, these two groups of people fostered bitter animosity toward each other.

On the slopes of Mount Gerazim, the mountain on which the woman says the Samaritans conducted their worship and at the base of which this dialogue takes place, had once been the Samaritans' temple. But in 128–129 B.C.E., a Jewish army led by John Hyrcanus destroyed it as part of their conquest of Samaria. Animosity ran deep. The Jews considered the Samaritans to be apostate, half-breed Jews whom God despised. The Samaritans considered themselves God's chosen people, believing that the temple should be on Mount Gerazim, not on Mount Moriah in Jerusalem. (This is clearly stated in Deut. 27:4 in the Samaritan version of the Pentateuch.) Notice in John 4 the reception the Samaritans give to Jesus the Jew and what title they ascribe to him.

1. What does the story reveal about the past of this woman? Why might she have come to draw water at noon instead of early morning or late afternoon with the rest of the village women?
2. How does Jesus arouse her curiosity in what he has to offer?
3. How is this dialogue similar to the Nicodemus dialogue, wherein Jesus speaks on one level but the hearer understands on another level?
4. What is the focus of Jesus' message to the woman?
5. In her response of faith, why do you think the woman left her water jar in 4:28?

In this discourse Jesus establishes the necessity for spiritual (= "true") worship (4:21–24). In the Fourth Gospel, Jesus is the truth and the way to God the Father (14:6). Furthermore, the Spirit reveals the truth to believers, teaching them about Christ (14:16–17, 25–26; 15:26; 16:12–15); and 7:38–39 states that the Spirit is received by those who believe and flows out of them like living water. John 1:12–13 states that those who place their faith in Jesus are born of God, and 3:3–8 explains that those who are born from above (experience the spiritual birth) are those who are born of the water and the Spirit.

John connects the Spirit and water closely, and receiving the Spirit is conditional on belief in Jesus (1:12–13; 7:38–39). Thus, when Jesus speaks of spiritual worship in John 4:24, he apparently designates the worship made possible by the spiritual transformation that people experience when they place their faith in him. Worshiping at particular places (Jerusalem temple for the Jews, Mount Gerazim for the Samaritans) is not the important dimension. God has sent his Son, and people must now acknowledge Jesus as the Christ. This forms the basis for "true," or "spiritual," worship.

John 4:31–42: The Savior of the World

1. How does the theme of confusion over the meaning of Jesus' words continue in 4:31–38?
2. What harvest does Jesus mean in 4:35? To what sort of harvest is he sending his disciples?
3. How does the Samaritans' belief in Jesus change over the two days during which he stays with them?
4. When expressing their belief in Jesus, what new title do the Samaritans add to those given by his Jewish followers in John 1:29–51?

Personal Worship
Where and under what conditions do you have the most meaningful experiences of worship or spiritual transformation? What conditions detract from your worship or spiritual experience? Why?

When do you find that you are like the woman in 4:19–20, preferring to talk about theological issues rather than personal issues that you would rather not face? What personal guidelines would help you achieve greater freedom and meaning in worship and in everyday life? How can you implement these?

John 4:43–54: Signs, Wonders, and Belief

1. What does this passage reveal about miraculous signs and belief in Jesus?
2. Both at the beginning and the end of the story of the healing of the official's son (4:46, 54), the author reminds us of the miracle Jesus performed at the wedding in Cana. What similarities are there between these two miracle stories?

John 4:44 seems confusing in light of 4:45, for the Galileans give Jesus a warm welcome. Perhaps the comment in 4:44 reflects the criticism Jesus voices in 4:48, but this interpretation is not assured (compare 2:23–24). As with 3:22, deciphering the intent of the comment is difficult.

John 5:1–18: "My Father is still working, and I also am working"

Jesus now returns to Jerusalem for an unspecified "festival of the Jews" (5:1). In the Fourth Gospel, the expression "the Jews" occurs frequently, sometimes in a neutral sense, merely indicating nationality (as in 5:1), but often in a derogatory sense, designating Jesus' opponents (as in 5:10, 16, 18). Later in the story, for example, Jesus, himself a Jew, while talking to his Jewish disciples, reminds them of what he said to "the Jews" (13:33). For the most part "the Jews" refuse to believe in Jesus, even as the prologue asserts: "He came to what was his own, and his own people did not accept him" (1:11).[7]

Unlike the Synoptic Gospels, which distinguish between different subgroups of Jewish people (primarily Pharisees and Sadducees), John makes no such distinction. Sometimes John speaks of Pharisees, but this is an imprecise equivalent for the main leaders of the Jewish people in 1:19–9:16, and thereafter he simply subsumes them under the category "the Jews." That the author of the Fourth Gospel saw no need to differentiate between various Jewish sects but merely combined all into a general heading, "the Jews," probably indicates that he wrote for people living outside Judea, and that he wrote long enough after the life of Jesus that he considered precise distinctions unnecessary. One normally does not use a designation such as "the Americans," for example, when writing from inside America to Americans. One is more likely to use such a title when speaking from outside the country. To put it another way, I would be much more prone to speak of "the French" if I were in the United States than if I were speaking to French people in France. The author of John does not appear to write within Judea for a Jewish audience. He addresses people who, for example, might not know that "Jews do not share things in common with Samaritans" (4:9).

John's Jesus

1. Unlike the previous miracle performed in Galilee (4:46–54), 5:8–9 makes no mention of the sick man by the pool in Jerusalem having any faith in Jesus. Why does healing this man get Jesus into trouble?
2. What differences do you see between how this handicapped man responds to Jesus and how the official responded in 4:46–54?
3. What highly significant claims does Jesus make about himself in this passage?

John 5:19–47: "If you believed Moses, you would believe me"

1. What is the major source of disagreement between Jesus and "the Jews" in this passage?
2. What new affirmations does Jesus make about himself? About eternal life? About coming judgment? About the scriptures?
3. To what four witnesses does Jesus appeal in 5:32–40? How is this concept of witnesses developed as an indictment against the Jews?

In some ways the Gospel of John functions like a trial narrative, in which the author presents evidence for Jesus' identity as Messiah and the reader must decide whether or not to accept his witness. Those who oppose Jesus in the Gospel are the enemies of God, although many of them are the religious leaders of the Jewish people. They interrogate, threaten, and finally eliminate Jesus, but the story reveals their verdict to be false. He is the Son of God, and life comes only through belief in him.

John 6:1–21: "This is indeed the prophet"

Jesus again leaves Jerusalem and heads north, to the eastern side of the Sea of Galilee (6:1).

1. Why are people following him at this point?
2. This story of the feeding of the five thousand is one of the few that John shares with the Synoptics. How does this version compare with that of Mark 6:30–52?
3. In John's account, what do those who ate the miraculous meal conclude about Jesus?

John 6:22–71: Looking for a Free Lunch

Miracles in John's Gospel provide opportunities for Jesus to reveal important things about himself. Frequently, therefore, discourses follow miracle stories as a means of elaborating on the significance of the events.

1. What criticism does Jesus level against those who follow him to Capernaum?

2. What images does Jesus apply to himself that flow from the story of the feeding of the five thousand?
3. What connection does Jesus make in 6:27–51 between believing in him and eternal life?
4. What other claims does Jesus make in 6:52–71 about his identity and work?
5. How does the standard Johannine strategy of having Jesus talk on a spiritual level and his audience hear on a physical level play a graphic role in this account? (Notice also how strong the descent/ascent motif is in this passage.)

The comments about eating in 6:49–53 employ forms of the normal Greek word for "eat" (*esthio*). But in 6:54–57, Jesus uses *trogo*, a word often used for the audible sound of gnawing and munching done by animals. This makes Jesus' words that much more difficult to swallow.

6. Why does Peter say he will not turn away from following Jesus, although many others left in disgust?

John 7:1–13: "My time has not yet come"

Jesus returns to Jerusalem for the Feast of Tabernacles (or Feast of Booths; 7:1, 10), continuing the Johannine cycle of movements back and forth between Galilee and Judea. This feast occurs in the fall, beginning on the fifteenth day of the month of Tishri (September–October), according to Leviticus 23:39. The Jews celebrate it for seven days by constructing little huts (booths) in which they stay to commemorate the forty years the Israelites dwelt in tents in the wilderness (see Lev. 23:33–36; Deut. 16:13–15).

1. What is the basis for conflict between Jesus and his brothers?
2. What different evaluations of Jesus do the people in Jerusalem make?

John 7:14–36: "How does this man have such learning?"

1. Where does Jesus claim to have received his theological training?

In the ensuing argument, Jesus asserts that the Jews are trying to kill him for the "one deed" he previously performed (7:21). This is a reference to the healing of the man by the pool and the resulting debate in 5:1–9.

2. What is the basis for the confusion over Jesus' identity in 7:25–27?
3. How does the Johannine strategy of Jesus speaking on one level

and his audience understanding on a different level enter into 7:32–36?

John 7:37–52: Many Believed in Him

During the Feast of Booths, the Jewish people held organized prayer for God to send rain upon the land so that their crops the next year would be abundant. Part of this process of interceding for rain involved a ceremony in which a priest dipped a pitcher full of water from the Gihon spring, which he took in a procession back to the altar in the temple, where he poured it out on the ground.[8] On the last day of the feast this ceremony was especially elaborate, and Jesus gives his speech about living water on the final day. God answers their prayer for water, but the answer comes on a spiritual instead of a physical level. Once again, the physical becomes a pointer to spiritual realities—to the fact that Jesus replaces the Jewish ceremonies, and only in him one truly comes to see God.

1. How is Jesus' teaching about himself here similar to what he said to the Samaritan woman in John 4?
2. What does Jesus explain about the activities of the Spirit?
3. What does the confusion after Jesus' assertion in 7:37–38 reveal about Jewish messianic expectations?

Note the irony in verse 42. The author assumes his readers already know Jesus was born in Bethlehem, for he does not explicitly recount this detail in the Gospel. The leaders unwittingly bear witness to Jesus.

4. Nicodemus, who first came to Jesus in 3:1, now reappears in the narrative to argue on Jesus' behalf. His fellow Pharisees ridicule him, however. What reason do they give for rejecting Jesus as the Messiah?
5. What themes in John 4—7 tie the stories together into a unity of purpose, showing the public declaration of the deity and messianic identity of Jesus?
6. How does this public proclamation of Jesus' deity compare with the portrait of Jesus in the Synoptics?

SECTION THREE: JOHN 8—12: RESULTS OF BELIEF AND UNBELIEF IN JESUS CHRIST

John 7:53–8:11: "Let anyone among you who is without sin be the first to throw a stone"

Most translations of the Bible indicate in a footnote or in some other way that none of the most important early Greek manuscripts for the text of John contains this story. Most likely it was not originally part of John's Gospel. When and where a scribe added the story is not known, but it was added at a fairly early date and might recount an actual event in the life of Jesus.

1. How does Jesus' attitude toward the woman differ from that of the scribes and Pharisees?

John 8:12–58: "I am the light of the world"

Chronologically, this story follows directly after 7:37–52, where Jesus proclaims himself to be the *source of living water*. Now he changes the imagery, claiming to be the *light of the world*. Both sets of imagery, however, play on events that occurred during the Feast of Booths. On the first night (at least) of the feast, temple officials standing in the Court of Women lit seven candles in golden candlesticks. This was the same part of the temple through which the priest with the pitcher of water from the spring of Gihon led the procession to the altar (see under 7:37–52). Jesus apparently delivers his address in 8:12–20 from the Court of the Women, since the temple treasury (8:20) adjoins the Court of the Women.[9]

The public debate with adversaries over the legitimacy of Jesus' witness continues in this passage (compare 7:14–24). Notice the increasing intensity of the accusations and counteraccusations. The narrative shows the hostility growing in magnitude as Jesus' opponents become more and more committed to their rejection of his claims, and Jesus becomes more pointed in his judgments of them.

1. What objection do the Pharisees raise to Jesus' claim to be the light of the world?
2. How does Jesus answer their objection?
3. What further claims does Jesus make about himself in 8:21–30?
4. How do the events that follow in 8:31–47 show that the belief mentioned in 8:30 is not sufficient for salvation?
5. Of what does Jesus accuse these people who had placed their faith in him? How do they respond to his accusations?
6. What kind of slavery does Jesus describe in 8:31–47? What kind of freedom? What kind of slavery do his listeners think he is describing?

Note again the irony of the two levels of understanding, and also how strongly Jesus asserts the theme of his descent from heaven.

7. What momentous claims does Jesus make about himself in 8:48–58?

Walking in the Light
What would it mean to say that actions and attitudes you have observed among some religious people make it seem like Satan, not God, is their Father? What would "stepping into the light" mean in these instances?

172

John's Jesus

John 9:1–40: "Who sinned, this man or his parents?"

Jesus' disciples, who have not played a role in the narrative since 6:69, now reappear to set the stage for another controversy story. In 9:2 they ask a question that reflects a mistaken belief about the origin of physical handicaps. Most of the Old Testament reveals the common belief that God punishes people for bad behavior and rewards them for good deeds during their lifetime.[10]

Evidently, on the basis of such passages as Exodus 34:7 (which states that God will by no means clear the guilty, "visiting the iniquity of the parents upon the children and the children's children, to the third and the fourth generation"), some in Jesus' day believed that the effects of sins committed by the parents could be manifested in their children through birth defects. Later writings by the rabbis also reflect the belief that infants could sin while still in the womb, and perhaps John 9:2 indicates that this idea was current in the first century.[11]

1. How does Jesus answer the mistaken question posed by his disciples?

Jesus, the light of the world (9:5), heals the blind man, an individual trapped in a world of darkness. But because he performed the miracle on the Sabbath, he again encounters severe criticism from the Pharisees.

2. From their treatment of the formerly blind man, what does the story reveal about the attitude of the Pharisees? Why does the miracle cause a division among them?
3. How does the blind man's response to Jesus differ from that of the handicapped man whom Jesus healed on the Sabbath in 5:2–18?
4. How does the blind man's understanding of Jesus differ from that of the Pharisees?

This story drips with irony. The Pharisees, on the one hand, have studied the scriptures and view themselves as those who know the will of God; but they are blind to the reality of God in their midst. The blind beggar, on the other hand, although he has no theological training, understands more about Jesus than they do. In great frustration he even gives them a theology lesson in 9:30–33, to which they respond with bitter sarcasm and intimidation, without answering his legitimate observation. Jesus is the light of the world (9:5; 1:4–5, 9; 8:12; 12:46), and he brings the blind man out of his darkness. The Pharisees, however, walk in darkness because they refuse to come to the light (3:19–20; 11:10; 12:35).

173

John 9 may provide a major clue for determining when the Gospel was written. Fear of excommunication from the synagogue plays an important role in the story, preventing the blind man's parents from answering the Pharisees' question (9:22) and causing the blind man to be cast out when he confesses faith in Jesus (9:34). Historically speaking, the situation described in 9:22, that anyone confessing faith in Christ should be "put out of the synagogue," could refer to the synagogue ban imposed by rabbis between 85 and 90 C.E. In the *Eighteen Benedictions,* or *Shemoneh `esreh,* recited in synagogues, the twelfth benediction (formulated ca. 85 C.E.) was a curse on heretics, largely directed toward Christian Jews. Some scholars argue that around 90 C.E. rabbis conducted a concerted attempt to drive Christian Jews from the synagogues, and this date becomes very important for the date they assign to the Fourth Gospel.

If John 9 reflects this later synagogue ban, the Gospel was probably written, at least in final form, after 90 C.E. But Shaye Cohen observes that there was no central governing authority over the synagogues during the first century. He argues that each community ran its own synagogue, and there is little possibility that rabbis could have imposed an empire-wide ban.[12] If the text of John 9 represents only a local intimidation of Jewish Christians, therefore, an earlier date for the Gospel may be postulated.

The Christology of John does not, by itself, demand a later date. The apostle Paul's letters are among the earliest documents we have in the New Testament, and his Christology also strongly emphasizes the deity of Christ. In Philippians 2:6–11, for example, Paul quotes an early hymn of praise to Christ that describes the eternal Son of God humbling himself to take on the form of a man, to die on the cross, and then to be exalted back to his glory in heaven. Paul wrote Philippians no later than 64 C.E., and the descent/ascent Christology employed so strongly in the Fourth Gospel differs little from that which Paul proclaimed long before the last decade of the first century. Being positive about when John was written remains an impossibility for scholars, although tradition has long maintained that it was composed in the 90s.

John 10:1–21: "I am the good shepherd"

This passage seems to continue Jesus' discourse from John 9, for there is no indication of a break between the sections. Yet the imagery takes a radical shift to that of shepherding. John 10:1–21 apparently functions as a bridge between the discourses associated with the Feast of Booths in John 7—9 and with the Feast of Dedication in 10:22–39. It continues the theme of showing the

Jewish religious leaders to be illegitimate representatives of God (10:1, 5, 8, 10, 12–13; cf. 9:16–34, 40–41), and its imagery of the sheep and the shepherd is continued in 10:26–29.

At night, when the sheep rested inside an enclosure, the shepherd slept in the opening through which the sheep entered and left the pen. Thus the shepherd became the "door" of the sheepfold. Once the shepherd lay down for the night, nothing entered or left without going over him.

Bedouin camp in Israel. Note the construction of the crude pen for keeping animals at night.

1. Jesus applies to himself the images of a good shepherd and a gate or door for a sheepfold. How does he say he differs from others who consider themselves to be shepherds over the sheep?
2. How do Jesus' words affect his listeners? (Note the similar mixture of responses described in John 7:40–43; 9:16–17.)

John 10:22–42: "The Father and I are one"

The Feast of Dedication, or Hanukkah, commemorates the cleansing of the temple in Jerusalem by Judas Maccabeus on the twenty-fifth of Chislev (1 Macc. 4:52–58; 2 Macc. 10:1–8), after Antiochus IV Epiphanes had defiled the altar of Yahweh by making it into an altar of Zeus and sacrificing pig flesh on it. Chislev (November–December) is a winter month (10:23), so Hanukkah occurs some three months after the Feast of Booths. Thus, although the events in 10:22–42 are tied thematically to the previous material through continuation of the sheep-shepherd imagery, a substantial period of time lies between them. Nevertheless, 10:26–29 seems to presuppose the same audience as 10:1–21, which presents another difficulty in the narrative (cf. 3:22; 4:44). The author here seems more interested in theological concerns than in accurate chronology.

1. Note that Jesus responds affirmatively when the Jews ask if he is the Messiah. What else does he claim about his identity in his response to them?
2. What do the Jews understand that Jesus is saying about himself, and how do they respond to his claim?
3. How does the people's response in 10:40–42 differ from that in 10:31–33?

John 11:1–53: "If you had been here, my brother would not have died"

This story begins with an assumption that the reader already knows its main characters. The narrator's comment in 11:2 identifies Mary as the woman who anointed Jesus with perfume, although this event does not occur in John's Gospel until 12:1–3.

1. If Jesus loves Lazarus (11:5), why does he wait until the man dies before going to Bethany?
2. Why are Jesus' disciples apprehensive about returning to Judea?
3. Is Thomas's comment in 11:16 an expression of bravery or exasperated sarcasm? (John 20:25 may help you decide.)
4. What do Martha's and Mary's responses to Jesus' delayed arrival indicate about what they believe and do not believe about Jesus at this point?
5. What does Lazarus's death allow Jesus to reveal about himself?
6. What different reactions does this miracle of raising Lazarus from the dead elicit from the onlookers?
7. What does the response of the Pharisees and chief priests to news of Jesus' raising Lazarus reveal about them?

In this story, the Jewish leaders decide that they would rather keep their temple and their identity as a people than risk believing in God's Son. They no longer seek to deny that Jesus performs miracles (11:47); they urgently seek to murder him, to eliminate the threat he poses. Ironically, the high priest, Caiaphas, explains the significance of Jesus' death, not only for the Jews but also for Gentiles who will place their faith in Jesus (11:49–53).

John 11:54–12:50: "While you have the light, believe in the light"

Ephraim (11:54) was presumably about twelve miles north of Jerusalem. There Jesus stays away from the Jewish leaders in Jerusalem until the next spring and the feast of Passover. Then he travels again to Bethany to stay with his good friends. There, in a gesture of love and gratitude, Mary anoints his feet with expensive ointment and wipes them with her hair.

1. What actions had the Jewish leaders taken in anticipation of Jesus' coming?
2. What does 12:6 indicate about Judas's duties and character flaws?
3. Why do the chief priests want to kill Lazarus?
4. When the majority of the people enthusiastically welcome Jesus into Jerusalem, how do the Pharisees respond?
5. What does 12:27–36 add to John's portrait of Jesus?
6. What reasons does 12:37–43 give for the unbelief of some of the Jews?

John 12:44–50 concludes the public ministry of Jesus with a short sermon in which Jesus asserts some of the main themes of chapters 1—12. Eternal life comes only through belief in Jesus, who has entered the world from above, as light penetrating the darkness. He does not seek his own glory by making claims for his deity; he merely speaks in obedience to what God, his Father, orders him to speak. To reject this heavenly message and the heavenly messenger is to experience the judgment of God. To believe in Jesus is to experience eternal life.

Since Jesus went into hiding in 12:36, there is no audience for the sermon he delivers in 12:44–50. It is the narrator's way of letting Jesus deliver one more statement to the reader that sums up the content of the previous twelve chapters. It is a sermon without a setting, but it expresses the major themes of the Gospel. As in 3:16–21 and 3:31–36, the narrator speaks to the readers through Jesus, seeking to convince them to "believe that Jesus is the Messiah, the Son of God, and that through believing [they] may have life in his name" (20:31).

SECTION FOUR: JOHN 13—17: THE FAREWELL DISCOURSE

In John 13—17, Jesus delivers final instructions to his beloved disciples, those who have responded by believing in him. This discourse is an extended farewell address by the eternal Son of God, who is now moving quickly toward his "hour" in which he will die and ascend back to his Father in heaven. No parallel exists for this material in the Synoptic Gospels. And contrary to the Synoptics, the supper Jesus and his disciples eat together before his arrest in John 13 is not a Passover meal, because it occurs the day *before* the Passover in this Gospel (see 13:1; 18:28; 19:14, 31, 42). There is no institution of the Lord's Supper in which the Lord says, "Take; this is my body" and "This is my blood of the covenant, which is poured out for many" (Mark 14:23, 24). The last supper in the Fourth Gospel focuses on Jesus washing his disciples' feet and beginning his final discourse to them. The trial-like narrative of chapters 1—12 is past. Jesus now speaks not to inspire belief but to instruct believers in how they are to live in a world that is hostile toward them.

John 13:1–20: "I have set you an example"

1. According to 13:1–3, what does Jesus know about himself and his disciples at this time? Notice that, in spite of this knowledge, he also washes Judas's feet.
2. How do Jesus' actions in 13:3–4, 12 dramatically symbolize the descent/ascent motif that so pervades John's Gospel?

"The task of washing feet was so menial that it was placed among work Jewish male slaves should not be required to do; such work is to be reserved for Gentile slaves, for wives, and for children (*Mekilta* on Exodus 21:2 [82a])."[13]

3. Why does Peter change his mind so drastically about Jesus washing his feet?
4. What are the disciples to learn from the foot washing?

Determining the significance of the brief dialogue between Jesus and Peter in 13:6–10 is difficult. *Water* and *Spirit* are closely connected in John's Gospel (see Jesus' comments to Nicodemus in 3:5–8; to the Samaritan woman in 4:10, 14, 23–24; and to the crowd in 7:37–39), and 13:8–10 indicates that experience of salvation requires being washed by Jesus.

The background for Jesus' comment in 13:10 is simple. According to Mediterranean custom, "a person invited to a dinner party takes a bath (at home or in the public baths) before coming to supper. Upon arrival, the individual needs only to have his feet washed before the meal."[14] However, the precise meaning of 13:10 is such an enigma that a multitude of interpretations exists in the scholarly literature. John's intended meaning in this statement is virtually impossible to assert with any confidence, but he closely ties it with the descent/ascent motif so vividly illustrated in the humble service performed in the foot washing. Jesus' coming death is for the salvation of those who believe in him (loving descent to serve others), and thereafter he will ascend back to the Father. His disciples are to learn humble service toward one another from Jesus' action (13:12–17). Thus, the main point is clear, even though the meaning of 13:10 remains obscure.

Self-Perception and Insecurity
People normally do not stand in line to do menial tasks. Especially when we feel somewhat insecure about our identity, we may want to avoid such things for fear of what others will think of us. What tasks do you feel are beneath you?

John 13:21–38: "And it was night"

The literary power of this passage is considerable. Jesus, the light of the world, knows full well that his betrayal is at hand. The forces of evil are at work, and when Judas leaves the room, the narrator says symbolically, "And it was night" (13:30). The scene is not despairing, however, for Jesus fully controls the situation. Like a stage director, the Son of God sets into motion events leading to his own death. And as soon as Judas leaves, Jesus says, "Now the Son of Man has been glorified, and God has been glorified in him" (13:31). Thus, the crucifixion in John becomes an event showing Jesus' glory and control, as he stated in 10:17–18: "For this reason the Father loves me, because I lay down my life in order to take it up again. No one takes it from me, but I lay it down of my own accord. I have power to lay it down, and I have power to take it up again. I have received this command from my Father."

1. How does 13:21–30 reveal that Jesus controls this situation?
2. What portrait of Judas do 12:4–6 and 13:26–30 paint?
3. How does the "new commandment" in 13:34–35 enhance the commandment given in 13:14–17?
4. What effect will love for one another have on the disciples' witness to the nonbelieving world?

The identity of the disciple "whom Jesus loved" (13:23) poses a problem. The narrative mentions him in 13:23–25; 19:26–27, 35; 20:2–10; 21:7, 20–24, and possibly 1:37–40 and 18:15. The beloved disciple reclines at the last supper beside Jesus (13:23), and his closeness to the Lord dominates the characterization of him in the Fourth Gospel. Unlike the other disciples, he never seems to misunderstand Jesus. Thus he provides the ideal vehicle for making Jesus known to others. Faithfully following Jesus to the cross (19:26–27), he observes the blood and water flow out of Jesus' pierced side (19:34). The narrator at this point indicates the significance of the beloved disciple for the Johannine community by saying, "He who saw this has testified so that you also may believe. His testimony is true, and he knows that he tells the truth" (19:35). As we will soon see, this man apparently stands behind the tradition recorded in the Fourth Gospel.

John 14:1–14: "I am the way, and the truth, and the life"

1. How does the disciples' confusion in 13:36–38 continue in this passage?
2. What does Jesus explain about himself in 14:1–11?
3. What does Jesus reveal about his followers in 14:12–14?

John 14:15–31: "I will not leave you orphaned"

1. As Jesus prepares to depart from the earth, he reassures his followers that he will not leave them destitute. By what means will he continue to be with them?

Jesus calls the Holy Spirit "the Spirit of truth" (14:17) and the Paraclete (14:16). Various versions of the Bible translate *Paraclete* in different ways, so your translation might read "Counselor," "Advocate," "Intercessor," or "Helper." Despite the difference in terms, the activities of the Spirit are clear.

2. What different roles does Jesus say the Spirit will play (14:17–28)?

3. According to 14:21–24, what role does love play in the life of the disciple of Jesus?

Jesus refers to the Spirit as *"another* Paraclete" (14:16), indicating that the Spirit will take over the position Jesus has held with his disciples while on earth. The roles of the Spirit in 14:18–28 duplicate and continue the ministry of Jesus in John's Gospel.

John 15:1–27: "I am the true vine"

The sequence of events becomes somewhat confusing at this point. In 14:31, Jesus commands his disciples to arise from the table around which they have been reclining and go with him out of the house. Yet he continues to teach them for two more chapters. Not until 18:1 do they go out to the garden, where Jesus is arrested. Commentaries offer a number of explanations of this difficulty; but as with other passages in the Gospel, the reason for it remains obscure. As with the sermon without an audience in 12:44–50, matters of chronology play a secondary role to the author's primary concern of presenting Jesus' teaching.

1. Jesus introduces a new set of symbols in John 15, describing his relationship with his disciples in terms of branches connected to a vine that provides the nutrients necessary for growth and health. What things are essential, in 15:1–8, for the follower of Jesus to "bear fruit"?
2. Jesus' teaching on love plays an important role in this passage, beginning with 15:9. What does he say is the relationship between love and "bearing fruit"?
3. Notice that Jesus moves from love among his disciples in verse 17 to the hatred of the world for them in verse 18. What reason does he give for the world's hatred of his followers?

Notice the distance the story places between Jesus and his Jewish opponents when, in reference to the scriptures, he speaks of what "is written in *their* law" in 15:25.

4. What further information does Jesus give about the role of the Holy Spirit in the world (15:26–27)?

John 16:1–33: "It is to your advantage that I go away"

The predicted synagogue ban in 16:1–4 echoes the punishment for confessing belief in Jesus that the Pharisees imposed in 9:22, 34; 12:42. Continually abiding in Jesus and following his commandments (John 15) will keep his followers from falling away from faith (16:1–4). The Holy Spirit will be extremely important in helping them remain faithful once Jesus returns to his Father (16:7–15). They are sorrowful at the thought of Jesus' leaving, but he assures them it is better that he does (16:7).

1. What does Jesus say the role of the Spirit will be after he (Jesus) departs from the world?
2. How will the way in which the disciples pray change after Jesus' departure?
3. When do the disciples understand that Jesus is talking about his departure from the world and return to the Father?

Jesus explains that after his coming arrest, the disciples will abandon him, leaving him alone; but he will not really be alone, "because the Father is with me" (16:32). Then he pronounces his victorious statement "But take courage; I have conquered the world!" (16:33). This portrait of Jesus as totally in control of his destiny fits beautifully the total thrust of the Gospel. Jesus does not struggle with his coming death; he is instrumental in bringing it about. When Jesus is gone, the Holy Spirit will guide his disciples into further truth about him (14:26; 16:12–15).

Jesus' teaching about the Spirit in this passage provides valuable background for how the author understands the role of the Holy Spirit in revealing the deeper insights into Jesus' identity that are recorded in this Gospel. The Spirit of truth has guided the author's community of believers into all the truth that Jesus' disciples were not capable of understanding while he was on the earth (16:12–13).

John 17:1–26: "Father, the hour has come"

This section is often called Jesus' high-priestly prayer. After completing his final discourse, he now prays for himself, his disciples, and those who will believe in him through their message.

1. What is the focus of Jesus' prayer for himself in 17:1–5?
2. What specific things does Jesus pray for his disciples in 17:6–19?
3. What does he affirm about the disciples' relationships with God and with the world in 17:6–19?
4. What is the focus of Jesus' prayer for those who will believe in him through his disciples' teaching? (17:20–21)
5. What role does glory play in all three sections of Jesus' prayer?
6. What does Jesus affirm about himself and his relationship with the Father in his prayer?

The farewell discourse begins with Jesus' knowledge of the glory he had with the Father before coming to earth (13:1, 3), and it ends with him speaking of this glory in his prayer to the Father.

But the concluding section of the discourse also makes some amazing claims about the glory of Jesus' disciples. The oneness and love experienced between Jesus and the Father are to characterize the fellowship of his people in this world (17:20–26). As they share the glory of the incarnate Son of God, the hostility directed toward them by the world (17:14) will not cause them to fall away from believing in him. Experiencing the glory and love of God in their lives, they live in the world, but they are not really part of the world (17:14–18). They have come to know some of the divine detachment of their heavenly Lord by being born "from above" through the Spirit.

Glory
How might understanding the glory that Jesus prays for his disciples (cf. the foot washing in John 13) empower you to do menial tasks unselfconsciously?

SECTION FIVE: JOHN 18—21: THE ASCENT OF THE ETERNAL LOGOS
John 18:1–27: "I have said nothing in secret"

At the conclusion of his prayer, Jesus leads his disciples out across the Kidron Valley to a garden. John makes no mention here of an agonized prayer by Jesus to be delivered from his coming death. Such a prayer would violate the portrait of Jesus in the Fourth Gospel (see 12:27). The cross is his moment of glorification, the beginning of his ascent.

1. In what ways does the arrest scene (18:1–11) make it clear that Jesus is totally in control of the situation?
2. How was Simon Peter able to get into the court of the high priest?

Note that in John's account, Peter denies that he knows Jesus (18:15–18, 25–27), but in contrast to the Synoptic accounts, John makes no mention of Peter leaving the courtyard weeping.

3. In the interrogation scene of 18:19–24, Jesus speaks defiantly to his accusers and answers that he has taught openly, not hiding anything. How does this scene compare with the Synoptic accounts of his trial before the Sanhedrin?

What Is Truth?
Many people in the world today share Pilate's cynical view that one cannot know truth. What effect can this belief have on one's view of how to treat others?

John 18:28–40: "My kingdom is not from this world"

John contains no reference to the nocturnal trial before the Sanhedrin. Jesus is taken to Annas (18:13), who questions him and sends him to Caiaphas (18:28), who in turn delivers him to Pilate. Throughout the Gospel, Jesus proclaims himself as the truth, and in this passage the Roman leader is forced to confront the truth as he judges Jesus.

Jesus' trial occurs on the day before the Passover (18:28;

19:14), a day earlier than in the Synoptic accounts, which have Jesus and his disciples eating the Passover meal just before his arrest and trial (e.g., Mark 14:12–25). For John's account, it is important that Jesus be offered up in sacrifice on the cross at the same time that the Passover lambs are being sacrificed. Like the Passover lamb, of which Exodus 12:46 specifies that none of its bones shall be broken, Jesus' leg bones are not broken (19:32–33). Pure and spotless, the one whom John the Baptist announced as the "Lamb of God who takes away the sin of the world" (1:29) offers himself for the sins of the world.

From a historical point of view, uncertainty exists over whether or not the Last Supper was a Passover meal. Each of the Gospels pursues a theological agenda in its passion narrative. The Synoptics have Jesus celebrating a deeply meaningful Passover meal with his disciples before his arrest and crucifixion, showing that his coming sacrifice will be like a Passover sacrifice through the Last Supper imagery "This is my blood of the covenant which is poured out for many" (Mark 14:24). John makes the same connection by having Jesus sacrificed on the day of the Passover. This beautifully fits the Johannine motif of showing how Jesus replaces Jewish religious feasts and institutions.

Although some people attempt to harmonize the accounts on the basis of complicated arguments concerning solar and lunar calendars,[15] these efforts have not gained widespread acceptance. Since the issues involved are rather complicated, the interested reader should consult commentaries and other secondary literature for detailed information.

1. Why do the Jews not want to enter Pilate's headquarters, the praetorium? Why is this extremely ironic?

The statement in 1:11, "He came to what was his own, and his own people did not accept him," now receives its final fulfillment. The Jews deliver Jesus to be crucified. Pilate wants nothing to do with the whole affair, but he is pressured into it.

2. On what issue does Pilate focus when he interrogates Jesus?
3. How does the story reveal that Jesus is still in control, even as he stands before the Roman ruler?
4. In some ways Pilate is on trial, forced to reach a conclusion on the claims of the condemned man before him. What does he conclude about Jesus' guilt or innocence?

John 19:1–30: King of the Jews

By having Jesus beaten and mocked, Pilate evidently attempts to inspire pity and change the Jews' minds so that they will drop their charges against Jesus. He repeats his verdict "I find no case against him" (20:4, 6), but the Jews refuse to be dissuaded.

1. What is Pilate's emotional response to the Jews' insistence on crucifixion?
2. How does Jesus' dialogue with Pilate in 19:9–11 again show that he is in control of his own destiny?
3. How do the Jews coerce Pilate into executing Jesus?
4. On what charge is Jesus crucified? (Pilate's sign on Jesus' cross serves as an ironic affirmation of Jesus' glory [19:19–22].)
5. Why do the soldiers cast lots for Jesus' tunic (a *chiton*, the garment Jewish men and women wore next to their skin)?
6. How do Jesus' pronouncements from the cross and the manner of his death reveal his control over the entire event? (Note that in 19:17, Jesus alone carries his cross. There is no mention of Simon of Cyrene; cf. Mark 15:21.)

In addition to the women, John says the beloved disciple was present to observe Jesus on the cross (19:25–26). The Synoptics make no mention of this (Matt. 27:55–56; Mark 15:40–41), but in John's account his presence is quite important, especially in 19:34–35. Since Jesus' brothers do not believe in him (7:5), they are not part of the family of God that Jesus establishes in the Fourth Gospel. The faithful beloved disciple therefore receives the responsibility to care for Jesus' mother (19:26–27). The spiritual family of those who have been "born from above" takes precedence over earthly institutions, even the biological family.

John 19:31–42: Blood and Water

1. Why is the Jews' concern to have the bodies removed from the crosses before sundown ironic?
2. How do the soldiers make sure that the crucified men are dead?

Joseph of Arimathea (also mentioned in Matt. 27:57; Mark 15:43; and Luke 23:50) and Nicodemus believed in Jesus but feared the opinions of others too much to follow him openly (19:38). They seem to represent those described in 12:42–43, who do not confess belief in Jesus because they fear being kicked out of the synagogue. Now they come forward to care for Jesus' body in a rather elaborate way, with one hundred pounds of myrrh and aloes (19:39).

3. Why do they bury Jesus in a garden tomb close to the site of crucifixion?

The beloved disciple watches the soldier thrust a spear into Jesus' side and sees blood and water flow from the wound

(19:34–35). From the perspective of the editor's comment in 19:35, this is a very important eyewitness report for bringing faith to those who hear his account. To the witness of John the Baptist (1:19–35; 3:27–30), of Jesus' miracles (e.g., 5:36), of God the Father (e.g., 5:32, 37; 8:18), and of the Holy Spirit (14:25–26; 16:8–15) the beloved disciple adds his witness to the truth of Jesus' identity. A similar statement appears in 1 John 5:6–9:

> This is the one who came by water and blood, Jesus Christ, not with the water only but with the water and the blood. And the Spirit is the one that testifies, for the Spirit is the truth. There are three that testify: the Spirit and the water and the blood, and these three agree. If we receive human testimony, the testimony of God is greater; for this is the testimony of God that he has testified to his Son.

Yet the significance of "blood and water" in 19:34 is obscure enough to have spawned numerous explanations. John's Gospel closely associates water with the work of the Holy Spirit (e.g., 3:5–7; 7:38–39), who was *with* the disciples during Jesus' time on earth but was to be *in* them after his glorification (14:17). But the precise meaning of 19:34 is extremely allusive. Perhaps it simply indicates that Jesus really did have a physical body (1:14) and experienced a physical death; or perhaps it symbolizes that Jesus' death brings about the era of the Spirit.[16] The attempts by some modern doctors to provide physiological explanations for how water could be separated

Reconstruction of a first-century tomb at the Biblical Resources Study Center in Jerusalem.

from the blood in Jesus' heart are no doubt sincere, but they fail to recognize the symbolic nature of the witness in 19:34–37.

John 20:1–31: "Receive the Holy Spirit"

1. After the women discover the empty tomb, who wins the race to the tomb: Peter or the beloved disciple?
2. Who first enters the tomb?
3. Who first "believes" when he sees the burial cloths?
4. How does the account in Luke 24:1–11 of the women coming to the tomb and then reporting back to Jesus' disciples compare with John's account in 20:1–10?

When Peter and the beloved disciple reach the tomb, they see the burial cloths lying on the stone bench where the body had lain.

Now empty, the cloths lie crumpled under the weight of the spices. The head cloth lies slightly separate from the body cloth, also empty. The body is simply no longer there to fill the wrappings.

The beloved disciple, not Peter, first realized the significance and "believed" (20:8). This adds further significance to his witness (19:34–35). He is the source of the information recorded in the Fourth Gospel (21:24), and his witness is extremely important.

5. What does Mary's encounter with Jesus in 20:11–18 reveal about Jesus' ascent to the Father?
6. What does Jesus' encounter with his disciples in 20:19–23 reveal about his resurrected existence?
7. What causes Thomas, the doubter, to believe that Jesus really did rise from the dead? In Thomas' confession of faith, what does he call Jesus?
8. How might Thomas serve as a model for some who have read the Gospel but find it difficult to believe all the claims made about Jesus?
9. How do Jesus' final words in 20:29 summarize the intent of the author in composing his Gospel? How does this affirmation compare in content with 20:30–31?

When Jesus appears to his disciples in the locked room in 20:19–23, he imparts to them the promised Holy Spirit. Although Jesus tells Mary not to touch him in 20:17, since he has *not yet ascended to God the Father*, in 20:27 he instructs Thomas to touch his hands and side. So we may conclude that Jesus has now been glorified and has returned to impart the Spirit, just as he promised in John 16:7–24 (see also 14:15–17, 25–29; 15:26–27). This seems to be the Johannine equivalent of the day of Pentecost, when the Holy Spirit descends on believers, in Acts 2.

John 21:1–25: "We know that his testimony is true"

The fact that 20:30–31 concludes the Gospel account presents problems in understanding the presence of John 21. It seems to be an *epilogue*, but determining whether the author of the Gospel or one of his associates made the addition is virtually impossible. All the oldest Greek manuscripts contain John 21, indicating that the epilogue was added quite early and that the Gospel apparently never circulated without it.

1. The scene shifts from Jerusalem to Galilee. How many disciples follow Peter as he returns to his profession of fishing?
2. When Jesus appears on the beach, who is the first to recognize him?

In verse 7, the word *naked* seems to mean "lightly clad." Jewish people in Jesus' time were quite modest, and complete nudity in the fishing boat is extremely dubious, especially in the cool of the morning (see v. 4). Yet to put on more clothes (as the NRSV translates the verb *diazonnymi* in v. 7) to swim to shore also seems peculiar, so it is better to translate *diazonnymi* with "to tie around" or "tuck in" (cf. Jesus' tying the towel around himself or tucking it in when he washed the disciples' feet in 13:4, where the same verb *diazonnymi* is used). To give greater freedom for swimming, Peter "tucks in" the light garment fishermen wore while working, jumps into the water, and swims to shore.[17]

3. After the others get to the beach with the fish and they all finish breakfast, Jesus quizzes Peter. What does the story reveal about Peter and his future ministry?
4. What does Peter learn about his own death, and how does he respond to this knowledge?
5. What does the author inform us about expectations versus reality concerning the death of the beloved disciple?
6. What does the conclusion of the epilogue (21:24–25) indicate about the selectivity involved in writing the Gospel?

The beloved disciple plays an important role in the Fourth Gospel. He is the one who leaned on Jesus' breast during the Last Supper and spoke with Peter about Judas the betrayer (13:23–25), who witnessed the crucifixion and was given charge of Jesus' mother (19:26–27), who saw the piercing of Jesus' side and the issue of blood and water (19:35), who first reached Jesus' tomb and believed when he saw the burial cloths (20:2–8), who first recognized Jesus from the fishing boat (21:7), who some Christians thought would not die before Jesus came again (21:20–23), and probably who knew Caiaphas and so was able to get Peter into the high priest's courtyard (18:15–16); he perhaps was also the "other disciple" in 1:37. Since 19:35 indicates that the author of the Gospel is not the beloved disciple (unless 19:35 is a later editorial insertion, which seems doubtful), the connection of the beloved disciple with the writing of the Gospel in 21:24 is problematic.

At first glance, John 21:24 seems to identify the beloved disciple either as the author of the Gospel as a whole or as the author of the epilogue, if 21:24–25 was added by his associates who were not involved in writing the Gospel. More likely, however, 21:24 strongly affirms the connection between the beloved disciple and the contents of the Gospel. His witness forms the basis for the Gospel's message, and thus his teaching lies behind the writing of the message, bringing its contents to life. His voice still lives as a witness in the Gospel pages, and his witness is central to the validity of the written message. In the epilogue, the author stands with the church community of the beloved disciple and asserts, "we know that his testimony is true" (21:24), even as the narrator states in 19:35, "He who saw this has testified so that you also may believe. His testimony is true, and he knows that he tells the truth."

The figure of the beloved disciple lies behind the teaching of the Fourth Gospel, therefore, although he is not himself the author. Throughout the Gospel, the author

> never refers to himself and the disciples as "we." In John, the first person plural seems to refer to a group or community which gathered around the Beloved Disciple (21:24–25). So, while the narrator's point of view at times approximates that of the disciples, he does not claim that position. At most, the narrative gives the impression that the narrator is a part of the group around Jesus because much of it deals with events that occurred within that group. In short, the story is presented by an omniscient observer.[18]

The beloved disciple was apparently a historical figure, but whether he was an apostle or a disciple of Jesus who was not one of the twelve apostles is unclear. He seems to have played a major role in founding the Johannine community (or the community of the beloved disciple), and he was the primary source for the Christology presented in the Fourth Gospel. The epilogue (John 21) seems to have been written at least partially to explain to concerned Christians why this influential leader died (21:23). Apparently, one who learned about Jesus from the beloved disciple wrote the Fourth Gospel, recording his elder's teachings; then he added John 21 as a further means of validating the eyewitness quality of the Gospel contents.

REVIEW OF JOHANNINE THEMES

The Gospel of John seems to have been written by an unknown follower of a man identified in the Gospel as the disciple whom Jesus loved. Apparently, during the time of writing, leaders in the Christian community that the beloved disciple founded and taught saw the need to write an account of Jesus' life that emphasized his identity as the Son of God who descended to earth and ascended back to heaven. One of these leaders composed the Fourth Gospel, recording stories the beloved disciple had told in order to demonstrate that Jesus, the Messiah, is the eternal Son of God, and that eternal life comes only through believing in him.

If 9:22 and 12:42 reflect the synagogue ban of 85–90 C.E., the

Gospel was written around 90–95 C.E., but this connection is speculative. The location of writing seems clearly to be outside Judea, with an intended audience of Gentile Christians. The portrait of Jesus is quite distinct from that found in the Synoptics and represents a careful interpretation of the story of Jesus in light of a Christology resulting from the witness of the Holy Spirit and the beloved disciple. Written for people who already know the story of Jesus, the Fourth Gospel forcefully argues not only that one must believe that Jesus is Messiah but that one's belief must also be based on acceptance of Jesus' deity, which leads to following him and his teachings unconditionally. Jesus is not merely the founder of a religious sect; he is the eternal Logos who descended into human history. One's eternal destiny depends on how one responds to the message of the Christ. To come to him is to walk in light and experience eternal life. To reject him is to remain in darkness and experience God's judgment.

FURTHER READING ON THE GOSPEL OF JOHN

Beasley-Murray, George. *John*. Word Biblical Commentary 36. Waco, Tex.: Word Books, 1987.

Brown, Raymond E. *The Gospel according to John*. 2 vols. Anchor Bible. Garden City, N.Y.: Doubleday & Co., 1966.

Bruce, F. F. *The Gospel of John*. Grand Rapids: Wm. B. Eerdmans Publishing Co., 1984.

Bultmann, Rudolf. *Gospel of John*. Philadelphia: Westminster Press, 1941.

Culpepper, R. Alan. *Anatomy of the Fourth Gospel: A Study in Literary Design*. Philadelphia: Fortress Press, 1983.

Dodd, C. H. *Historical Tradition in the Fourth Gospel*. Cambridge: Cambridge University Press, 1963.

Ellis, E. E. *The World of St. John*. Grand Rapids: Wm. B. Eerdmans Publishing Co., 1984.

Kysar, Robert. *John's Story of Jesus*. Philadelphia: Fortress Press, 1984.

Nicholson, Godfrey. *Death as Departure: The Johannine Descent-Ascent Schema*. Chico, Calif.: Scholars Press, 1984.

Schnackenburg, Rudolf. *The Gospel according to St. John*. 3 vols. New York: Seabury Press, 1980–1982.

Smith, D. Moody. *Johannine Christianity: Essays on Its Setting, Sources and Theology*. Columbia: University of South Carolina Press, 1984.

———. *John*. Proclamation Commentary. Philadelphia: Fortress Press, 1976.

Talbert, Charles H. *Reading John: A Literary and Theological Commentary on the Fourth Gospel and the Johannine Epistles*. New York: Crossroad, 1992.

Westcott, B. F. *The Gospel according to St. John*. London: James Clarke & Co., 1958.

What Portrait Will You Hang on Your Wall?

Early in the history of the church, Christians noticed differences among the four Gospels; and responses to this diversity varied then even as they do now. Some celebrated the diversity and others chafed at it. In the second century, for example, a scholar named Tatian produced a sort of scissors-and-paste harmony of the Gospels called the *Diatessaron* (Greek meaning: "through four") that was quite popular for a while among the Syrian churches. For the most part, however, Christian leaders have endorsed the four Gospels as authoritative in spite of their diversity. Four are better than one.

Constructing a harmony of the Gospels typically ends up weakening or even destroying the uniqueness and significance of each. Therefore, a foundational part of our study of the Gospels has been a commitment to take each Evangelist seriously, seeking to see how each portrayed Jesus of Nazareth and attempting to ascertain some of the reasons why the Evangelist wrote as he did. To do so involves not only doing careful detective work on each Gospel but also trying to interpret all four in light of ancient Mediterranean culture. The primary orality of the cultures in which the Evangelists wrote serves as a reminder that standards of writing and literary conventions then differed from what readers in most modern cultures would take as "normal" or even as "acceptable."

As we recognize the distance between our own time and first-century Palestine, we realize the necessity of reading documents from the ancient Mediterranean world that are not included in the Bible, for they provide helpful clues to our biblical interpretation. Caution is a necessary component to interpreting the Gospels, but overt skepticism is unnecessary. Although our perception is limited and our conclusions are continually in need of evaluation, we are quite capable of comprehending much of the message of the Gospels. In spite of time and cultural barriers, we can read the Gospels with substantial understanding; and the rewards are immense. Reading the Gospels inductively, observing their unique portraits of Jesus come increasingly into view, is very rewarding. Not only is it intellectually stimulating to do such literary detective work, but it is also personally challenging to ponder the significance of Jesus' teachings and actions. But what would it be like if we were limited to only one Gospel?

Mark's depiction of Jesus is stimulating and fast-paced. Events rush from scene to scene, often leaving the bewildered disciples behind. Jesus is the deeply emotional, miracle-working Son of God, who insists on secrecy. Religious leaders ridicule him; his own family questions his sanity; and his disciples are painfully unaware of the meaning of his ministry. Not until halfway through the Gospel story does Peter confess that Jesus is the Christ, and then he immediately finds himself in conflict with Jesus over the coming crucifixion. He and the other eleven are busy arguing with one another over who is the greatest even as Jesus gives his second passion prediction. Old ideas die slowly, and the messianic expectations that dominated their thinking left no room for the cross. The disciples find themselves actually resisting Jesus even as they confess him to be the Messiah.

Jesus' repeated successes at humiliating religious leaders in verbal combat only encourage his disciples to believe that he is going to establish himself as ruler in Jerusalem, and the overt attempt by James and John to gain the right and left positions of power when Jesus comes in his glory reveals what the rest also envision. So when the powerful yet secret Messiah comes in his glory on a cruel cross, his disciples have deserted him. In the poignant crucifixion scene, Jesus cries out in agony, asking why even God has abandoned him. Faithful women come to care for his body and are terrified when the angel speaks encouragement to them. Mark's story ends with the women running in fearful silence from the tomb.

What if this were our only primary account of Jesus? How would the church's theology be shaped? What portraits of Jesus would hang on our walls? What would be our view of discipleship?

What Portrait Will You Hang on Your Wall?

Although Luke uses much material from Mark's Gospel, his portrait of Jesus is more stoic, with a visible lack of expressions of emotion. Jesus is always the one under control of his feelings and calmly walking toward God's chosen destination. Luke's stress on Jesus' humble beginnings (birth in a manger and adoration by shepherds) is balanced by the remarkable predictions of angels and pious humans that this child is God's royal Son, chosen to sit on the throne of King David. Yet a major focus in the birth narrative is that this child will mean the fall of the rich and powerful and the rise of the poor and oppressed. Messiah has come, and Zechariah and his son, John, both proclaim that the Messiah will liberate Israel from foreign oppressors and fulfill the promises God gave to Abraham, Isaac, and Jacob.

Consequently, when Jesus announces the focus of his ministry in Luke 4 as bringing good news to the poor and letting the oppressed go free, confusion follows. His miracles are impressive, but he associates with the wrong people, and the way in which he reverses expectations in the Sermon on the Plain in Luke 6 creates further tension. In Luke 7, John sends messengers to ask if Jesus is the Messiah or if they should be looking for another. Yet, within this confusion, the apostles show much greater understanding than they do in Mark's account. They are, after all, the leaders of the early Christian movement, and portraying them as imbeciles would not fit well with Luke's goals in telling the story. When they do not understand, there are often good reasons, as in 9:45: " But they did not understand this saying; its meaning was concealed from them, so that they could not perceive it."

Luke records numerous parables of Jesus, placing more emphasis on his teaching than does Mark. These parables often contain colorful characters who sometimes do outrageous things, and entering into the narrative world of these creative stories engages us on multiple levels. In parabolic teaching and in his own actions, Jesus reverses the power structures of society, challenging accepted norms and exhibiting deep compassion for lost and wayward people. Repeatedly, tax collectors and sinners accept Jesus' teachings while the religious grumble and reject his words. Jesus insists that God deeply loves Gentiles, does outrageous things such as making a Samaritan the hero of a story, and in general upsets the status quo.

In the passion narrative, Jesus exhibits remarkable self-control. Modifying Mark's account of the prayer in Gethsemane, Luke has Jesus pray only once and then move on with his commitment to do God's will. Unlike Mark's picture of Jesus abandoned on the cross, Luke indicates that "all his acquaintances, including the women who had followed him from Galilee, stood at a distance, watching these things" (23:49). Jesus' words as he approaches Golgotha and as he hangs on the cross betray no pain or feelings of abandonment. His words express concern for those who mourn his execution, those who crucify him, and the thief on a cross beside him. His final words are triumphant. He is an ideal martyr, unflinchingly following God's will. And in the final chapter, Jesus appears to his understandably confused disciples and preaches to them extensively from the scriptures in order to explain the significance of his ministry and death and resurrection. Unlike the unsettling ending of Mark, Luke's Gospel ends in triumph, with Jesus ascending to heaven.

What if Luke were our only Gospel? We would have marvelous examples of Jesus' teachings, a portrait of an emotionally controlled (almost emotionless) Jesus, and a relentless presentation of the theme of the great reversal. How would Christian theology be formulated with only this picture? What images of Jesus would hang on our walls?

Unlike the Gentile-oriented presentation of Jesus in Luke, Matthew's Gospel is written for a Jewish-Christian audience; and his portrait of Jesus is very Jewish, a Messiah committed to fulfilling the law in its entirety. Contrary to Mark 7:19, which states, "Thus he declared all foods clean," Jesus does not challenge the validity of Mosaic laws in Matthew's version. Indeed, Matthew portrays Jesus as the authoritative interpreter of the law, and the very structure of his Gospel (alternating narrative and discourse sections) reveals the seriousness with which he pursues this agenda. Although he uses a great deal of Mark's material in his telling of the story, he persistently modifies it in ways that emphasize Jesus' words instead of his actions. Matthew typically reduces the number of narrative details and adds material on what Jesus said in the various situations.

Furthermore, whenever critics challenge any of Jesus' actions, Matthew is quick to vindicate Jesus with Old Testament quotations. When criticized for not properly keeping the Sabbath, for example, Jesus justifies his action and then explains, "But if you had known what this means, 'I desire mercy and not sacrifice,' you would not have condemned the guiltless" (12:7). Matthew relentlessly shows, in story after story, that the other teachers in Jewish society (usually Pharisaic scribes) are ignorant of the true meaning of the law and do not keep it properly. His redaction of Mark and his use of Q consistently single out the Pharisaic teachers for charges of ignorance and evil intentions. All of chapter 23 is a sustained attack on their teachings and motives. They are blind guides, and all who follow them do so at their own peril. To please God, one must follow the authoritative teaching of Jesus Messiah.

Unlike Luke, who traces Jesus' genealogy back to Adam, Matthew inaugurates his Gospel with a genealogy that begins with Abraham. And unlike Luke's emphasis on Jesus' birth under modest conditions, Matthew's birth account is fitting for a king, with foreign dignitaries, not shepherds, coming to pay homage. The focus on Joseph, not Mary, stresses the godliness of Jesus' father; and the flight into Egypt and return to resettle in Galilee contain echoes of the account of Moses in Exodus. Jesus Messiah in Matthew is above all the teacher/Christian lawgiver, and he delivers his authoritative commandments from a mountain in chapters 5—7, not on a plain as in Luke 6. In this sermon Jesus asserts the abiding validity of the law of Moses, contrasts his teaching with that which the audience hears from others, affirms the three pillars of Jewish piety (almsgiving, prayer, and fasting), and insists that true disciples are those who hear his teaching, obey, and bear fruits of righteousness.

Because of the emphasis on Jesus' teaching, the apostles in Matthew's account comprehend much more than those in Mark. If disciples do not understand and follow their master's words, this brings dishonor to the master, and the apostles are in fact "scribes trained for the kingdom" in Matthew's Gospel. Whereas Mark stresses the disciples' bewilderment, Matthew affirms, "Blessed are your eyes, for they see, and your ears, for they hear" (13:16), contrasting Jesus' followers with outsiders who do not understand (13:13–15, 19). True disciples follow Jesus' teachings and bear fruit, and they may be distinguished from those who claim to be disciples but do not bear good fruit. Therefore, final judgment will be based on whether or not people have kept the commands, as the parables of judgment in Matthew 25 make clear.

Like Luke, Matthew concludes his Gospel with Jesus victoriously ascending to heaven; but in contrast to Luke's account, this occurs in Galilee instead of near Bethany, just east of Jerusalem. Adding material to refute the charge that Jesus' disciples stole his body, Matthew ends his story of Jesus by emphasizing the necessity of teaching people what the authoritative teacher taught his disciples: "Go therefore and make disciples of all nations, baptizing them in the name of the Father and of the Son and of the Holy Spirit, and teaching them to obey everything that I have commanded you. And remember, I am with you always, to the end of the age" (28:19–20).

What if Matthew were our only first-century account of Jesus? If our only portrait of Jesus were this very Jewish version of the authoritative teacher of the law of Moses, how would this shape the church's theology? What effect would it have on the portraits of Jesus that we would hang on our walls? What would be the view of discipleship transmitted by missionaries who preach the Gospel message in various cultures around the world?

And what pictures of Jesus would we have if we relied only on the Gospel of John for our images of Jesus? The portrait of Jesus in the Fourth Gospel is quite different from those of the Synoptics. Whereas their differences are often matters of emphasis, as the three share many of the same stories, John blazes a new path christologically. He focuses not on Jesus Messiah preaching the kingdom of God but on Jesus the eternal Word, God incarnate forcefully arguing for acceptance of his deity as a prerequisite for having eternal life. Opponents are no longer differentiated with some degree of precision, as in the Synoptics, but are typically lumped together under the category "the Jews." How radically different is the picture that emerges in this Gospel from Matthew's depiction of Jesus as the observant Jew who forcefully argues for righteousness in obedience to his teaching of the Torah! What if we only had John?

In John's account, there is no emphasis on Jesus' earthly lineage. The focus is on his eternal existence, and hardly any mention is made of his parents. From the beginning, his followers understand his deity and heavenly mission. John the Baptist proclaims him to be the Lamb of God (1:29, 36), already understanding the sacrificial nature of Jesus' coming death (cf. his confusion in Luke 7:18–23). At the beginning of Jesus' ministry, his followers ascribe to him such titles as "Messiah" (1:41), "him about whom Moses in the law and also the prophets wrote" (1:45), "Son of God," and "King of Israel" (1:49). Nothing is secret about Jesus' identity in John's account. Even Jesus' enemies clearly understand who Jesus claims to be. The only question is whether people will believe in him and have eternal life or refuse to believe in him and live in darkness.

If we had only the Gospel of John, we would not have any of Jesus' parables; instead, we would have to rely on the extended discourses of the Johannine Christ for our understanding of how Jesus taught and the content of his message. Jesus has a body in John, but he is not nearly as human as in Mark. Indeed, he is so otherworldly that his disciples have difficulty understanding his highly symbolic words. Continually he speaks on a spiritual plane, expressing spiritual truths, while his listeners hear his words on an earthly plane, misunderstanding the true meaning. The Johannine Christ is understandable only in retrospect, from a later time when the Spirit of truth guides disciples into the truth. And this later truth fundamentally shapes the account of Jesus recounted in John. It is the story of Jesus retold in light of later christological reflection, bringing to light the previously incomprehensible meaning of his being and mission. He is scarcely human in this version.

Portraits of Jesus based on John's Gospel would be primarily ethereal, emphasizing his deity, not his humanity. In John, Jesus stresses that discipleship primarily involves believing in him and loving one another. He provides no moral and ethical teaching in John 1—12 but proclaims his divine origin. Later, in the farewell discourse, he urges his followers to sacrificial love for one another (esp. John 13; 15). Outsiders in John are dwellers in darkness, who openly hate Christians because they do not belong to God. This is particularly true of "the Jews," whom John castigates for their willful disbelief in God's Son. Unlike Matthew, who attacks certain groups within Judaism, John lumps these factions together; and in the history of church, this has been rather problematic. Some Christians have combined Matthew 27:25, in which a Jewish group says, "His blood be on us and on our children," with John's "the Jews" to produce a vitriolic anti-Semitic bias. John's Christology, therefore, although representing an exalted view of the nature of Christ, is insufficient by itself.

Four Gospels are truly better than one. A single perspective on the central figure of Christian faith is inadequate for a religion that transcends geographical, cultural, and ethnic boundaries. Multiple perspectives are healthy for evaluating the significance of Jesus of Nazareth, Son of God, and these must not be naively explained away. To say that the Gospel accounts differ in description only as accounts of some event differ because witnesses saw it from different vantage points is deficient. Evidence strongly suggests that the Evangelists were not eyewitnesses to the ministry of Jesus. They took what was delivered to them and creatively shaped it to address the needs of those for whom they wrote. Needs vary in different communities, and distinct groups will tend to gravitate more toward one Gospel than to the others. This is always a danger, although sociologically this tendency is understandable. The fourfold Gospel witness to Jesus needs to remain, with all the tensions that this creates. We tend to be drawn to the image that best fits our own cultural norms and theological tendencies, so the other images are necessary to challenge us to rethink our views and arrive at ever more adequate portraits of Jesus.

Appendix A
Jewish Religious Groups in the Time of Jesus

For the most part, groups such as the Pharisees and the Sadducees oppose Jesus and his apostles in the Gospel accounts, so the information contained about them in these stories tends to be negative. Because most Christians read about these Jewish groups only from the New Testament, they conclude, for example, that *Pharisee* is synonymous with *hypocrite*. This unfortunate stereotype does not take into account important information available from other ancient sources that describe the Pharisees in very positive terms. Reading these other accounts brings a broader perspective and greater degree of understanding of the issues involved in the first-century world in which Jesus lived than does restricting oneself to the New Testament.

Pharisees, Sadducees, Zealots, scribes, and chief priests play important roles in the story of Jesus, but we cannot learn the history of these parties by limiting our reading to the Gospels. Each group came into existence as a response to social and political forces and formed part of the complex fabric of Jewish society. Although there remains much we do not know about the history of each of these groups, we have enough information to understand some of the important elements of each. For our purposes, their stories begin at the time of the exile.

Before the destruction of Jerusalem by the Babylonian king Nebuchadnezzar in 587 B.C.E. (see 2 Kings 25:1–26), the temple in Jerusalem was central to the religious life of the Israelite people. The main religious functionaries were the *priests*, who offered sacrifices in the temple on behalf of the rest of the people, and the *prophets*, who spoke forth the word of the Lord. A tremendous emphasis was not placed on reading the sacred books. In other words, although many Hebrews held the laws of Moses in high esteem, the magnitude of the importance accorded this legislation was less before than after the exile.

The destruction of Jerusalem changed all that. In 597 B.C.E., Nebuchadnezzar conquered Judah and exiled to Babylon many of the elite in Hebrew society (2 Kings 24:10–17). Ten years later, after the revolt of Judah against his rule, Nebuchadnezzar completely demolished Jerusalem and the surrounding countryside, carrying

Appendix A

off into exile all but the poorest of the Hebrews (2 Kings 25:1–26). He humiliated them and forced them to march the long journey from Jerusalem to Babylon. Psalm 137 reflects a poet's reaction to this bitter ordeal:

> By the waters of Babylon—
>   there we sat down and there we wept
>   when we remembered Zion.
> On the willows there
>   we hung up our harps.
> For there our captors
>   asked us for songs,
> and our tormentors asked for mirth, saying,
>   "Sing us one of the songs of Zion!"
> How could we sing the LORD's song
>   in a foreign land?
> If I forget you, O Jerusalem,
>   let my right hand wither!
> Let my tongue cling to the roof of my mouth,
>   if I do not remember you,
> if I do not set Jerusalem
>   above my highest joy.
>
> (Ps. 137:1–6)

These words graphically portray the central role played by the Jerusalem temple in the life of the Hebrew people. In Babylonian exile, however, they were forced to restructure their religious and cultural existence. The Hebrews became a people of the book, and this profoundly affected their religious experience.

Tremendous literary activity occurred in Babylon. Hebrew scholars compiled the history of their people in final form. They edited and published the oracles of the prophets. They pondered the question "Why did God allow his chosen people to suffer defeat and be dragged away from their homeland?" And they found the answer in the covenant between God and his people in the Deuteronomic law: They had failed to observe God's laws; they had broken the Mosaic covenant (or treaty) established between God and the Israelites. Thus they concluded that God sent the Babylonians to conquer this rebellious people as punishment for their sins of apostasy.

Deciding that the road back to God's favor lay in careful obedience to the laws of Moses, these leaders sought diligently to teach the laws to the Hebrew people. The office of *scribe* became more than simply one who recorded business transactions or correspondence. In exile, Hebrew scribes devoted themselves to copying and studying Torah, the sacred writings. Life increasingly revolved around the book, and this replaced the centrality of the temple in Hebrew life.

In 539 B.C.E. the Persian king Cyrus conquered Babylon, and this new lord of the ancient Near East espoused a different idea of how to maintain loyalty among subjugated peoples. The Babylonians believed that the way to crush rebellions was to eliminate national identity by removing people from their homelands. In another land they would lose their incentive to fight, since they would have no homeland to protect. The Persians, however, thought that allowing people to stay in their own land and practice their own customs would inspire gratitude and loyalty.

According to the book of Ezra, Cyrus issued the following official decree in 539 B.C.E.:

> The LORD, the God of heaven, has given me all the kingdoms of the earth, and he has charged me to build him a house at Jerusalem in Judah. Any of those among you who are of his people—may their God be with them!—are now permitted to go up to Jerusalem . . . and rebuild the house of the LORD, . . . and let all survivors, in whatever place they reside, be assisted by the people of their place with silver and gold, with goods and with animals, besides freewill offerings for the house of God in Jerusalem. (Ezra 1:2–4)

After forty-eight years in Babylon, however, the majority of Hebrews had no desire to return to what was now a foreign land, Judah. They had homes and businesses. Aramaic, the official language of Babylon, was now their native tongue; most could not speak Hebrew. The actual number of Hebrews who returned to Judah, therefore, was only a small fraction of the total population. Most were content to stay in Babylon and help finance the expedition.

Ezra and Nehemiah recount the difficulties that those who ventured off to Judah faced. The returning exiles suffered considerable hardships and opposition from the residents of the area. And transforming into a temple the charred heap of rocks the Babylonians had left behind forty-eight years earlier was a task that took twenty-two years to finish (completed 516 B.C.E.). Yet, in spite of opposition, discouragement, and hardships, these Hebrews were given freedom by the Persians to have their own *high priest* and to live under the Mosaic laws. While they struggled for existence in Judah, however, far away to the northwest boiled a situation destined to influence the world's history profoundly.

For years, Persian kings sought to conquer the Greek city-states, and the Greek people hated these foreign intruders. Finally, a brilliant young leader called Alexander the Great avenged the Greeks. In 333 B.C.E., at the age of twenty-three, he crushed the Persian army of Darius III at Issus. Alexander devastated some significant Persian cities as his army swept away all opposition. His conquests reached all the way to India, where a combination of factors, including powerful defending armies and dissension among his own ranks, forced him to terminate his eastward push. On his return west, he contracted an illness and died in Babylon in 323 B.C.E., at the age of thirty-three. Alexander's military victories were truly amazing, but his historical significance involved much more than military conquest.

Alexander brought doctors, architects, artists, and philosophers with him to propagate what he saw as the superior culture of the Greeks. As a child, his personal teacher was the great philosopher Aristotle, and this training exercised a profound influence on Alexander. He sponsored the building of great cities, beautiful works of art, and libraries such as the one at Alexandria (a city named after himself).

Greeks considered anyone unable to speak Greek to be a barbarian (someone whose words sounded like *bar bar*). Alexander believed he could raise the standard of other civilizations by exposing them to Greek ways, and he industriously attempted this. He also recognized that language exercises an important influence on how people think. Under Alexander's influence, Greek became the standard language over a vast empire. The impact of speaking Greek upon Mediterranean cultures was enormous.

Under Greek rule, the educated people of many cultures adopted Greek ways of thinking. We call this infiltration of ideas the hellenization process (an expression arising from Hellas, the Greek word for Greece). When people assumed Greek speech and ways of living, they were hellenized. Judah (Judea) did not escape this process. Many of the more affluent and well educated became very Hellenistic, choosing the Greek manner of life over that of loyalty to the Mosaic law. Considerable strife erupted between these Hebrews and those who remained faithful to Mosaic Torah, and other historical events exacerbated this.

After Alexander's death in 323 B.C.E., some of his main generals divided the empire, each grabbing for himself as substantial a portion as he could defend. Ptolemy, whom Alexander had made governor of Egypt, sent troops and occupied Palestine. For the next one hundred years Ptolemy and his heirs ruled Palestine from Alexandria. To the north, the descendants of another general, called the Seleucids, ruled over Asia Minor and Persia from their capital in Syria. They posed a constant threat to Ptolemaic rule over Palestine; and because of the strong economic and cultural ties between Hebrews in Judea and Babylon, a significant number of Hebrews preferred the idea of Syrian rule.

When Alexander was conquering the Mediterranean region, because Palestine offered no resistance to his armies, he allowed the Hebrews to maintain the way of life the Persians had permitted. The Hebrews continued their religious observances in the temple. Their high priest, who was responsible not only for religious ritual but also for conveying the yearly payment of taxes to the Persians, remained the central figure of authority in the community. Along with the chief priest was a council of elders, and together they maintained order in the community. This council was composed of the heads of influential Jerusalem families and significant priests, and it developed into what was known by New Testament times as the *Sanhedrin*.

During Ptolemaic rule of Palestine, this Hebrew governing system remained largely intact. But the high priesthood increasingly became a political position, with considerable economic power due to the profits gained from collecting taxes from the people. Such power invited corruption. And while wealthy men competed with each other, courting the Egyptian rulers for the high priest's office, the common people continued to chafe under their taxation.

In 223 B.C.E. the Syrian king Antiochus III wrestled Palestine away from Egypt. But Syrian domination proved worse than Egyptian, and their harsh treatment of the Hebrews finally led to rebellion. Antiochus IV Epiphanes, a power-crazy individual with demented tendencies, ruled from 175 to 164 B.C.E. He considered the Hebrews a "detestable nation" whose superstitions hindered them from learning the splendors of Greek culture (Tacitus, *Historiae* 5.8), and he tried to eliminate Jewish faith through forced hellenization. To make them more civilized, he attempted to eliminate the Hebrews' ancestral religion. The result was war, and ironically, the preservation of the Jewish faith.

Many Hebrews were already sympathetic with total adoption of Greek ways. For example, a Hebrew priest named Jason purchased the office of high priest by offering Antiochus IV a large sum of money and subsequently using his authority to build a gymnasium in Jerusalem. Since the Greek gymnasium functioned as an educational center as well as a place for exercise, its presence was profound. The word *gymnasium* stems from the Greek word *gumnos*, meaning "naked," and that is how the participants exercised! First Maccabees, a historically valuable, second-century document located in the Old Testament Apocrypha, reports:

Appendix A

In those days certain renegades came out from Israel and misled many, saying, "Let us go and make a covenant with the Gentiles around us, for since we separated from them many disasters have come upon us." This proposal pleased them, and some of the people eagerly went to the king, who authorized them to observe the ordinances of the Gentiles. So they built a gymnasium in Jerusalem, according to Gentile custom, and removed the marks of circumcision, and abandoned the holy covenant. They joined with the Gentiles and sold themselves to do evil. (1 Macc. 1:11–15)

The book of 2 Maccabees, also found in the Apocrypha, describes the situation with more detail:

When Seleucus died and Antiochus, who was called Epiphanes [= "God manifest"], succeeded to the kingdom, Jason the brother of Onias obtained the high priesthood by corruption, promising the king at an interview three hundred and sixty talents of silver, and from another source of revenue eighty talents. In addition to this he promised to pay one hundred fifty more if permission were given to establish by his authority a gymnasium and a body of youth for it, and to enroll the people of Jerusalem as citizens of Antioch. When the king assented and Jason came to office, he at once shifted his compatriots over to the Greek way of life.

He set aside the existing royal concessions to the Jews, secured through John the father of Eupolemus, who went on the mission to establish friendship with the Romans; and he destroyed the lawful ways of living and introduced new customs contrary to the law. He took delight in establishing a gymnasium right under the citadel, and he induced the noblest of the young men to wear the Greek hat. There was such an extreme of Hellenization and increase in the adoption of foreign ways because of the surpassing wickedness of Jason, who was ungodly and no true high priest, that the priests were no longer intent upon their service at the altar. Despising the sanctuary and neglecting the sacrifices, they hurried to take part in the unlawful proceedings in the wrestling arena after the signal for the discus-throwing, disdaining the honors prized by their ancestors and putting the highest value upon Greek forms of prestige. . . .

When the quadrennial games were being held at Tyre and the king was present, the vile Jason sent envoys, chosen as being Antiochian citizens from Jerusalem, to carry three hundred silver drachmas for the sacrifice to Hercules. (2 Macc. 4:7–15, 18–19)

Thus, the movement toward hellenization gained considerable momentum from within the Israelite community. Jason's term as high priest (174–171 B.C.E.), epitomized by the construction of a gymnasium near the temple, where Hebrew priests preferred to pursue Greek learning and exercise rather than perform their duties in the temple, shows how far the process extended. If Antiochus Epiphanes had left Jerusalem alone, the Hebrew Hellenists might have obliterated the traditions of their fathers, giving up completely the laws of Moses.

But Antiochus was unsatisfied with such developments. A Hebrew from nonpriestly descent by the name of Menelaus offered a larger bribe than Jason did to Antiochus and thus obtained the high priesthood. This further infuriated faithful Hebrews, who considered this a desecration of the office of high priest. In addition, Jason did not give up his claim to the office. While Antiochus was invading Egypt in 169 B.C.E., rumor spread that he had been killed (2 Macc. 5:5). Jason responded to the news by launching a surprise attack on his adversaries in Jerusalem, to regain his position of high priest by force.

> When news of what had happened reached the king, he took it to mean that Judea was in revolt. So, raging inwardly, he left Egypt and took the city by storm. He commanded his soldiers to cut down relentlessly everyone they met and to kill those who went into the houses. Then there was massacre of young and old, destruction of boys, women, and children, and the slaughter of young girls and infants. Within the total of three days eighty thousand were destroyed, forty thousand in hand-to-hand fighting; and as many were sold into slavery as were killed.
>
> Not content with this, Antiochus dared to enter the most holy temple in all the world, guided by Menelaus, who had become a traitor both to the laws and to his country. He took the holy vessels with his polluted hands, and swept away with profane hands the votive offerings that other kings had made to enhance the glory and honor of the place. (2 Macc. 5:11–16)

Not only did Antiochus brutally murder many Israelites, but he also violated their religious sensibilities by entering the temple, an act strictly forbidden for any Gentile, and plundered gold and silver from it to pay his war debts. Several years later, he embarked on an empire-wide policy of enforced hellenization that exploded Hebrew opposition into the Maccabean rebellion:

> Then the king wrote to his whole kingdom that all should be one people, and that all should give up their particular customs. All the Gentiles accepted the command of the king. Many even from Israel gladly adopted his religion; they sacrificed to idols and profaned the sabbath. And the king sent letters by messengers to Jerusalem and the towns

of Judah; he directed them to follow customs strange to the land, to forbid burnt offerings and sacrifices and drink offerings in the sanctuary, to profane sabbaths and festivals, to defile the sanctuary and the priests, to build altars and sacred precincts and shrines for idols, to sacrifice swine and other unclean animals, and to leave their sons uncircumcised. They were to make themselves abominable by everything unclean and profane, so that they would forget the law and change all the ordinances. He added, "And whoever does not obey the command of the king shall die."

In such words he wrote to his whole kingdom. He appointed inspectors over all the people and commanded the towns of Judah to offer sacrifice, town by town. Many of the people, everyone who forsook the law, joined them, and they did evil in the land; they drove Israel into hiding in every place of refuge they had.

Now on the fifteenth day of Chislev, in the one hundred forty-fifth year, they erected a desolating sacrilege on the altar of burnt offering. They also built altars in the surrounding towns of Judah, and offered incense at the doors of the houses and in the streets. The books of the law that they found they tore to pieces and burned with fire. Anyone found possessing the book of the covenant, or anyone who adhered to the law, was condemned to death by decree of the king. They kept using violence against Israel, against those who were found month after month in the towns. And on the twenty-fifth day of the month they offered sacrifice on the altar that was on top of the altar of burnt offering. According to the decree, they put to death the women who had their children circumcised, and their families and those who circumcised them; and they hung the infants from their mothers' necks.

But many in Israel stood firm and were resolved in their hearts not to eat unclean food. They chose to die rather than to be defiled by food or to profane the holy covenant; and they did die. Very great wrath came upon Israel. (1 Macc. 1:41–64)

The book of 2 Maccabees describes this tragedy even more graphically:

Not long after this, the king sent an Athenian senator to compel the Jews to forsake the laws of their ancestors and no longer to live by the laws of God; also to pollute the temple in Jerusalem and call it the temple of Olympian Zeus. . . .

Harsh and utterly grievous was the onslaught of evil. For the temple was filled with debauchery and reveling by the Gentiles, who dallied with prostitutes and had intercourse with women within the sacred precincts, and besides brought in things for sacrifice that were unfit. (2 Macc. 6:1–4)

Hebrews who refused to deny their faith paid dearly:

> For example, two women were brought in for having cir-
> cumcised their children. They publicly paraded them about
> the city, with their babies hanging at their breasts, and then
> hurled them down headlong from the wall. Others who had
> assembled in the caves nearby, in order to observe the sev-
> enth day secretly, were betrayed to Philip and were all
> burned together, because their piety kept them from de-
> fending themselves, in view of their regard for that most
> holy day. (2 Macc. 6:10–11)

In the intensity of this situation, many faithful Hebrews dispersed from the city to the surrounding countryside. Among
them was a priest by the name of Mattathias, who moved his family to the town of Modein. But he could not escape the problem.
"The king's officers who were enforcing the apostasy came to the
town of Modein to make them offer sacrifice. Many from Israel
came to them; and Mattathias and his sons were assembled" (1
Macc. 2:15–16). The officer asked Mattathias to sacrifice, but the
old priest defiantly objected.

When another Jew came forward to sacrifice, Mattathias flew
into a rage and killed the man on the altar. Then he killed the
king's officer, tore down the altar, and cried out, "Let every one
who is zealous for the law and supports the covenant come out
with me!" (1 Macc. 2:27). He fled to the hills, leaving behind all
his possessions. Although not alone in fleeing to the hill country,
Mattathias's family fared better than many others:

> At that time many who were seeking righteousness and jus-
> tice went down to the wilderness to live there, they, their
> sons, their wives, and their livestock, because troubles
> pressed heavily upon them. And it was reported to the
> king's officers, and to the troops in Jerusalem the city of
> David, that those who had rejected the king's command
> had gone down to the hiding places in the wilderness.
> Many pursued them, and overtook them; they encamped
> opposite them and prepared for battle against them on the
> sabbath day. They said to them, "Enough of this! Come out
> and do what the king commands, and you will live." But
> they said, "We will not come out, nor will we do what the
> king commands and so profane the sabbath day." Then the
> enemy quickly attacked them. But they did not answer
> them or hurl a stone at them or block up their hiding
> places, for they said, "Let us all die in our innocence;
> heaven and earth testify for us that you are killing us un-
> justly." So they attacked them on the sabbath, and they
> died, with their wives and children and livestock, to the
> number of a thousand persons.

Appendix A

> When Mattathias and his friends learned of it, they mourned for them deeply. And all said to their neighbors: "If we all do as our kindred have done and refuse to fight with the Gentiles for our lives and for our ordinances, they will quickly destroy us from the earth." So they made this decision that day: "Let us fight against anyone who comes to attack us on the sabbath day; let us not all die as our kindred died in their hiding places."
>
> Then there united with them a company of Hasideans, mighty warriors of Israel, all who offered themselves willingly for the law. And all who became fugitives to escape their troubles joined them and reinforced them. They organized an army, and struck down sinners in their anger and renegades in their wrath; the survivors fled to the Gentiles for safety. And Mattathias and his friends went around and tore down the altars; they forcibly circumcised all the uncircumcised boys that they found within the borders of Israel. (1 Macc. 2:29–46)

This Israelite revolt against Syrian rule started by the old priest Mattathias in 168 B.C.E. is called the Maccabean rebellion. Mattathias died shortly after the beginning of the war, and his son Judas Maccabeus was appointed to lead the rebellion. He was a fearless leader who experienced considerable success against the Syrians, although he finally died in battle. In the decades that followed, one after the other of his brothers commanded the insurrection when the previous leader was killed in battle or treacherously murdered. The cost was high, but they finally succeeded in ridding Judea of Syrian rule, and this brief independence fostered Hebrew nationalism and loyalty to biblical faith.

With victory, however, came inter-Hebrew power struggles, as various factions fought for dominance. Some evidence suggests that the Pharisees were one of the groups seeking political power for propagation of their religious views. They may have arisen from among the ranks of the Hasideans mentioned in 1 Maccabees 2:42, the valiant men zealous for the law, although this cannot be asserted with certainty. *Hesed* in Hebrew means "faithful," and the plural noun *hasidim* (translated "Hasideans" in the NRSV) means "faithful ones." Quite likely various subgroups combined to comprise the larger group of *hasidim*, and perhaps the beginnings of the Pharisaic movement may be found here.

Flavius Josephus, an important Jewish historian born in 37/38 C.E., provides several accounts of the activities and beliefs of the Pharisees in his two major works *The Jewish War* (written ca. 75 C.E.) and *Jewish Antiquities* (ca. 93 C.E.). Josephus was commander in chief of the army in Galilee during the Jewish revolt against Rome that began in 66 C.E. After suffering defeat in 67 C.E., he decided that the rebellion was futile and gave himself up to the Roman commander Vespasian. He then endeared himself to Vespasian by predicting that the general would one day become emperor. When this actually happened in 69 C.E., Vespasian granted Josephus his freedom as a gesture of gratitude. The Roman commander Titus stayed in Palestine to finish the war against the Hebrews, and Josephus helped him by risking his life as he tried to convince the resistance forces in Jerusalem to surrender. When the war was over, Josephus accompanied Titus to Rome, and there Vespasian gave him a yearly pension for living expenses, making it possible for him to devote his time to writing.

Josephus first mentions the Pharisees while describing the reign of the Maccabean monarch Jonathan, 160–143 B.C.E., so perhaps by this time they had emerged as a recognizable party. Here he recounts some of their beliefs, and we shall return to these shortly, after reading further about the political involvements of the Pharisees.

Because the Maccabean leaders were successful in war against the Syrians in spite of overwhelming odds, many Hebrews believed that God had ordained this family to rule over Israel. Consequently, in 140 B.C.E. a large assembly of Hebrew leaders and common people appointed Simon, the current Maccabean leader, to be both their high priest and their military commander (1 Macc. 14:25–40):

> The Jews and their priests have resolved that Simon should be their leader and high priest forever, until a trustworthy prophet should arise, and that he should be governor over them and that he should take charge of the sanctuary and appoint officials over its tasks and over the country and the weapons and the strongholds, and that he should be obeyed by all, and that all contracts in the country should be written in his name, and that he should be clothed in purple and wear gold. (1 Macc. 14:41–43)

The Pharisees may have been among those who conferred both kingly and priestly honors on Simon. Some of the *hasidim,* however, were infuriated that a man of war, stained with the blood of many battles, should function as the high priest.

After the murder of Simon and his two oldest sons by an ambitious son-in-law, Simon's son John Hyrcanus assumed the throne in 134 B.C.E. Hyrcanus, himself a follower of the Pharisees, came into direct conflict with this religious party over an issue of purity. According to Josephus, a Pharisee falsely charged that Hyrcanus's mother had been captured during the reign of Antiochus IV and placed in prison. Since a woman could be defiled in prison, this man said Hyrcanus should not function as high priest. Enraged against the Pharisees because of this, Hyrcanus joined the Sadducees (*Ant.* 13.10.4–6 [§§288–98]).

Hyrcanus became a tyrannical leader, alienating himself from the Hebrew people by his brutality and despotism (*Ant.* 13.13.3–5). In the same way, his son who ruled after him, Alexander Janaeus (reigned 103–76 B.C.E.), revealed a propensity for brutality. Because of the despotic rule of these Maccabean leaders, more and more people followed the Pharisees, who became a formidable opposition party. During the Feast of Tabernacles one year, Janaeus massacred six thousand Hebrews because they taunted him while he offered sacrifice, saying that he had no right to be high priest (*Ant.* 13.13.5 [§§372–73]; *War* 1.4.3 [§88]). Open rebellion followed, in which about fifty thousand Hebrews were killed. In the end Janaeus prevailed, and his revenge so shocked and demoralized his opponents that he momentarily broke the political aspirations of the Pharisaic party:

> His rage was grown so extravagant, that his barbarity proceeded to a degree of impiety: for when he had ordered eight hundred to be hung upon crosses in the midst of the city, he had the throats of their wives and children cut before their eyes; and these executions he saw as he was drinking and lying down with his concubines. Upon which, so deep a surprise seized on the people, that eight thousand of his opposers fled away the very next night, out of all Judea, whose flight was only terminated by Alexander's death. (*War* 1.4.6 [§§96–98]; see also *Ant.* 13.15.2 [§§389–91])

These eight hundred crucified men were Pharisees, and the tyrant's barbarous behavior deeply impressed the Hebrew people. Gone were the days of trust and respect for Maccabean leadership. Josephus claims, however, that when Janaeus died, his widow, Alexandra Salome, regained favor with the populace by courting the favor of the Pharisees.

> Now the Pharisees joined themselves to her, to assist her in the government. These are a certain sect of the Jews that appear more religious than others, and seem to interpret the laws more accurately. Now, Alexandra hearkened to them to an extraordinary degree, as being herself a woman of great piety towards God. But these Pharisees artfully insinuated themselves into her favor by little and little, and became themselves the real administrators of the public af-

fairs; they banished and loosed [men] at their pleasure; and, to say all at once, they had the enjoyment of the royal authority, whilst the expenses and the difficulties of it belonged to Alexandra. . . . Accordingly, they themselves slew Diogenes, a person of figure, and one that had been a friend to Alexander: and accused him as having assisted the king with his advice, for crucifying the eight hundred men [before mentioned]. They also prevailed with Alexandra to put to death the rest of those who had irritated him against them. (*War* 1.5.2–3 [§§110–13])

Josephus gives a longer account of this event in *Antiquities* 13.15.5–16.5 (§§398–429), but it is not as critical of the Pharisees. Written in 93 C.E., after the Pharisees had emerged as the dominant leaders in Judaism, Josephus's second version differs somewhat from that in *War* 1.5.1–3, which was written shortly after the war. By this time Josephus claims to be a Pharisee (*Life* 9—12), and the modifications of the story of Alexandra Salome may be politically motivated to increase that group's stature before the Romans. In other words, political agendas played an important role in how Josephus depicted the Pharisees and other Jewish groups. He did not attempt to give an unbiased historical account.

The Pharisees gradually gave up their political aspirations and devoted themselves to matters of personal piety, praying that God would usher in his kingdom with the promised messiah and end the rule of evil men. During the time of Jesus, however, a group of radical political activists known as the Zealots aggressively sought direct overthrow of Roman rule. A Zealot named Sadduc maintained that paying taxes to the Romans was no better than slavery and insisted that God would defend the Jews if they revolted. His words excited a number of Jews, and they incited the rebellion against Rome that swept many into this disastrous endeavor (*Ant.* 18.1.1 [§§3–10]). Josephus calls them the fourth philosophical sect among the Jews. (He uses philosophical terms common among his Roman readers when describing Jewish parties.)

The Jews had for a great while three sects of philosophy peculiar to themselves; the sect of the Essenes, and the sect of the Sadducees, and the third sort of opinions was that of those called Pharisees. . . . Now, for the Pharisees, they live meanly, and despise delicacies in diet; and they follow the conduct of reason; and what that prescribes to them as good for them, they do; and they think they ought earnestly to strive to observe reason's dictates for practice. They also pay a respect to such as are in years; nor are they so bold as to contradict them in anything which they have introduced; and, when they determine that all things are done by fate, they do not take away the freedom from men of acting as they think fit; since their notion is, that it hath pleased God to make a temperament, whereby what he wills is done, but so that the will of men can act virtuously or viciously. They also believe that souls have an immortal vigor in them, and that under the earth there will be rewards or punishments, according as they have lived virtuously or viciously in this life; and the latter are to be detained in an everlasting prison, but that the former shall have power to revive and live again; on account of which doctrines, they are able greatly to persuade the body of the people; and whatsoever they do about divine worship, prayers, and sacrifices, they perform them according to their direction; insomuch that the cities gave great attestations to them on account of their entire virtuous conduct, both in the actions of their lives and their discourses also.

But the doctrine of the Sadducees is this: That souls die with the bodies; nor do they regard the observation of anything besides what the law enjoins them; for they think it an instance of virtue to dispute with those teachers of philosophy whom they frequent; but this doctrine is received but by a few, yet by those still of the greatest dignity; but they are able to do almost nothing of themselves; for when they become magistrates, as they are unwillingly and by force sometimes obliged to be, they addict themselves to the notions of the Pharisees, because the multitude would not otherwise bear them.

The doctrine of the Essenes is this: That all things are best ascribed to God. They teach the immortality of souls, and esteem that the rewards of righteousness are to be earnestly striven for; and when they send what they have dedicated to God into the temple, they do not offer sacrifices, because they have more pure lustrations of their own; on account of which they are excluded from the common court of the temple, but offer their sacrifices themselves. . . . They exceed all other men that addict themselves to virtue. . . . This is demonstrated by that institution of theirs which will not suffer anything to hinder them from having all things in common; so that a rich man enjoys no more of his own wealth than he who hath nothing at all. There are about four thousand men that live in this way, and neither marry wives, nor are desirous to keep servants; as thinking the latter tempts men to be unjust, and the former gives the handle to domestic quarrels.

But of the fourth sect of Jewish philosophy, Judas the Galilean was the author. These men agree in all other things with the Pharisaic notions; but they have an inviolable attachment to liberty; and say that God is to be their only Ruler and Lord. They also do not value dying any kind of death, nor indeed do they heed the deaths of their relations and friends, nor can any such fear make them call any man Lord. (*Ant.* 18.1.2–6 [§§11–25])[1]

Jewish Religious Groups in the Time of Jesus

Sorting Out the Differences

1. What does Josephus emphasize about the beliefs and practices of the Pharisees?
2. How do they differ from the priestly Sadducees? From Essenes?

The history of the Pharisees chronicles a movement from intense political activism to introspective piety. During this time the Pharisaic scribes, the more highly educated members of the group, debated matters of how one lives piously. The Pharisees preserved teachings of their more famous scribes in the memory of their community, gradually collecting these into an oral tradition called the "traditions of the fathers." Josephus mentions these oral laws in his accounts, stressing their great importance to the Pharisees. By the time of Jesus these traditions occupied a level of importance almost equal to that of the scriptures, and the Pharisees believed these laws had been passed down orally since the time of Moses.

Originally, these oral laws offered contemporary explanations of the meaning of Mosaic legislation, providing a service to the common people. The obscure nature of many Mosaic laws made obeying them difficult, and even laws that were clear were sometimes hard to apply. For example, the law commands no work be done on the Sabbath. But what connotes work? Obviously, people should not labor in the fields on the Sabbath; but how far could they walk to visit friends? Gradually the number of specifications to clarify such matters grew, lest someone break the law ignorantly and incur God's displeasure.

The Pharisees reasoned that if God raised up Babylon to defeat Judah because their ancestors broke the law, future defeat of the nation might be avoided by careful adherence to the commandments of Moses. They therefore built a fence around the law so that people would not violate it unwittingly.

Apparently, the originators of the Pharisaic movement were priests; and as their ranks expanded to include those from non-priestly families, they applied to all members of the party the Old Testament ceremonial laws that pertain only to priests. Thus they came to hold a concept of the priesthood of all true believers. They wanted to establish a nation of pure Israelites, each remaining in a condition of purity and thus qualified to serve God. This route would lead to a nation truly blessed and protected by God. Their initial goals were noble enough, but the Gospels accuse them of becoming so focused on obeying individual laws that many forgot the larger purpose lying behind these mandates.

In summary, the Maccabean rebellion profoundly affected

Appendix A

Hebrew theologies. Before the rebellion, the main influence toward hellenization came from among the ranks of the priestly aristocracy. After the success of the revolt, priests under the Maccabees were far more conservative and took their duties pertaining to temple worship seriously. The name Sadducees most likely comes from Zadokites, meaning "descendants of Zadok." Zadok was a ruling priest under David and supported Solomon to be king after David (2 Sam. 15:24–35; 19:11–15; 1 Kings 1—2). Many years later Ezekiel prophesied:

> The [temple] chamber that faces north is for the priests who have charge of the altar; these are the descendants of Zadok, who alone among the descendants of Levi may come near to the LORD to minister to him. (Ezek. 40:46)

> But the levitical priests, the descendants of Zadok, who kept the charge of my sanctuary when the people of Israel went astray from me, shall come near to me to minister to me. . . . It is they who shall enter my sanctuary, it is they who shall approach my table, to minister to me. (Ezek. 44:15–16)

The Sadducees considered themselves the descendants of Zadok and therefore the legitimate priests. They rejected the Pharisees' oral law and refused to develop doctrine except from the books of Moses, the Pentateuch. So, whereas Pharisees believed in angels, demons, and the resurrection of the body, the Sadducees rejected such beliefs as modern innovations that went beyond the limits of Mosaic teaching.

Pharisees, by contrast, while very faithful to the laws of Moses, also believed that the other books of the Hebrew scriptures (the Prophets and the Writings) were inspired by God and authoritative. In addition, they revered their oral traditions and believed all Israelites should follow them. This difference fostered hostilities between Sadducees and Pharisees. Sadducees considered the Pharisees too rigorous in their interpretation of how people must live lawfully. Another group, however, viewed the Pharisees as too lenient.

The Dead Sea Scroll community was more zealous than the Pharisees, separating themselves from society for matters of purity. Many scholars believe that when the founder of this sect, the Teacher of Righteousness, speaks in his writings of those who make things too easy for people by their interpretation of the laws, he refers to the Pharisees: "I thank Thee, O Lord, for Thou hast . . . saved me from the zeal of lying interpreters, and from the congregation of those who seek smooth things" (*Hymn* 3).[2]

The members of this sect also rejected the Sadducees' claim to be the rightful priests in the temple, believing instead that these opponents had polluted the temple to such an extent that only the messiah could purify it again. So they withdrew from Jerusalem and waited in the wilderness for the messiah to come and lead them into battle against those whom they considered to be perverters of the true faith.

SECTARIAN JUDAISM AND
THE GOSPEL ACCOUNTS OF JESUS

Understanding more about the Jewish religious groups in the first century provides many fascinating insights into the Gospel stories of conflict between these people and Jesus. If you would like to read more detailed information about these groups than is contained in this brief historical summary, additional resources are provided in the following bibliography. Also, descriptions of their beliefs and practices are located throughout the chapters on the Gospels, where such information is helpful in understanding particular encounters between Jesus and his disciples and members of these groups.

FURTHER READING ON JEWISH RELIGIOUS GROUPS IN JESUS' TIME

Cohen, Shaye J. D. *From the Maccabees to the Mishnah.* Philadelphia: Westminster Press, 1987.

Jeremias, Joachim. *Jerusalem in the Time of Jesus: An Investigation into Economic and Social Conditions during the New Testament Times.* Philadelphia: Fortress Press, 1969.

Lohse, Eduard. *The New Testament Environment.* Nashville: Abingdon Press, 1976.

Neusner, Jacob. *From Politics to Piety: The Emergence of Pharisaic Judaism.* Englewood Cliffs, N.J.: Prentice-Hall, 1973.

———. *The Rabbinic Traditions about the Pharisees before 70.* 3 vols. Leiden: E. J. Brill, 1971.

Rivkin, Ellis. *A Hidden Revolution: The Pharisees' Search for the Kingdom Within.* Nashville: Abingdon Press, 1978.

Roetzel, Calvin J. *The World That Shaped the New Testament.* Atlanta: John Knox Press, 1985.

Safrai, S., and M. Stern, eds. *The Jewish People in the First Century.* 2 vols. Compendia rerum iudaicarum ad novum testamentum. Philadelphia: Fortress Press, 1974, 1976.

Schürer, Emil. *The History of the Jewish People in the Age of Jesus Christ.* 3 vols. Revised and edited by Geza Vermes, Fergus Millar, and M. Black. Edinburgh: T. & T. Clark, 1973.

Tcherikover, Victor. *Hellenistic Civilization and the Jews.* Translated by S. Applebaum. Philadelphia: Jewish Publication Society, 1966.

Appendix B
How to Write an
Exegesis Paper on a Gospel Passage

The word *exegesis* comes from the Greek word *exegeomai,* which basically means "to lead out of." When applied to the interpretation of written texts, it means "to read out" or "to explain the meaning of." Any time you interpret the meaning of a statement you hear or a sentence you read, you are involved in the task of exegesis. The following guidelines are designed to sharpen your skills in interpreting Gospel passages, as well as to make clear how to go about writing an exegesis paper.

RESEARCHING THE PAPER

After deciding on the passage you intend to explain the meaning of, take the following approach to studying the text:

1. Describe what form the story represents. If a saying, is it a parable, an apocalyptic discourse, a teaching on a matter pertaining to Jewish law, a symbolic discourse (in John's Gospel primarily), a type of wisdom saying, or some other form? If a narrative, is it a miracle story (if so, describe whether it is a healing, an exorcism, or a nature miracle) or another kind of story, such as a description of his birth, baptism, or calling of his disciples? Why might the story have been preserved in the oral tradition of the church before its use in the Gospel?

2. Observe carefully how the passage fits into the larger context of its Gospel. What role does the passage play in the narrative, and how does the larger context provide information necessary for understanding it?

3. Study carefully the component parts of the passage, seeking to determine how they fit together to form the whole. Writing down the passage often facilitates this endeavor, for in the process of writing you will often observe aspects of the story that you miss otherwise. Watch for repeated words and phrases, because repetition usually indicates something of importance. Does the passage employ irony, a chiastic structure, or poetry? Does it use metaphors, similes, forms of overstatement, or a proverb?

4. Determine the significant words in your passage and

look these up in several Bible dictionaries in the library's reference room. Understanding the meaning of particular words can substantially influence your interpretation of some passages, although you must be careful of interpreting your text on the basis of dictionary articles. Determine which meaning of the word best fits the context. Consult standard reference works such as *The Interpreter's Dictionary of the Bible, Theological Dictionary of the New Testament* (Kittel), and *The New International Dictionary of New Testament Theology.*

5. Determine whether the passage is from Mark, Q, M, or L. If it is Markan material, is it used in Matthew, in Luke, or in both? Study how Matthew or Luke has redacted the story. If it is from Q, compare the ways in which Matthew and Luke present the passage. Do the Gospels that include the story place it in the same context or in different ones?

6. After carefully studying the passage yourself, read what others have written about it in commentaries, journal articles, and books dealing with specific topics. If your passage addresses the issue of divorce, for example, check the card catalog for books on divorce and look in their indexes to see which pages deal with your passage. Use at least seven commentaries in your study, but do not count ones that cover the entire Bible in one volume. For example, if your passage is in Mark, use commentaries that devote their entire contents to Mark. Try to find volumes from recognized series such as New International Commentary on the New Testament, International Critical Commentary, Hermeneia, New Century Bible, Tyndale New Testament Commentary, Anchor Bible, Harper's New Testament Commentary.

Do not limit your research to reading works that state the position you presently hold. You will strengthen your case by reading opposing views, for they will help you think through your position and bring greater clarity to your thought.

Maintain an openness to the biblical material. Do not merely seek to prove what you already believe; that is a dishonest approach to research. Study the text carefully; become aware of the issues involved; formulate your conclusions; and then write your paper to demonstrate what you have discovered.

Do not simply report what someone else has written on your biblical text. Researching and writing the paper will help develop your ability to read carefully, sift the evidence, and reach your own conclusions. Your paper should demonstrate that you have considered the data presented in the secondary literature and formulated your own conclusions on the meaning and implications of the passage.

ORGANIZING AND WRITING

After reflecting on the significance of your passage and mentally dialoging with the explanations of it presented in the secondary literature, you will begin to formulate your own ideas on what the text means. Before you compose these into a formal paper, however, construct an outline of what you want to communicate, sketching out the sequence and content. This outline will help your thoughts flow smoothly in the exegesis paper, for you will know your direction and avoid figuring out where you are going as you write.

Performing your research in advance and establishing your conclusions before you begin to write your paper will greatly improve the quality of your work. If you are not familiar with elements of effective writing, consult a standard work such as W. Strunk and E. B. White, *The Elements of Style* (inexpensive in paperback). Use the following format for writing your exegesis paper.

1. *Introduction:* Explain concisely the central theme of your paper, stating what is most important in your passage and why it is significant in the document in which it is located. Avoid procedural language such as "I will do this, and then I will . . ."

2. *Form and Literary Setting:* Explain what form of teaching or narrative the story represents, as well as the significance of the location of the passage in its larger literary context. Briefly show how the story fits into its narrative setting, and explain the importance of the material immediately preceding and following it for interpreting the passage.

3. *Analysis of the Passage:* As you explain the meaning of your passage, give attention to matters such as the following (not in any preset order; use them as they best fit):

   A. The significance of its literary structure. Are certain words or groups of words repeated? Is antithetical or synonymous parallelism used? Is there a chiastic structuring of the contents? Is poetry included? Are metaphors or irony employed?

   B. Use of rhetorical techniques to strengthen the message. Does the biblical author use rhetorical questions? Does he begin a series of statements in the same manner for emphasis, such as "Blessed are the . . ." (Matt. 5:3–10) or "You have heard it said . . . , but I say to you . . ." (Matt. 5:21–48). Does he use plays on words, such as "You blind guides, straining out a gnat [*qalma*] and swallowing a camel [*gamal*]" (Matt. 23:24)? (Commentaries will point these out for you.)

219

Does the passage use techniques such as arguing "from the lesser to the greater"? (For example, in Matt. 12:11–12, Jesus argues that if pulling a sheep out of a pit to save its life is legal on the Sabbath, surely healing a man with a paralyzed hand on the Sabbath is legal.)

C. Words that need to be defined carefully for a proper understanding of the passage.

D. Quotations of or allusions to Old Testament passages or other ancient literature. Where is the quotation from? How does your passage use it, and why? If the quotation changes its Old Testament source, why does it do so?

E. Historical information that is important for understanding your passage.

F. Comparisons with the ways in which other Gospels use the story and formulate its contents (redaction criticism).

G. Theological significance of the passage. Of what value is its teaching for today?

4. *Conclusion:* Summarize the content of your paper and forcefully state the significance of the study.

Your goal is to explain as best you can what the biblical author meant when writing the passage and to elucidate, if possible, why he included it and how he modified it for his purposes. To do this, you need to study the structure of the passage, the context in which it is located, and the significant words it employs. Be careful, however, not to make your paper a word study in which your passage is merely one of many texts you consider to explain the meaning of a particular term. Also avoid merely giving your testimony as a means of reflecting on the passage. The assignment is an exercise in delving into a Gospel story, coming to grips with it on its own terms.

The paper should be typed, double-spaced, on one side of the page, and should include a title page, notes, and bibliography. Use a spell-checker! Proper grammar and spelling, a good writing style, and correct form on notes and bibliography dramatically strengthen your work.

CITING PRIMARY AND SECONDARY SOURCES

When quoting or referring to a biblical passage, you need not use a footnote. Merely place the needed information in parentheses: "It was because you were so hard-hearted that Moses allowed you to divorce your wives" (Matt. 19:8). (Note the placement of the period after the citation in parentheses.) When quoting or providing information taken from a secondary source, however, you must show where you obtained the material. *When relying on the work of another, even if you do not quote his or her words exactly, you must give credit to that person.* If you fail to do so, you are committing plagiarism. For example, if you were studying Mark 10:2–12 on divorce, you could take my book *Sex in the Bible,* note in the index where I address this passage, and then read that material. If you decided to use some of my information in your paper, you would indicate this in a note either at the bottom of the page (footnote) or at the end of your paper (endnote). Parenthetical notes, although popular in some disciplines, are not beneficial in exegesis papers, where careful documentation of sources may involve lengthy lists of data that can clutter the main body of the text. With word processors, the construction of footnotes is easy.

Make it your habit, when citing as evidence the argument of an author of a commentary, journal article, or other publication, to include in your footnote or endnote a listing of any primary sources he or she used to argue for a particular viewpoint. This helps the reader evaluate the strength of the viewpoint without having to locate and read the book cited.

FOOTNOTES OR ENDNOTES

Use the following as guides:

For a Commentary in a Commentary Series

Note that the title of the individual commentary is italicized or underlined, but the series title is not.

1. William L. Lane, *The Gospel according to Mark,* New International Commentary on the New Testament (Grand Rapids: Wm. B. Eerdmans Publishing Co., 1974), p. 41.

2. Raymond E. Brown, *The Gospel according to John, I—XII,* vol. 1, Anchor Bible (Garden City, N.Y.: Doubleday & Co., 1966), p. 90.

For a Book on a Biblical Topic

3. Michael R. Cosby, *Sex in the Bible: An Introduction to What the Scriptures Teach Us about Sexuality* (Englewood Cliffs, N.J.: Prentice-Hall, 1984), pp. 17–20.

For a Dictionary Article

Note that the name of the author of the article comes first and the main editor of the dictionary later. Look at the end of the article for the name of its author.

Appendix B

4. O. J. Baab, "Divorce," in *Interpreter's Dictionary of the Bible,* vol. 1, ed. G. A. Buttrick (Nashville: Abingdon Press, 1962), p. 859.

For a Journal Article

5. B. Vawter, "Divorce and the New Testament," *Catholic Biblical Quarterly* 39 (1977): 528–42.

6. Michael R. Cosby, "The Rhetorical Composition of Hebrews 11," *Journal of Biblical Literature* 107 (1988): 257–73.

7. Michael R. Cosby, "Hellenistic Formal Receptions and Paul's Use of APANTHSIS in 1 Thessalonians 4:17," *Bulletin for Biblical Research* 4 (1994): 15–33.

For an Article in a Book of Collected Essays

8. Michael R. Cosby, "Paul's Persuasive Language in Romans 5," in *Persuasive Artistry: Studies in New Testament Rhetoric in Honor of George A. Kennedy,* Journal for the Study of the New Testament—Supplement Series 50, ed. Duane F. Watson (Sheffield: Sheffield Academic Press, 1991), pp. 209–26.

BIBLIOGRAPHY

Alphabetically arrange according to the last name of the author. (Do not number bibliography entries.) For the same works as above you would type:

Baab, O. J. "Divorce." P. 859 in *Interpreter's Dictionary of the Bible,* vol. 1, ed. G. A. Buttrick. Nashville: Abingdon Press, 1962.

Brown, Raymond E. *The Gospel according to John, I—XII,* vol. 1, Anchor Bible. Garden City, N.Y.: Doubleday & Co., 1966.

Cosby, Michael R. "Hellenistic Formal Receptions and Paul's Use of APANTHSIS in 1 Thessalonians 4:17." *Bulletin for Biblical Research* 4 (1994): 15–33.

———. "Paul's Persuasive Language in Romans 5." Pp. 209–26 in *Persuasive Artistry: Studies in New Testament Rhetoric in Honor of George A. Kennedy.* Journal for the Study of the New Testament—Supplement Series 50. Edited by Duane F. Watson. Sheffield: Sheffield Academic Press, 1991.

———. "The Rhetorical Composition of Hebrews 11." *Journal of Biblical Literature* 107 (1988): 257–73.

———. *Sex in the Bible: An Introduction to What the Scriptures Teach Us about Sexuality.* Englewood Cliffs, N.J.: Prentice-Hall, 1984.

Lane, William L. *The Gospel according to Mark.* New International Commentary on the New Testament. Grand Rapids: Wm. B. Eerdmans Publishing Co., 1974.

Vawter, B. "Divorce and the New Testament." *Catholic Biblical Quarterly* 39 (1977): 528–42.

How to Write an Exegesis Paper on a Gospel Passage

THINGS TO NOTE

1. Any quotation of five or more lines should be indented and single-spaced in your paper. Do not put quotation marks around such *block quotations.*
2. When *quoting* a source, be careful to reproduce the exact wording.
3. All foreign words (e.g., *Heilsgeschichte*) and terms transliterated into English (e.g., *agape*) should be italicized or underlined.

Avoid such common unfavorable practices as

1. the use of clichés and other overly informal means of expression. What is acceptable in everyday conversation is not always desirable in a formal paper.
2. concluding a sentence with a preposition: "Whom are you going with?" Instead say, "With whom are you going?"
3. the use of contractions, such as "can't," "don't," "won't."
4. confusing the spelling of "its" and "it's"; "accept" and "except"; and "affect" and "effect." Know the differences between the meanings of such words.

Appendix C
Quests for the Historical Jesus

The focus of study in this book is on the literary portraits of Jesus in the four Gospels, and it is outside the scope of this work to delve into the quests for the historical Jesus. Studying the ways in which the Evangelists modify their sources to create their own theologically oriented presentations, however, results in the legitimate question "What was Jesus of Nazareth actually like?" Scholars answer this in a variety of ways. Some maintain a firm belief in the overall historical veracity of the Gospels and argue that in Jesus, God supernaturally entered the world to redeem humanity. Others respond with historical skepticism, rejecting the Gospel claims that Jesus performed miracles and was in fact Deity in human form. In between are those who represent a variety of differing approaches to and evaluations of historical and theological issues. Arriving at mutually agreed-upon methods for studying the life of Jesus continues to be extremely problematic. Indeed, one must search hard to find a more contentious area of study.

The different presuppositions that people bring to the endeavor to re-create what Jesus actually said and did result in substantial differences in conclusions. The issues raised by life-of-Jesus research are extremely problematic and sufficiently taxing that few dare to dive into it extensively. It has also been a painful pursuit for some who have sought to dig behind the post-Easter portraits of Jesus that the Evangelists present in order to uncover the Jesus of history. Caution and honesty are needed when probing into this subject.

From our study of the Gospels, we have seen that the Evangelists arranged the individual stories about Jesus into the orders they desired to produce their own distinct portraits of Jesus. Early in the twentieth century, Karl Ludwig Schmidt compared these individual units of tradition to pearls on a string. In his analogy, the pearls, representing incidents in the life of Jesus, were on the string in a certain order as events unfolded in their historical sequence. But Schmidt concluded that after Jesus' death, the string was cut; the pearls fell to the floor, and no one knows how they were originally arranged on the string.[1]

In 1901, Albert Schweitzer brilliantly synthesized several

centuries of life-of-Jesus research in his *The Quest of the Historical Jesus: A Critical Study of Its Progress from Reimarus to Wrede.*[2] Schweitzer chronicled the development of ideas on the historical Jesus, sifting through thousands of pages to present a distillation of the main viewpoints of the major figures in this endeavor. He comments in his introductory chapter that in the past, various people attempted to formulate their portraits of Jesus based on one Gospel in preference over the others. But such attempts resulted in a stalemate. Many scholars finally concluded that they must study each story as an independent unit, for, from a historical perspective, there was no guarantee of its connection to the surrounding context. This ominous evaluation of the absence of connections between the Gospel stories led to considerable skepticism over the possibility of finding the historical Jesus, and for a number of years many scholars gave up the quest.

We are presently witnessing what is called the Third Quest, in which studies tend to focus on the social setting of first-century Palestine. Older works take different approaches, and describing the history of the three quests requires much more space than is allowable in this book. The following bibliography provides some of the many books written on the historical Jesus.

BRIEF BIBLIOGRAPHY
ON THE LIFE OF JESUS

Borg, Marcus. *Jesus: A New Vision: Spirit, Culture, and the Life of Discipleship.* New York: Harper & Row, 1987.

Borg, Marcus, and N. T. Wright. *The Meaning of Jesus: Two Visions.* San Francisco: Harper Collins, 1999.

Bornkamm, Günter. *Jesus of Nazareth.* Translated by I. McLuskey and G. McLuskey. New York: Harper & Brothers, 1960.

Boyd, Gregory A. *Cynic Sage or Son of God: Recovering the Real Jesus in an Age of Revisionist Replies.* Wheaton, Ill.: Victor Books, 1995.

Bultmann, Rudolf. *Jesus and the Word.* Translated by L. P. Smith. New York: Charles Scribner's Sons, 1934.

Charlesworth, James H. *Jesus within Judaism.* New York: Doubleday, 1988.

Conzelmann, Hans. *Jesus.* Philadelphia: Westminster Press, 1973.

Crossan, John Dominic. *The Historical Jesus: The Life of a Mediterranean Peasant.* San Franscisco: Harper Collins, 1991. (This is a good example of the Third Quest. The first half of the book is devoted to explaining significant dimensions of Mediterranean societies, such as honor/shame, slavery , social strata, patron-client relationships, and popular messianic movements.)

Dodd, C. H. *The Founder of Christianity.* New York: Macmillan Co., 1970.

Dunn, James D. G. *The Evidence for Jesus*. Philadelphia: West-minster Press, 1985.

Fitzpatrick, James K. *Jesus Christ: Before He Became a Super-star*. Harrison, N.Y.: Roman Catholic Books, 1977.

Fosdick, H. E. *The Man from Nazareth*. New York: Harper & Brothers, 1949.

Gerhardsson, B. *Memory and Manuscript*. Lund: C. W. K. Gleerup, 1961.

Goergen, Donald. *The Mission and Ministry of Jesus*. Wilming-ton, Del.: Michael Glazier, 1986.

Harvey, A. E. *Jesus and the Constraints of History*. Philadelphia: Westminster Press, 1982.

Hayes, John. *Son of God to Superstar*. Nashville: Abingdon Press, 1976.

Johnson, Luke T. *The Real Jesus: The Misguided Quest for the Historical Jesus and the Truth of the Traditional Gospels*. San Francisco: Harper Collins, 1996. (Johnson attacks the meth-ods and conclusions of scholars like Borg and Crossan.)

Marshall, I. H. *I Believe in the Historical Jesus*. Grand Rapids: Wm. B. Eerdmans Publishing Co., 1977.

Meier, John P. *A Marginal Jew: Rethinking the Historical Jesus*. New York: Doubleday, 1991.

Sanders, E. P. *Jesus and Judaism*. Rev. ed. London: SCM Press, 1987.

Sanders, E. P., and Margaret Davies. *Studying the Synoptic Gospels*. London: SCM Press, 1989. (See esp. pp. 301–44, "Research into the Life and Teaching of Jesus: The Quest and Its Methods.")

Schweitzer, Albert. *The Quest of the Historical Jesus: A Critical Study of Its Progress from Reimarus to Wrede*. Translated by W. Montgomery. New York: Macmillan Co., 1968.

Segundo, Juan Luis. *The Historical Jesus of the Synoptics*. Mary-knoll, N.Y.: Orbis Books, 1985.

Stanton, Graham. *Gospel Truth? New Light on Jesus and the Gospels*. Valley Forge, Pa.: Trinity Press International, 1995.

Tatum, W. Barns. *In Quest of Jesus: A Guidebook*. Atlanta: John Knox Press, 1982.

Vermes, Geza. *Jesus the Jew*. New York: Macmillan Publishing Co., 1973.

Witherington, Ben III. *The Christology of Jesus*. Minneapolis: Fortress Press, 1990.

———. *The Jesus Quest: The Third Quest for the Jew of Nazareth*. Downers Grove, Ill.: InterVarsity Press, 1995. (This work rep-resents an evangelical challenge to more skeptical scholarship on the historical Jesus.)

Wright, N. T. *Jesus and the Victory of God: Christian Origins and the Question of God*. Vol. 2. Minneapolis: Fortress Press, 1997. (As do Johnson and Witherington, Wright challenges historical Jesus research conducted by scholars like Crossan and provides an explanation of Jesus that is more compatible with historic ex-pressions of Christian faith.)

———. *Who Was Jesus?* Grand Rapids: Wm. B. Eerdmans Pub-lishing Co., 1993.

Appendix D
The Rewards of Teaching Inductively

A major emphasis in research in higher education today is the area of active learning. Professors in all disciplines are engaged in significant attempts to enhance learning by getting students actively involved in their subject matter. Many of us are experimenting with various uses of computer technology to facilitate learning through visual aids and information access through the Internet. The percentage of those who rely strictly on classroom lecturing as a means of educating has drastically dwindled in the past decade. Although some teachers seem to have largely abandoned course content in favor of classroom activities that I would label "shared ignorance," most responsible educators are searching for good tools to enhance their students' understanding of their discipline.

In Biblical Studies, however, there is simply no substitute for learning to read the text carefully, seeking to understand it in light of ancient Mediterranean culture. To motivate students raised in a video-oriented society to read carefully, doing textual detective work, requires creativity and diligence. This book is designed to help people see for themselves the complexities of the Gospels and to experience the pleasure of discovering the riches contained in these stories about Jesus.

Acquiring a taste for such discovery requires time and effort, and most students need assistance to develop this appetite. When merely asked to read a portion of the Gospels, they do not initially know what kinds of questions to ask of the text. Unless they are guided in this search, they will not notice many of the details that are necessary for them to see before they can begin to apprehend Mark's literary style, or Matthew's and Luke's redactions of Markan material, or the distinctive elements of John's portrait of Jesus. Thus, the questions asked in this textbook are an integral part of the discovery process. By no means busywork, they are a necessary step toward responsible interpretation of stories about Jesus that were written in an ancient Mediterranean setting. Without these questions, most students begin to interpret too quickly and end up drawing invalid conclusions.

Appendix D

The approach this book takes is to encourage careful observation of the contents of each Gospel; and the quotations from other ancient sources, explanations of cultural norms, and so forth are all designed to facilitate this process. Consequently, the reading assignments for each segment are not lengthy, for the goal is to read in depth, learning to notice details. And instead of answering questions that students have not yet asked, this book allows critical issues to arise from actual study of the Gospels. This approach is methodologically superior, because we all understand things much better when we see them for ourselves than we do when simply taking someone else's word for it.

The questions in the chapter on Mark train students in literary analysis of the text, helping them see significance in the existing sequence of the stories and learn to interpret the Gospel accordingly. In the chapters on Luke and Matthew, the questions train students to do redaction criticism, because in order to complete many of the assignments, they must use a synopsis and compare parallel accounts in the Gospels. When they see for themselves the differences between these accounts, they are much more likely than otherwise to listen carefully to source theories and see why scholars postulate various redactional hypotheses. In the chapter on John, they discover the radical differences in structure and content of the Fourth Gospel. As they compare Jesus' combative approach and lengthy monologues on his Deity with his parabolic teaching about the kingdom of God in the Synoptics, they begin to appreciate some of the difficulties faced by scholars doing life-of-Jesus research.

After comparing accounts and seeing the differences, the students are able to grasp scholarly methods and theories as real responses to viable questions, and bibliographies become helpful tools for pursuing issues further. In addition, when students write down their observations in this book, they learn more. Responding to thought-provoking questions forces them to slow down enough to analyze the text carefully. As a result, they come to class better prepared, which greatly improves the quality of classroom discussions and improves their insights into the significance of the Gospel accounts.

Students, whether enrolled at Christian or at secular institutions, typically take Bible classes because they are interested in knowing what scripture has to say about issues they face in their own lives. They want to ask the "So what?" kinds of questions that enable them to apply the content of biblical stories, particularly the teachings of Jesus. Therefore, in addition to observation and interpretation questions, this book is filled with questions that focus on personal application. Professors in secular institutions who are concerned about issues pertaining to separation of church and state may choose not to assign these application questions or discuss them in class. But most students enrolled in these classes will be interested in such issues, and they will be grateful that their textbook helps them to contemplate their significance. The vast majority of people using this book will have a vital interest in asking what influence the teachings and actions of Jesus should have on their lives. So, although the textbook is academically oriented and will lead students to see things that might initially be unsettling, the devotional aspects of Gospel study also play a vital role.

Reading the Gospels should be an adventure of discovery, and explorers benefit from having a map and a guide. This book provides the map; the professor functions as the guide. By helping students see firsthand the ways in which the authors of the Gospels tell their stories, we equip them to read the Bible responsibly, to learn new questions to ask of the text, to find out how to answer these questions. Or, to use another image, this book is like a shovel, giving students the tool they need to dig into the Gospels to find the riches that await them there.

Notes

Chapter One: The Rewards of Inductive Study of the Gospels

1. Although some of Irenaeus's explanations sound archaic today, they reveal an awareness of the differences among the Gospels. Concerning why there are four Gospels he says, "It is not possible that the Gospels can be either more or fewer in number than they are. For, since there are four zones of the world in which we live, and four principal winds, while the Church is scattered throughout the world, and the 'pillar and ground' of the Church is the Gospel and the spirit of life; it is fitting that she should have four pillars" (*Against Heresies* 3.11.8). Of the four cherubim of Revelation 4:6–7 he says, "For the cherubim, too, were four-faced, and their faces were images of the dispensation of the Son of God. For, [as the scripture] says, 'The first living creature was like a lion,' symbolizing His effectual working, His leadership, and royal power; the second [living creature] was like a calf, signifying [Jesus'] sacrificial and sacerdotal order; but 'the third had, as it were, the face as of a man,'—an evident description of His advent as a human being; 'the fourth was like a flying eagle,' pointing out the gift of the Spirit hovering with His wings over the Church. And therefore the Gospels are in accord with these things, among which Christ Jesus is seated. For that according to John relates to His original, effectual, and glorious generation from the Father. . . . But that according to Luke, taking up [Jesus'] priestly character, commenced with Zecharias the priest offering sacrifice to God. . . . Matthew, again, relates His generation as a man, saying, 'The book of the generation of Jesus Christ, the son of David, the son of Abraham. . . . ' This, then, is the Gospel of his humanity. . . . Mark, on the other hand, commences with [a reference to] the prophetical spirit coming down from on high to men, saying, 'In the beginning of the Gospel of Jesus Christ, as it is written in Esaias the prophet,'—pointing to the winged aspect of the Gospel" (3.11.8). Quotations of Irenaeus are from *The Ante-Nicene Fathers,* vol. 1, ed. by A. Roberts and J. Donaldson (reprint; Grand Rapids: Wm. B. Eerdmans Publishing Co., 1977).

2. The great Christian scholar Jerome switched the symbols for Mark and John, and his assignment became standard for the church, although others, like Augustine, have provided alternative explanations. Jerome gave John the symbol of the eagle

because his Gospel begins "In the beginning . . . " and causes the hearer to soar to the heavens, while Mark begins with John the Baptist roaring like a lion in the wilderness and so should be symbolized by the lion (*Commentary on Ezekiel* 1.1).

Augustine critiques previous assignments of the symbols from Rev. 4:7 to the Gospels, because they "have chosen to keep in view simply the beginnings of the books, and not the full design of the several evangelists in its completeness, which was the matter that should, above all, have been thoroughly examined. For surely it is with much greater propriety that the one who has brought under our notice most largely the kingly character of Christ, should be taken to be represented by the lion. . . . For in Matthew's narrative the magi are recorded to have come from the east to inquire after the King, and to worship Him whose birth was notified to them by the star" (*Harmony of the Gospels* 1.6.9). He goes on to explain that Luke begins with Zechariah offering sacrifice; Jesus is taken to the temple for circumcision in obedience to the law; and many other details in the Gospel indicate that "Luke's object was to deal with the part of the priest." Mark did not give anything specific about kingship or priesthood, so the symbol of the man most appropriately applies to him. "John, on the other hand, soars like an eagle above the clouds of human infirmity, and gazes upon the light of the unchangeable truth with those keenest and steadiest eyes of the heart" (1.6.9). Quotations from Augustine, *Harmony of the Gospels,* in *Nicene and Post-Nicene Fathers,* vol. 6, ed. Philip Schaff (Peabody, Mass.: Hendrickson, 1994; reprint of 1888 edition by Christian Literature Publishing Co.).

Chapter Two: Mark the Evangelist

1. Augustine (354–430 C.E.) says, concerning the order of the writing of the Gospels, "first Matthew, then Mark, thirdly Luke, lastly John. . . . For Matthew is understood to have taken it in hand to construct the record of the incarnation of the Lord according to the royal lineage, and to give account of most of his deeds and words as they stood in relation to this present life of men. Mark follows him closely, and looks like his attendant and epitomizer" (*Harmony of the Gospels* 1.2.3–4; translation from *Nicene and Post-Nicene Fathers,* vol. 6, ed. by Philip Schaff [Peabody, Mass.: Hendrickson, 1994; reprint of 1888 edition by Christian Literature Publishing Co.]). Such assessments can be seen in many books written over the centuries.

2. See Walter Ong, *Orality and Literacy: The Technologizing of the Word* (New York and London: Methuen, 1982); and Werner Kelber, *The Oral and the Written Gospel: The Hermeneutics of Speaking and Writing in the Synoptic Tradition, Mark, Paul, and Q* (Philadelphia: Fortress Press, 1983).

3. From Eusebius, *The History of the Church from Christ to Constantine,* trans. G. A. Williamson (Minneapolis: Augsburg Publishing House, 1975), 3.39, p. 150.

4. Also *2 Baruch* 22:1 says, "And afterward it happened that, behold, the heaven was opened, and I saw, . . . and a voice was heard from on high which said to me . . . " (translations from J. H. Charlesworth, ed., *The Old Testament Pseudepigrapha,* vol. 1: *Apocalyptic Literature and Testaments* [Garden City, N.Y.: Doubleday & Co., 1983]).

5. A few scholars do not believe that in Jesus' day there were any specific buildings called synagogues. They argue that this term simply designates a gathering of people (as James 2:2 uses the word), which might occur in someone's home or in another type of structure, such as a basilica (multipurpose building). Howard Clark Kee, "The Transformation of the Synagogue after 70 C.E.: Its Import for Early Christianity," *New Testament Studies* 36 (1990): 1–24, argues that past scholars have erred in assuming there were buildings called synagogues in the first century. See also *The Synagogue: Studies in Origins, Archaeology and Architecture,* ed. J. Gutmann (New York: KTAV Publishing House, 1975).

6. See, for example, C. Colpe, *"Ho huios tou anthropou"* in *Theological Dictionary of the New Testament,* vol. 8, ed. G. W. Bromiley (Grand Rapids: Wm. B. Eerdmans Publishing Co., 1972), pp. 400–477; O. Michel, "Son of Man," in *The New International Dictionary of New Testament Theology,* vol. 3, ed. C. Brown (Grand Rapids: Zondervan Publishing House, 1978), pp. 613–34; and I. H. Marshall, *The Origins of New Testament Christology* (Downers Grove, Ill.: InterVarsity Press, n.d.), pp. 63–82, for detailed analyses and extensive bibliographies.

7. "As I watched in the night visions, I saw one like a human being ['son of man' in the Aramaic] coming with the clouds of heaven. And he came to the Ancient One ['Ancient of Days' in the Aramaic] and was presented before him. To him was given dominion and glory and kingship, that all peoples, nations, and languages should serve him. His dominion is an everlasting dominion that shall not pass away, and his kingship is one that shall never be destroyed" (Dan. 7:13–14; note that Dan. 7:18 identifies Israel ["the holy ones of the Most High"] with this figure). "After seven days I dreamed a dream in the night. . . . And I looked, and behold, this wind made something like the figure of a man come up out of the heart of the sea. And I looked, and behold, that man flew with the clouds of heaven; and wherever he turned his face to look, everything under his gaze trembled" (4 Ezra 13:1–4). "This Son of Man whom you have seen is the One who would remove the kings and the mighty ones from their

comfortable seats and the strong ones from their thrones. He shall loosen the reins of the strong and crush the teeth of the sinners" (*1 Enoch* 46:4). The "Son of Man was given a name in the presence of the Lord of Spirits . . . before the creation of the stars. . . . He is the light to the Gentiles. . . . All those who dwell on earth shall fall and worship him" (*1 Enoch* 47:2–5).

8. W. Wrede, *Das Messiasgeheimnis in den Evangelien* (1901), trans. J. C. G. Greig as *The Messianic Secret* (Cambridge: James Clarke & Co., 1971).

9. Colpe, *"Ho huios tou anthropou,"* pp. 420–29; Michel, "Son of Man," pp. 614–17; and Marshall, *Origins of New Testament Christology,* pp. 63–69.

10. Eusebius, *History of the Church from Christ to Constantine,* 3.39.15, p. 152.

11. Bruce J. Malina, *The New Testament World: Insights from Cultural Anthropology,* rev. ed. (Louisville, Ky: Westminster/John Knox Press, 1993), p. 104.

12. For a brief historical survey of the various Jewish religious parties at the time of Jesus, see Appendix A. For detailed studies, see, for example, Jacob Neusner, *From Politics to Piety: The Emergence of Pharisaic Judaism* (Englewood Cliffs, N.J.: Prentice-Hall, 1973); and idem, *The Rabbinic Traditions about the Pharisees before 70,* 2 vols. (Leiden: E. J. Brill, 1971); Ellis Rivkin, *A Hidden Revolution: The Pharisees' Search for the Kingdom Within* (Nashville: Abingdon Press, 1978); S. Safrai and M. Stern, eds., *The Jewish People in the First Century,* vol. 1, Compendia rerum iudaicarum ad novum testamentum (Philadelphia: Fortress Press, 1974); Emil Schürer, *A History of the Jewish People in the Age of Jesus Christ (175 B.C.–A.D. 135),* vol. 2, rev. and ed. G. Vermes and F. Millar (Edinburgh: T. & T. Clark, 1979).

13. From S. E. Johnson, *A Commentary on the Gospel according to Mark* (London: Adam and Charles Black, 1960), p. 61. Unfortunately, Johnson does not specify the location of this passage.

14. For more information see Aharon Oppenheimer, *The 'Am Ha-Aretz: A Study in the Social History of the Jewish People in the Hellenistic-Roman Period* (Leiden: E. J. Brill, 1977).

15. "Let not your fasts be with the hypocrites, for they fast on Mondays and Thursdays, but do you fast on Wednesdays and Fridays" (Didache 8:1; from *The Apostolic Fathers,* vol. 1, trans. K. Lake [Loeb Classical Library; Cambridge, Mass.: Harvard University Press, 1945], p. 321).

16. *The Mishnah,* trans. Herbert Danby (London: Oxford University Press, 1933), p. 106.

17. The reference to Abiathar as high priest (Mark 2:26) does not coincide with 1 Samuel 21:1, which specifies Ahimelech as the head priest to whom David spoke. Abiathar was Ahimelech's son who escaped Saul's slaughter of the priests at Nob (1 Sam. 22:20). Note that Matthew 12:4 and Luke 6:4 correct the problem by deleting the reference to Abiathar. Scholarly commentaries on Mark provide good discussions of this matter.

18. Danby, trans., *The Mishnah*, p. 172.

19. See W. E .M. Aitken, "Beelzebul," *Journal of Biblical Literature* 31 (1912): 34–53.

20. In Matthew's retelling of the story, the disciples' understanding is the key (Matt. 13:11), but this fits Matthew's agenda, not Mark's.

21. In chapter 3, section 8, "Interpreting the Parables of Jesus," we investigate the problem of not knowing the original context in which Jesus spoke many of his parables.

22. There might also be a reflection on Ps. 107:23–32 in this passage. The description of the events in this psalm closely resembles Mark 4:35–41.

23. For a similar reference to sending demons out of the region to where they cannot harm people (5:10), see Tobit 8:3.

24. See C. E. B. Cranfield, *The Gospel according to Saint Mark* (Cambridge: Cambridge University Press, 1963), p. 195.

25. It is also interesting that Matt. 10:10 modifies the account so that Jesus tells them *not* to take a staff. This lends further credibility to understanding Mark's reference to the staff as having significance for the disciples' ministry as shepherds.

26. Mark calls these men apostles only in 3:14 and 6:30.

27. They do not get to Bethsaida until 8:22.

28. William L. Lane, *The Gospel according to Mark* (Grand Rapids: Wm. B. Eerdmans Publishing Co., 1974), p. 251.

29. Jesus was in contact with many sick people in marketplaces (6:56), and the Pharisees consider going to the marketplace defiling (7:4).

30. Mishnah *Gittin* 9:10; in Danby, trans., *The Mishnah*, p. 320.

31. Martin Kähler, *The So-Called Historical Jesus and the Historic Biblical Christ*, trans. and ed. by Carl E. Branton (Philadelphia: Fortress Press, 1964; 1964 translation of the 1896 German edition), p. 80, n. 11.

32. See V. Eppstein, "The Historicity of the Gospel Account of the Cleansing of the Temple," *Zeitschrift für die Neutestamentliche Wissenschaft* 55 (1964): 42–58.

33. For the theory that Jesus had been in Jerusalem for about six months, entering the city (11:1–11) during the Feast of Tabernacles in the fall of the year, see C. W. F. Smith, "No Time for Figs," *Journal of Biblical Literature* 79 (1960): 315–27; and idem, "Tabernacles in the Fourth Gospel and Mark," *New Testament Studies* 9 (1963): 130–46.

34. See Michael Cosby, "Mark 14:51–52 and the Problem of Gospel Narrative," *Perspectives in Religious Studies* 11 (1984): 219–32.

35. Scholars are currently debating how much authority the Sanhedrin had in the first century.

36. Such meaning would largely be lost to the Greek-speaking audience of Mark, however, unless the public reader were to add a comment on it. Mark does not provide an editorial comment, as he does elsewhere when clarifying the meaning of words or customs for his audience (see 5:41; 7:3–4; 15:34).

37. Lane, *Gospel according to Mark,* p. 557.

Chapter Three: Luke's Jesus: Reversing Social Expectations

1. Translation from *New Testament Apocrypha,* vol. 1, ed. E. Hennecke and W. Schneemelcher (Philadelphia: Westminster Press, 1963), p. 43.

2. Irenaeus (ca. 180 C.E.) says, "Luke, the companion of Paul, recorded in a book the Gospel preached by him" (*Against Heresies* 3.1.1; in *The Ante-Nicene Fathers,* vol. 1, ed. A. Roberts and J. Donaldson [reprint; Grand Rapids: Wm. B. Eerdmans Publishing Co., 1977]). The heretic Marcion (ca. 150 C.E.), who was quite committed to Pauline theology, may have given canonical status only to the third Gospel because he believed that Luke was a traveling companion of Paul; we do not know this for sure.

3. Henry J. Cadbury's *The Making of Luke-Acts* (London: SPCK, 1958) remains one of the most important studies on this topic. See also Ernst Haenchen, *The Acts of the Apostles: A Commentary* (Philadelphia: Westminster Press, 1971), pp. 72–80.

4. For a wealth of information on this topic, see Charles Talbert, *Literary Patterns, Theological Themes, and the Genre of Luke-Acts* (Missoula, Mont.: Scholars Press, 1974); idem, *What Is a Gospel? The Genre of the Canonical Gospels* (Philadelphia: Fortress Press, 1977) (Talbert argues that they are all biographies); and idem *Luke-Acts: New Perspectives from the SBL Seminar* (New York: Crossroad, 1984).

5. Translation from *The Old Testament Pseudepigrapha,* vol. 2, ed. James H. Charlesworth (Garden City, N.Y.: Doubleday & Co., 1985), pp. 667–69. See also *1 Enoch* 46:4–5; *2 Esd.* 11:37–46; 12:31–34, for material on the messiah.

6. Emil Schürer, "Excursus I—The Census of Quirinius," in *The History of the Jewish People in the Age of Jesus Christ,* vol. 1, rev. and ed. G. Vermes and F. Millar (Edinburgh: T. & T. Clark, 1973), pp. 399–427.

7. The King James Version (KJV), which says in 2:6 that Mary was "great with child," is inaccurate. The Greek text says no such thing.

8. See, for example, Kenneth E. Bailey, "The Manger and the Inn: A Middle Eastern View of the Birth Story of Jesus," *Presbyterian Outlook* (January 4–11, 1988): 8–9; or Bruce Malina and Richard Rohrbaugh, *Social-Science Commentary on the Synoptic Gospels* (Minneapolis: Fortress Press, 1992), pp. 296–97.

9. The full text of the *Protevangelium of James* may be read in a book found in most college and university libraries: *New Testament Apocrypha,* vol. 1, ed. Hennecke and Schneemelcher, pp. 374–88.

10. James Barr, "Abba Isn't Daddy," *Journal of Theological Studies* 39, n.s. (1988): 28–47; idem, "Abba and the Familiarity of Jesus' Speech," *Theology* 91 (1988): 173–79; J. Fitzmyer, "Abba and Jesus' Relation to God," in *A cause de l'evangile: Études sur les Synoptiques et Actes offertes à Jacques Dupont O.S.B. à l'occasion de son 70e anniversaire* (Lectio divina 123; Publications de Saint-André; Paris: Cerf, 1985), pp. 14–38.; and Mary Rose D'Angelo, "*Abba* and 'Father': Imperial Theology and the Jesus Traditions," *Journal of Biblical Literature* 111, 4 (1992): 611–30. Much earlier, G. F. Moore argued in *Judaism in the First Centuries of the Christian Era* (New York: Schocken Books, 1927), pp. 201–11, that pious Jewish people of Jesus' time used the title "Father" for God.

11. The reference to "proclaiming the message in the synagogues of Judea" in Luke 4:44 seems odd, since Jesus' ministry at this point is in Galilee (cf. Mark 1:39). Hans Conzelmann sees this as indicative of Luke's ignorance of Palestinian geography, a view that I. H. Marshall contests: "Conzelmann's picture of Jesus moving to and fro across an imaginary Judaean-Galilean frontier proves to be an illusion. Rather Luke uses 'Judaea' as a term which includes Galilee, and the reason for this usage may lie in the fact that he does not ascribe theological importance to Galilee; it is the place where the Gospel 'begins' (Acts 10:37) but not its main theatre" (*Luke: Historian and Theologian* [Grand Rapids: Zondervan Publishing House, 1970], p. 71). For Conzelmann's view, see *The Theology of St. Luke* (New York: Harper & Brothers, 1960; English translation of *Die Mitte der Zeit,* 1954), pp. 18–94, esp. p. 69. Whatever the answer to the problem, it reveals that Luke modifies material used from Mark to fit his own agenda.

12. For a translation of the *Gospel of Thomas,* see James M. Robinson, ed., *The Nag Hammadi Library in English* (New York: Harper & Row, 1977).

13. Acts 1:21–22 specifies "apostles" as those who have witnessed the entire career of Jesus. This will be important when selecting a replacement for Judas in Acts 1.

14. Since Nain is in Galilee, the statement in 7:17 that word "spread throughout Judea" is problematic (cf. 4:44). Perhaps it merely leads in to 7:18, since John was in prison in the south, and is meant to show why John's disciples hear about Jesus' actions.

15. Luke 10:21–22 sounds very much like the theology we will see later in the Gospel of John. This has caused commentators to give this statement such titles as the "Johannine Thunderbolt," saying that it comes like a lightning bolt out of the Johannine sky.

16. The origin and development of the Levites is a matter of intense debate among Old Testament scholars. Yet to say that in Jesus' day the Levites were a group with responsibilities for such things as assisting priests, taking care of the temple grounds, cleaning sacred vessels, and functioning as gatekeepers, musicians, and leaders of liturgy is not controversial. They did not have as privileged a position as the priests, but they were an important part of the sacrificial (i.e., cultic) system.

17. Translation by Geza Vermes, *The Dead Sea Scrolls in English,* 4th ed. (New York: Penguin Books, 1995), p. 109.

18. Ibid.

19. Herbert Danby, trans., *The Mishnah* (London: Oxford University Press, 1933), p. 172.

20. See Bruce J. Malina, *The New Testament World: Insights from Cultural Anthropology,* rev. ed. (Louisville, Ky.: Westminster/John Knox Press, 1993), pp. 90–94; Richard Rohrbaugh, "The Pre-Industrial City in Luke-Acts: Urban Social Relations," in *The Social World of Luke-Acts*, ed. Jerome H. Neyrey (Peabody, Mass.: Hendrickson, 1991), pp. 137–47; and J. Neyrey, "Ceremonies in Luke-Acts: The Case of Meals and Table Fellowship," in Neyrey, ed., *Social World of Luke-Acts*, pp. 361–87.

21. Bruce Malina and Richard Rohrbaugh, *Social-Science Commentary on the Synoptic Gospels* (Minneapolis: Fortress Press, 1992), p. 366.

22. Since the goal in this book is to see the portrait of Jesus that each of the four Evangelists presents, we normally do not delve into the difference between the life setting of Jesus and the life setting of the Evangelist in an effort to reconstruct the exact words of the historical Jesus. This is not to say such endeavors are unimportant but merely that they predominantly lie outside our sphere of inquiry.

23. Helpful bibliographies are available in such books as William R. Herzog II, *Parables as Subversive Speech: Jesus as Pedagogue of the Oppressed* (Louisville, Ky.: Westminster John Knox Press, 1994), pp. 282–90.

24. See, for example, John Dominic Crossan, *In Parables: The Challenge of the Historical Jesus* (New York: Harper & Row, 1973), for a somewhat radical view of the parables as world-shattering devices.

25. Gordon Fee, *How to Read the Bible for All Its Worth*, 2d ed. (Grand Rapids: Zondervan Publishing House, 1993), pp. 138–39.

26. E.g., Malina and Rohrbaugh, *Social-Science Commentary*, pp. 373–75.

27. See Joachim Jeremias, *The Parables of Jesus*, 2d ed. (New York: Charles Scribner's Sons, 1963), pp. 74–76.

Chapter Four: Matthew's Jesus:
Authoritative Interpreter of the Law

1. See R. H. Gundry, *The Use of the Old Testament in St. Matthew's Gospel* (Leiden: E. J. Brill, 1967), for a complete study.

2. David L. Barr, "The Drama of Matthew's Gospel: A Reconsideration of Its Structure and Purpose," *Theology Digest* 24 (1976): 353.

3. Extensive comparisons of these two genealogies abound in the secondary literature. A good starting point for further research on this topic is Raymond E. Brown's *The Birth of the Messiah: A Commentary on the Infancy Narratives in Matthew and Luke* (Garden City, N.Y.: Doubleday & Co., 1977).

4. Translation by Geza Vermes, *The Dead Sea Scrolls in English*, 4th ed. (New York: Penguin Books, 1995), pp. 340–41.

5. See Krister Stendahl, *The School of St. Matthew and Its Use of the Old Testament* (Philadelphia: Fortress Press, 1968).

6. The attack might even begin in 2:3–6, in which the Jerusalem leaders know where the Messiah will be born but are frightened by the news of the star reported to them by the Gentile wise men from the East. They do not go to adore the child.

7. Bruce Malina and Richard Rohrbaugh, *Social-Science Commentary on the Synoptic Gospels* (Minneapolis: Fortress Press, 1992), p. 38.

8. W. D. Davies, *The Setting of the Sermon on the Mount* (Cambridge: Cambridge University Press, 1964), pp. 157–58.

9. From Martin Hengel, *Judaism and Hellenism*, vol. 1 (Philadelphia: Fortress Press, 1974), p. 171.

10. Davies, *Setting of the Sermon on the Mount*, pp. 147–49; see the Qumran documents 1QS iv 18–26; ix 9–11; CD vi 14.

11. The use of "Most High" instead of "God" is motivated by the same Jewish tendency that causes Matthew to say "kingdom of heaven" instead of "kingdom of God."

12. Translations from Herbert Danby, *The Mishnah* (London: Oxford University Press, 1933).

13. Robert H. Gundry, *Matthew: A Commentary on His Literary and Theological Art* (Grand Rapids: Wm. B. Eerdmans Publishing Co., 1982), p. 334.

14. Translation by Danby, *The Mishnah*, p. 227.

15. For an excellent survey of the history of interpretation of Revelation, see Arthur W. Wainwright's *Mysterious Apocalypse: Interpreting the Book of Revelation* (Nashville: Abingdon Press, 1993).

Chapter Five: John's Jesus:
The Descent and Ascent of the Eternal Logos

1. An investigation of the many uses of *logos* in antiquity lies outside the scope of this book, but you may consult a wealth of information by reading articles in the *Theological Dictionary of the New Testament*, ed. G. Kittel, and *The New International Dictionary of New Testament Theology,* ed. Colin Brown, or explanations in commentaries such as "Appendix II: The 'Word,' " in Raymond E. Brown, *The Gospel according to John,* 2 vols. (Anchor Bible; Garden City, N.Y.: Doubleday & Co., 1966), vol. 1, pp. 519–24. Keep in mind, however, that the Word *becomes flesh* in John 1:14, and this radically distinguishes the content of the Fourth Gospel from Gnostic redeemer myths of a divine revealer and Docetic beliefs that the Christ never actually had a physical body. The eternal Word dwells on earth for a time in human form, even though John's Gospel presents a more spiritual portrait of Jesus than do the other Gospels.

2. Brown, *The Gospel according to John,* vol. 1, p. 98.

3. Translation from *The Old Testament Pseudepigrapha,* vol. 1, ed. James H. Charlesworth (Garden City, N.Y.: Doubleday & Co., 1983).

4. See R. Alan Culpepper, *Anatomy of the Fourth Gospel: A Study in Literary Design* (Philadelphia: Fortress Press, 1983), pp. 70–73.

5. Ibid., pp. 26–49, esp. 39–42.

6. Ibid., p. 41.

7. See ibid., pp. 125–31.

8. Mishnah *Sukkah* 5.2–5; see Herbert Danby, trans., *The Mishnah* (London: Oxford University Press, 1933), pp. 179–80.

9. Brown, *Gospel according to John,* vol. 1, p. 344.

Notes to Appendix A

10. For a good summary of the development of this theology of retribution and its gradual modification to reward and punishment in the afterlife, see Shaye J. D. Cohen, *From the Maccabees to the Mishnah* (Philadelphia: Westminster Press, 1987), pp. 87–92.

11. See Hermann L. Strack and Paul Billerbeck, *Kommentar zum Neuen Testament aus Talmud und Midrasch,* vol. 2 (Munich: C. H. Beck, 1926), pp. 528–29.

12. Cohen, *From the Maccabees to the Mishnah,* pp. 114–15, 227.

13. Charles H. Talbert, *Reading John: A Literary and Theological Commentary on the Fourth Gospel and the Johannine Epistles* (New York: Crossroad, 1992), p. 191.

14. Ibid., p. 192.

15. E.g., A. Jaubert, *The Date of the Last Supper* (Staten Island, N.Y.: Alba House, 1965); and E. Ruckstuhl, *Chronology of the Last Supper* (New York and Paris: Desclée de Brouwer, 1965).

16. See Brown, *Gospel according to John,* vol. 2, pp. 946–52, for a good summary of the various options proposed by scholars.

17. See ibid., vol. 2, p. 1072.

18. Culpepper, *Anatomy of the Fourth Gospel,* p. 27.

Appendix A: Jewish Religious Groups in the Time of Jesus

1. An earlier passage found in *War* 2.8.1–14 (§§117–66) also describes these three groups, but there Josephus is interested far more in describing the Essenes than the Pharisees or Sadducees. He devotes considerable space to describing their beliefs and customs, but since the Gospels do not mention the Essenes, we will not study this quotation. Translations from Josephus are from *The Works of Josephus,* trans. Wm. Whiston (updated edition Peabody, Mass.: Hendrickson Publishing, 1987).

2. Translation by G. Vermes, *The Dead Sea Scrolls in English,* 2d ed. (Baltimore: Penguin Books, 1975), p. 156.

Appendix C: Quests for the Historical Jesus

1. Karl Ludwig Schmidt, *Der Rahmen der Geschichte Jesus* (The framework of the story of Jesus) (Berlin: Trowitsch, 1919).

2. Albert Schweitzer, *The Quest of the Historical Jesus: A Critical Study of Its Progress from Reimarus to Wrede,* trans. W. Montgomery (New York: Macmillan Co., 1968); original German edition titled *Vom Reimarus zu Wrede* (1901).

Index

Index

Index

Index

Index